R∞ster
TOWN

R∞ster
TOWN

EVELYN PETERS, MATTHEW STOCK, AND ADRIAN WERNER
WITH LAWRIE BARKWELL

The History of an Urban
Métis Community, 1901–1961

UNIVERSITY OF MANITOBA PRESS

Rooster Town: The History of an Urban Métis Community, 1901–1961
© Evelyn Peters, Matthew Stock, and Adrian Werner 2018

22   21   20   19   18   1   2   3   4   5

University of Manitoba Press
Winnipeg, Manitoba, Canada
Treaty 1 Territory
uofmpress.ca

Cataloguing data available from Library and Archives Canada
ISBN 978-0-88755-825-2 (PAPER)
ISBN 978-0-88755-568-8 (PDF)
ISBN 978-0-88755-566-4 (EPUB)

Cover design by Frank Reimer
Interior design by Jess Koroscil
Cover image: *Winnipeg Free Press* reporter outside 1145 Weatherdon
Avenue in Rooster Town, March 1959. Photo by Gerry Cairns, *Winnipeg
Free Press* Collection, Archives of Manitoba.

Printed in Canada

This book has been published with the help of a grant from the
Federation for the Humanities and Social Sciences, through the Awards
to Scholarly Publications Program, using funds provided by the
Social Sciences and Humanities Research Council of Canada

The University of Manitoba Press acknowledges the financial support for
its publication program provided by the Government of Canada through
the Canada Book Fund, the Canada Council for the Arts, the Manitoba
Department of Sport, Culture, and Heritage, the Manitoba Arts Council,
and the Manitoba Book Publishing Tax Credit.

Funded by the Government of Canada | Canadä

CONTENTS

LIST OF TABLES

LIST OF ILLUSTRATIONS

PREFACE

THIS BOOK RESULTED FROM SEVERAL YEARS OF RESEARCH to reconstruct the history of a largely Métis community that lived on the outskirts of the developed area of southwest Winnipeg from 1901 to 1961. Drawing on a wide variety of sources, this study counters the silence around urban Métis histories and geographies, and exposes the role colonial institutions, attitudes, and practices played in shaping Métis inhabitants' urban experiences.[1] It also brings to light the common but largely ignored history of Métis communities that grew up near prairie and British Columbia cities, in western Canada's early years of settlement. In the process, the book illustrates specific urban experiences of Métis people—a topic that has received very little scholarly attention to date.

The academic literature focusing on communities that emerged on the fringes of urban areas in North America between the early to mid-twentieth century is sparse. Probably most well-known is geographer Richard Harris's research on the emergence of working-class suburbs in Toronto between 1900 and 1950.[2] Harris found that, at the turn of the twentieth century, the lack of municipal regulations had made it possible for immigrant, working-class families to achieve their goals of owning a house and a plot of land by building their own houses, or self-building. Because the land at the fringe of the city did not receive municipal services, the cost of the land was within reach of less well-off households. With the Great Depression and resultant job losses, many working-class families moved back into the inner city where casual employment was more accessible. The extension of services and transit routes in the 1930s increased taxes, leading to tax debt for many remaining suburban working-class residents, and many lost their land as a result. Federal mortgage legislation and minimum building standards also discouraged suburban self-building during this time, and working-class suburbs declined. The severe housing shortages that emerged after the Second World War brought in a short second boom of working-class suburbanization by veterans who engaged in self-building like the immigrants before them. By the mid-1950s the corporate land development process, supported by municipal and federal government urban renewal initiatives, swept away the last of the unplanned working-class suburbs.

While Harris's research focused on Toronto, he argues that there were similar developments "around almost every city in North America."[3] These communities were heterogeneous. Economist Richard Andrews's examination of large American cities identified different kinds of settlements at the edges of the city, including high-cost modern developments, moderate-income neighbourhoods, low-income areas, trailer and cabin communities, and shack towns.[4] Andrews found that low-income areas included households attempting to better their lot through self-building, like those householders documented in Harris's work.[5] Historian Jill Wade's research on marginal housing in Vancouver describes squatters in shacks along Burrard Inlet, False Creek, and the Fraser River that the city razed repeatedly from the 1890s to the 1950s, with the shack residents rebuilding again and again.[6]

Africville is probably the most well-known fringe community in Canada. Settled in the mid-1700s, it began as a poor rural community of about fifty people, primarily escaped slaves from the Thirteen Colonies.[7] Later, more people moved there, drawn by jobs in industries and in the related facilities that developed nearby. Africville residents owned their properties and they paid taxes, although they did not receive city services. From the mid-nineteenth century onward, the city of Halifax moved its least desirable facilities to the Africville area, including a landfill located there in 1958. While Africville was regarded as a "slum" by city councillors and many urban residents, it was, like other fringe communities documented by Wade, a place where residents forged social and cultural ties.[8] For the residents of Africville, the settlement represented an opportunity to escape from the racism and discrimination of the white urban population and provided a place where families could afford to own land. The dissolution of Africville was part of urban renewal initiatives popular in the 1950s and 1960s. Despite Africville residents' desire to stay in the community and improve their living conditions, the Halifax City Council voted in 1962 to disperse the community and move residents to other locations, many of them to public housing. By 1969 all of the houses and the community church had been razed and the 400 residents moved away. In that year, former residents formed the Africville Action Committee to press for remuneration and to devise strategies to preserve community memory. In 2010, as a result of their attempts, the Halifax mayor apologized for the destruction of Africville and promised that the city would build a replica of the church on the former site of the community.

Much lesser-known are the numerous Métis communities that formed near urban settlements on the prairies and in British Columbia as settlement and urbanization increased in the twentieth century. Sociologist Arthur Davis, who came to Saskatchewan to work at the Centre for Community Studies in 1958 and later became a professor at the University of Calgary, studied the economies and housing conditions of Métis and First Nations households between 1960 and 1962 in three urban centres, Prince Albert, North Battleford, and Meadow Lake.[9] He found Métis and First Nations households in all areas of these cities, but noted that the largest clusters were at the city fringes. Called "The Fox Den" in Prince Albert, "Glenora" in North Battleford, and "Moccasin Flats" and "Little Chicago" in Meadow Lake, these clusters on the urban fringes, states Davis, had "a predominantly shantytown appearance. Water was usually drawn from wells or delivered by city trucks," and these settlements had the "lowest level-of-living scores and the highest indices of overcrowding."[10] Social scientist Jean H. Lagassé's study, commissioned by the Manitoba government in 1956, also found Métis communities at the edges of cities in Manitoba.[11] His 1959 study reported that, of the 253 Métis communities he had studied, twenty-six of them, comprising 2,535 people, were on the fringes of urban settlements, and ranged in population from eight to 434 people.[12] He noted, "each White community has labelled its fringe settlement with a colorful appellation. Melonville, Rooster Town, Smokey Hollow, Bannock Town, Fort Tuyau (French for Pipe), Fort Rouge, Little Chicago, Mud Flats, Shaughenessy Heights, Pumpville, Tintown, and La Coulee are some of the terms used in referring to Metis fringe settlements."[13] Although Lagassé mentioned Rooster Town on the edge of Winnipeg, he did not give its population figure or include it on his list of twenty-six Métis communities, suggesting that more Métis settlements may have existed than those he identified. Included in his list of the main differences between the Métis communities and the nearby urban settlements were: "different standards of housing," "different standards of law enforcement," and "disparity of community services and public utilities."[14] Lagassé also identified racial prejudice in many urban settlements. He wrote that some urban areas were unwilling to provide housing for the Métis, some passed legislation preventing the creation of fringe communities, and that "the white population in several communities consistently refuse[d] to provide the Metis with adequate schooling by voting against money bylaws and sending their own children to be educated elsewhere."[15]

To date, the history and characteristics of only one Métis settlement, similar to Rooster Town, have been documented, that of Island Cache at the edge of Prince George, British Columbia.[16] Using interviews and a range of data sources, researchers Mike Evans and Lisa Krebs found that the settlement began in the 1920s when a small group occupied an island, just outside of Prince George, separated from the city by a flood channel.[17] By 1970 approximately 40 percent of residents were Métis, 20 percent were non-Status Indians, and most of the remaining families were immigrants.[18] These families—just fewer than 600 people—were intensely poor.[19] In language reminiscent of that used by Halifax city officials and social services to describe Africville, the Island Cache community was viewed as a slum and as hazardous to the health of residents both of Prince George and Island Cache.[20] After the community was annexed by Prince George in 1970, the city began a series of initiatives to move the community's residents.[21] However, many inhabitants valued their residency, and they organized to protest, to explore mechanisms for flood prevention, and to advocate for streets, social services, and facility improvements.[22] In 1972, nevertheless, after severe flooding, Prince George began to condemn and demolish Island Cache houses so that by 1981, the community was completely gone.[23]

Despite the number of Métis settlements that existed at the edges of urban areas on the prairies and in British Columbia, and despite the fact that some lasted for many decades, their presence has been almost completely ignored in prairie urban geography and history, as well as in Métis history. In the chapters that follow, we attempt to remedy this oversight. We present a history of Rooster Town, a Métis community that existed in southwest Winnipeg on the fringes of urban development for at least six decades. This account was reconstructed by compiling information from a wide variety of administrative databases, newspaper records, and Métis genealogies and scrip records. The administrative archive included the 1901 to 1921 manuscript censuses, Manitoba and Henderson's Directories for the city of Winnipeg, municipal and federal voter lists, the First World War military records, Manitoba Vital Statistics, and City of Winnipeg assessment rolls, collectors' rolls, and building permits. City Council minutes and documents from several city departments provided the municipal policy context. Aerial photos

from various years as well as Winnipeg fire insurance maps helped locate
dwelling units where addresses were not clear and suggested the size of buildings. Sources for Métis genealogies included Gail Morin's 2001 *Métis Families: A Genealogical Compendium* and Douglas Sprague and R.P. Frye's *The
Genealogy of the First Metis Nation*.[24] Stories, obituaries, and the descriptions
of some houses were collected from the *Manitoba Free Press*, which became
the *Winnipeg Free Press* in 1931, and the *Winnipeg Tribune*. A few interviews
with individuals living nearby who remembered Rooster Town, and some
with people who had lived there as children, helped round out the Rooster
Town story. The result was a database with a great amount of information
that almost certainly still misses some people, events, and features, but al-
lows us to sketch out the general characteristics of kin relationships, family
and household formations, socio-economic conditions, movements, housing arrangements and strategies, and employment patterns. The database
and the genealogy of Rooster Town residents are available on the University
of Manitoba Archives and Special Collections website.[25]

We are conscious of the risks of cultural appropriation when non-Indigenous people research and write aspects of Indigenous history. Our decision
to pursue the story of Rooster Town rests on several factors. The first was
timing—if there was any chance of interviewing individuals who had lived
in Rooster Town, the research needed to be conducted very soon. Second, a
project of this nature is extremely expensive and time-consuming. In consequence, it needed to be undertaken by a mature scholar with resources to
hire researchers and pay for documents, and also one in a secure position and
not under constant pressure to quickly write up research for publication. Dr.
Peters's Canada Research Chair award provided financial resources and the
time to conduct the research. Third, although we do use the available socio-
economic and demographic data to describe community characteristics, we
are not attempting to provide an account from Métis perspectives on the experience of Rooster Town. We believe that this work is appropriately left to
Indigenous scholars. This research reconstructs the history of a Métis community from settler records, using evidence from these records to challenge
colonial interpretations. The story of Rooster Town illuminates an aspect of
settler colonialism that has been inadequately documented in the available
scholarship and needs to be told.

Our continued use of the name "Rooster Town" also requires some com-
mentary. There is no clear explanation of how this name came into being,

but it has a very long history, with the first media reference to the community by this name occurring in 1909, and this was what the community was called when it was dissolved in the late 1950s.[26] The name is similar to other fanciful names for Métis fringe communities in other locations, described above. Recently there has been some discussion about using the term "Pakan Town" to reflect what Métis themselves called the community. "Pakan" is the Michif word for hazelnut, and likely refers to the hazelnuts Métis harvested from the surrounding bush.[27] We have decided to continue to use the term "Rooster Town" for three reasons. First, that is the term employed in the settler records on which this account draws. Second, it is familiar both to Métis people and to settlers. Finally, the city understood "Rooster Town" to refer to the entire community that we describe, while it is not clear that "Pakan Town" did—for example the houses west of Cambridge Street were sometimes referred to as "Tintown."[28]

We contacted the Manitoba Métis Federation (MMF) when we began the research and, through Lawrie Barkwell, kept the MMF informed about our project. Lawrie Barkwell and Evelyn Peters attended several MMF annual meetings to relay the progress of the research. In October 2016, we gave three public lectures on the topic, inviting all of the former Rooster Town residents we had spoken to.

A project of this nature involves the work of many people. We wish, first of all, to express our gratitude to the individuals who took time to tell us what they remembered of Rooster Town—some grew up in Rooster Town, and some lived nearby and had friendships with or memories of Rooster Town residents. In alphabetical order, they are: Mike Bell, Dwili Burns, Susan Campbell, Bill Cardinal, Candace Hogue, Donald Laramee, Sharon Munro, Warren Mills, Doreen Pound, Frank and Darrell Sais, Loretta Smith, Audrey Walder, Dan Wiwchar, and Sonya Wright. Frank Sais, in particular, had many interesting stories about living in Rooster Town, and we are grateful that his son, Darrell, introduced him to us. Lawrie Barkwell and the staff of the Louis Riel Institute at the MMF were unfailingly supportive. Dr. Evelyn Peters also wishes to acknowledge the skills, dedication, and enthusiasm that research associates Matt Stock and Adrian Werner brought to their tasks. Without Adrian's superior map-making skills and dogged attention to detail, and Matt's excellent abilities in genealogical and manuscript census research, this book would not have been possible. Matt and Adrian appreciate the opportunity Dr. Peters gave them to participate in this project. Other researchers who brought their strong abilities to the undertaking included Nicola Schaefer, Campbell McClean, Paul Schram, and Sarah Hibbert, and we thank them for their work. As well, we owe thanks to the people at the University of Manitoba Press, whose skills, enthusiasm, and positive suggestions made the publication process much easier.

Research of this nature always involves individuals working at various libraries and archives. The staff at the City of Winnipeg Archives and Research Centre suggested possible record sources and cheerfully brought out box after box of heavy records, many of which contained only one or two documents we needed. Thank you, especially, to Sarah Ramsden and Martin Comeau for their assistance. The staff at the Manitoba Legislative Library similarly provided access to many reels of microfiche, and the personnel at the Archives of Manitoba helped us access ownership patterns for river lots in St. Boniface West, so that we could understand patterns of Métis dispossession in the area. We are also obliged to Louis-Philippe Bujold from the Winnipeg Public Library, Virginia Platt from the Harrow Street United Church, and Dr. Niigaanwewidam Sinclair from the Department of Native Studies at University of Manitoba, who organized lectures so that we were able to disseminate our research. The project could not have been undertaken without the Social Sciences and Humanities Research Council support of the Canada Research Chairs Program. Finally, we express our appreciation for our colleagues and the many friends and family members who listened to us talk about the project as it unfolded. Dr. Peters remembers with pleasure the afternoon she spent in Hamilton discussing the project with David Burley, who had previously published some research on Rooster Town. His interest and support was very much valued.

The reader's entry point into Rooster Town is Chapter 1, which provides a context for our research in the broader academic literature. It argues that the existing work focuses on the impacts of settler colonialism on urban First Nations, but largely ignores the unique processes and situations of Métis people in cities. Past research also fails to fully acknowledge Indigenous resistance to and subversion of colonial power in urban spaces. Then the chapter turns to the history of the Manitoba Métis. It includes discussion of the dispossession of Métis from their lands in Fort Rouge—the city ward where Rooster Town eventually formed—to help us understand the probable motivation for the establishment of the settlement. The formation and consolidation of the community are the subjects of Chapter 2. By way of context, the chapter describes Winnipeg's economic and housing background and the economic situation and location of other Métis individuals and households in the city. The focus then turns to Rooster Town in 1901, 1906, and 1911. While the First Nations experience of emerging settler cities was largely characterized by removal and confinement, the continuing presence of Métis living and working in Winnipeg and the establishment of Rooster Town demonstrate some of the differences of the Métis experience. Chapter 3 describes the settlement between 1916 and 1921. The situation in Winnipeg included the twin pressures of depression and inflation, chronic housing shortages, and a spotty social support network. Challenging common stereotypes of Métis inability to adapt to urban conditions, the economic and housing strategies of Métis families in Rooster Town showed resilience and innovation in the face of poverty and discrimination. Chapter 4 focuses on 1931 to 1946, years when Rooster Town grew rapidly. The absence of census data for these years means that there is much less information available about socio-economic conditions, family composition, and tenure and housing characteristics. There were very few First Nations people living in Canadian cities during these years, and Rooster Town's growth demonstrates that Métis experiences of settler colonialism differed from those of First Nations inhabitants. Chapter 5 describes the decade between 1951 and 1961, which brought about the end of Rooster Town. Newspaper depictions show how stereotypes of Métis inability to adapt to modern urban life shaped what reporters saw, despite plentiful evidence of decades-long participation of Métis residents in wage employment and in efforts to gain secure housing. The conclusion supports the arguments that urban Métis experiences of settler colonialism were different from those of First Nations and that the establishment of Rooster Town destabilizes colonial narratives that depict Indigenous cultures as out of place in modern urban society.

CHAPTER ONE

Settler Colonialism and the Dispossession of the Manitoba Métis

THE STORY OF ROOSTER TOWN CONTRIBUTES to and broadens our understanding of settler cities and Indigenous people, especially in the Canadian context. Since 2004, when geographer Nicholas Blomley[1] noted the lack of scholarship on the city as a postcolonial space, a number of studies have begun to explore how settler cities have defined perceptions of Indigenous[2] peoples' places and identities in relation to urban areas. The existing work, while claiming to explore settler colonialism and Indigenous people, really focuses on First Nations people and primarily on those who were registered under the Indian Act.[3] Métis people were defined differently in legislation and administrative practices and, while some of their experiences were similar to those of First Nations people, some were radically different. Research on specific Métis experiences of urbanization helps to complicate the theoretical frameworks of settler colonialism. In addition, current criticism's emphasis on settler colonial attitudes, mechanisms, and processes hides the way Indigenous people in Canadian cities have challenged dominant practices—sometimes through explicit resistance, and sometimes simply by attempting to make better futures for themselves, their families, and their communities. Although there were and continue to be power differentials between Indigenous people and the dominant society, our work illustrates that past social and spatial patterns were also co-constructed, and Indigenous

1

people and communities were able to assert some agency over their lives in relation to the city.

Studies on settler colonialism and urban Indigenous peoples point out that the contrast between civilization and savagery are central to colonial definitions of Indigenous identities in Canada, the United States, Australia, and New Zealand.[4] A substantial amount of research on white settler attitudes has documented their views of Indigenous peoples as primitive, backward, and often savage.[5] For settlers, authentic Indigenous cultures were associated with the past, or with places distant from the metropolitan centres of society. Literary critic Anne McClintock adds that Indigenous cultures are seen as existing in "anachronistic space—prehistoric, atavistic and irrational, inherently out of place in the historical time of modernity."[6]

Cities have been key in translating these stereotypes into spatial arrangements, which, in turn, have cemented ideas about the incompatibility of Indigenous people and urban space.[7] In the process of transforming Indigenous lands into private property and replacing Indigenous residents with settlers, municipal, provincial, and federal governments made self-invested decisions about where Indigenous people belonged in relation to the developing city. As historian Penelope Edmonds noted, the "tension between ideas about savagery and civilization played itself out spatially in the townscape."[8] Because colonial landscapes varied between different urban settings, the focus here will be on Canadian urban areas. The existing literature suggests that, as Canadian cities grew, they employed three main strategies to address the issue of Indigenous people in cities: containment, expulsion, and erasure. These strategies primarily focused on First Nations people.

Containment was probably the most widely used mechanism to keep people of First Nations away from urban spaces. In Canada, parcels of land known as reserves were set aside for their communities through legislation and administration. With respect to British Columbia, historical geographer Cole Harris wrote that "the allocation of reserves . . . defined two primal spaces, one for Native people and the other for virtually everyone else" based on a "racialized juxtaposition of civilization and savagery."[9] Reserves were purposefully located away from urban areas, in part, to give First Nations people access to hunting and gathering and to reduce subsistence costs to the Department of Indian Affairs. In some areas, however, reserves were located within urban boundaries, or cities grew to surround them. Attitudes toward these reserves reinforced ideas about Indigeneity and urban space. For instance, land use on reserves was seen as unproductive and wasteful.[10] Historian Jordan Stanger-Ross summarizes attitudes toward reserves in Vancouver in the 1930s as follows: "Aboriginal people failed to possess property in a fashion that settlers were bound to respect."[11] Beyond the idea of wastefulness, reserves were also viewed as a threat to urban development. The view of the city as a living organism emerged in city planning theory in the 1920s; because municipal officials could not control the reserves' use or appearance, these areas were presumed to pose a danger to the other healthy parts of the city.[12] Reserves were seen as places of disease, bedlam, and disorder.[13] As a result, reserve lands were surrendered, reserves were moved, and reserve boundaries were redrafted to shift them away from the borders of planned or expanding towns.[14] In 1911, claiming to be acting in Indigenous peoples' interests, the Government of Canada passed legislation to move reserves when growing towns came close because "such a situation, apart altogether from its accompanying irritation, is fraught with great danger to the Indians."[15]

As reserves were segregated from developing townscapes, First Nations people were increasingly expelled through a variety of strategies. Edmonds notes that "the settler-colonial order, which made them landless, also constructed Indigenous people as inconvenient, anomalous, and vagrant."[16] Her examination of Indigenous people in the settler city of Victoria documented some of the strategies through which they were expelled from town sites. These included their forceful removal by the police, receiving municipal orders to leave at night or obtain a pass from their employers if they were needed, and eviction through nuisance and sanitation laws.[17] Indigenous scholar Jaimy Miller documented the illegal surrender of the Pappaschase reserve in downtown Edmonton in 1881—through the dispersal of the band to other reserves and Métis settlements—to make way for settlers.[18] Historian Coll Thrush found that as Seattle developed between 1880 and 1920, nearby Indian settlements were gradually removed and resettled.[19] On the Canadian prairies, Indian Affairs officials at various levels enforced a pass system introduced after 1885, which required First Nations individuals to obtain permission from the Indian agent before they could leave their reserves. The purpose of this system was, in part, to keep First Nations people away from emerging prairie towns.[20]

According to Blomley, the erasure of Indigenous people in urban spaces happened in two ways.[21] First was the ideological removal of Indigenous people from cities so that they were viewed as being out of place there—this was achieved by colonial narratives of empty lands, expectations that Indigenous people would die out, and when they did not, assumptions about their inevitable assimilation. Conceptual removal also occurred through settlers' urban histories that do not acknowledge prior Indigenous occupation.[22] The second element of erasure involved the material or physical removal of Indigenous people and the emplacement of a settler society.

However, the existing research on Canadian settler colonialism and Indigenous urbanity has focused almost entirely on First Nations people. And while there is a significant body of work that has explored the emergence of the Métis as a "new peoples" on the Canadian Prairies,[23] there is virtually no research that, like our Rooster Town study, explores the links between the establishment of cities and Métis spaces and identities.[24]

Colonial legislation and administrative practices affected differently the experiences of First Nations and Métis people in relation to the city. First, the Métis were not acknowledged to have collective Indigenous rights to land like First Nations, whose rights were dealt with through treaties. Instead, Métis land rights were (supposedly) extinguished on an individual basis through a variety of mechanisms depending on time and place. Second, in connection with the non-recognition of Métis Indigenous rights to land, no reserves were established for Métis people. Historian Renisa Mawani has shown that in British Columbia the right of Métis people to live with their relatives on reserves was questioned.[25] Reserves, with their unique administration by band councils and the federal government—including the Crown's distinct process required to alienate reserve land, were important spatial anchors for the construction of First Nations identities. Métis people did not have reserves. Their legal status was also different from that of First Nations. First Nations people were wards of the federal government, governed by the provisions of the Indian Act, with distinct voting rights, limited access to alcohol, and eligibility for particular federal government services. As a result, First Nations were more "fully knowable to authorities."[26] Métis people were considered to be the responsibility of the provinces, and not differentiated from non-Indigenous people by legislation or legal status.[27] Conflating prairie Métis history in the city with that of First Nations homogenizes colonial processes of Indigenous displacement from, and dispossession of, urban spaces. In examining early- to mid-twentieth-century Métis histories in the prairie city of Winnipeg, we are following Cole Harris's suggestion that researchers should examine the functioning of colonial practices and discourses in specific times and places.[28]

A second shortcoming of current literature on urban Indigenous people and settler colonialism is the focus on the processes and mechanisms of colonial displacement and dispossession. This body of work largely ignores evidence of the ways Indigenous people challenged colonial processes, either through explicit resistance or as a by-product of their attempts to make a living and a future for themselves, their families, and their communities. In her work on the colonization of Colombo, Ceylon, urban planner Nihal Perera points out that "Indigenization," which she defines as the ways Indigenous people "adapt daily practices within their own perception of colonial society," and colonization are "simultaneously complicit and conflictual: these processes are neither separate nor direct opposites."[29] While the ways Indigenous peoples resisted colonial processes and institutions is not an emphasis in the existing research, there is nevertheless some evidence of Indigenous agency and resistance to colonizers' attempts to remove them from urban spaces and dispossess them of their lands. Edmonds documents the negotiation of the Coast Salish First Nations in Victoria to retain the reserves that the municipal officials wished to dissolve—they resisted police arrests, and they continued to use the city for a myriad of needs.[30] Mawani documents two court cases in Vancouver where mixed-race households went to court to protest their dispossession from their residences, in which they had lived for three decades, in Stanley Park.[31]

More recently, a number of authors have addressed the ways Indigenous people make physical and conceptual space for themselves in urban areas, despite continued perceptions of the incompatibility of urban and Indigenous space. Geographers Kathi Wilson and Evelyn Peters describe how First Nations people living in Toronto create sites of cultural safety where they can practise ceremonies by identifying compatible conditions in urban Indigenous organizations, nature, and in their own homes.[32] Native Studies scholar David Newhouse addresses the co-construction of urban Indigenous identities, arguing that, in the city, Indigenous identity is being examined on both an individual and collective basis, and it is being deliberately reconstructed by Indigenous institutions, educators, communities, and band leaders to be as reflective of Indigenous interests as possible.[33] For Newhouse, the existence of urban Indigenous organizations is key in this process, as they reflect the "presence of urban Aboriginal people who are interested in creating and participating in healthy vibrant communities and who see the city as an opportunity and renewal rather than a place of cultural erosion."[34] Evelyn Peters and Carol Lafond document the ways in which First Nations people in Saskatoon, Saskatchewan, make for themselves cultural spaces of belonging in Indigenous organizations through the celebration of Indigenous cultural events, through friendship networks, by practising their cultures in the privacy of their homes, and within the micro-spaces of shared Indigenous languages.[35] In these ways, intentionally or simply by following taken-for-granted ways of living and interacting, they have subverted dominant perceptions about where Indigenous people and cultures belong. Geographer Jay Johnson found that urban powwow celebrations allowed urban American Indians to create temporarily bounded Indigenous spaces in the city.[36] Geographers Ryan Walker and Sarem Nejad present a number of international case studies of contemporary Indigenous people's resistance to planning and ideas about their appropriate place in the city, as they create communities, institutions, cultural meeting places, and infrastructure in cities of commonwealth countries.[37]

The community of Rooster Town similarly challenges colonial expectations about the incompatibility of urban lifeways and Métis people and culture. Some aspects of the colonial construction of Métis cultures and identities parallel the discourses that consign First Nations people to history and to nature. The "Canadian Party," early Ontario settlers in what would later be called Winnipeg, viewed the interaction of incomers and Métis communities as a clash between civilized and primitive cultures. They predicted that Métis people would inevitably be swept away because they would be unable to adapt to settler society.[38] Marcel Giraud, the French ethnologist who, in the 1940s, wrote a monumental social history of the Métis of western Canada, argued that the dispersal of the Métis was caused by their own inferiority. In his opinion, the Métis were "incapable of understanding any plan of life other than nomadism."[39] Even as late as the 1950s, Lagassé noted in his research that the requests to the Manitoba government for the removal of Métis communities were often predicated on the premise that they should be located in isolated, natural areas, close to fish and wild game, where they would be "free to live as children of nature."[40] Conversely, in their attempts to access urban employment and provide educational opportunities for their descendants, Rooster Town householders moved from the rural parishes of the Red River Settlement to the edge of the growing city of Winnipeg. At the same time, they created a separate community, preferring not to integrate into the lower-cost housing areas in north Winnipeg. High levels of discrimination could be used to explain their settlement on the fringes, but, as we show in the next chapter, and as researchers Walter and Jean Boek found in the 1950s, a number of Métis people were also dispersed in various parts of the city.[41] Discrimination is therefore not a sufficient explanation for the emergence of a largely Métis community on the fringes of Winnipeg's southwest. Neither does poverty rationalize the occurrence. Although Winnipeg experienced chronic housing shortages, there was low-cost housing north of the railway tracks in Winnipeg's North End. Instead, it is likely that the Métis of Winnipeg used this settlement pattern to create a place of cultural safety within the hostile, white-settler, urban environment.

Red River Métis History and Métis Dispossession

Descended from European fur traders and First Nations women, the Métis created a unique cultural, economic, and political identity in western Canada. Historian John Foster argues that Métis communities did not emerge from the blending of European and First Nations cultures, but occurred as a result of changes in the fur trade. These changes allowed the Métis to take on key roles in providing pemmican to the fur-trading companies, organize complex buffalo hunting societies, and eventually challenge the Hudson's Bay Company's (HBC) control of the fur trade.[42] To provide a context for understanding the emergence of Rooster Town and its social, economic, and cultural characteristics, we sketch a brief history of the key Métis settlement of Red River, the Métis objectives in negotiating the 1870 Manitoba Act, and their subsequent dispossession from their land.

From the settler perspective, the watershed of Hudson's Bay, known as Rupert's Land, had been deeded by colonial Britain to the HBC in 1670, and for decades the company controlled the lucrative fur trade in the area. With the creation of the North West Company (NWC), a fur-trading business headquartered in Montreal in 1779, the HBC faced increasing competition. Métis worked as employees of both the NWC and the HBC. Others were free traders, or buffalo hunters supplying pemmican to the fur trade. Competition and conflict led to the amalgamation of the HBC and the NWC in 1821, and as a result fewer Métis were needed in the fur trade.

In 1811, the HBC had granted Scottish philanthropist Lord Selkirk 116,000 square miles centred in what is now southeastern Manitoba to settle Scottish crofters displaced from their holdings.[43] A condition of the grant to

Selkirk had been that one-tenth of the area should be set aside for HBC employees.[44] The HBC encouraged Métis laid off at the merger to move to this area known as the Red River Colony, fearing that their settlement in other parts of the country would interfere with trade.[45] The HBC also needed the Métis supply of pemmican produced from the buffalo hunt.[46] Consequently, according to early Winnipeg residents Alexander Begg and Walter Nursey, after 1824 "the Métis would exceed in numbers the members of other ethnic groups in the colony."[47] When the HBC bought out Lord Selkirk's estate in 1835, the census of the Red River Settlement showed that Métis with Indigenous and French or French Canadian ancestry, classified as "French Métis," occupied lots to the south and west of the forks of the Assiniboine and Red Rivers, and represented 55 percent of the population. The rest of the Métis, whose fathers came primarily from the British Isles, were classified as "English Métis" and they made up 30 percent of the population and settled north of the forks, toward Lake Winnipeg. The Selkirk settlers at Kildonan made up 8 percent of the population, and Saulteaux and Swampy Cree at St. Peter's represented 7 percent of the colony's population.[48] Figure 1.1 shows the extent of the parishes of the Red River Settlement.

Most of the Métis in the settlement participated in an economy based on farming, buffalo hunting, and freighting, for themselves or the HBC. According to Foster, "late in the spring, most Metis left their river lots, along with small plots planted with root vegetables and barley, harnessed oxen or horses to their two-wheeled Red River carts, and set out south to the rendezvous point near Pembina, on the border with United States territory. Only the elderly, the sick and the crippled remained at home."[49] The pemmican and dried meat cured after a successful summer buffalo hunt were sold to the HBC and provided a steady source of income for the Red River Métis. Upon the return to the settlement in fall, the Métis harvested what grew on their small plots of cultivated land and collected hay for the winter.[50]

In 1869, the HBC sold Rupert's Land to Canada, without consultation with the Red River residents. The sale created suspicion and anger, especially among Métis residents. According to Stanley, there was no systematic land tenure in the settlement, and few Métis had obtained titles to their lots from the HBC, which administered land assignment and record keeping.[51] In addition, a small group of traders from eastern Canada, who had established themselves close to Fort Garry to serve the Métis and the Selkirk colonists, agitated for the annexation of the settlement to Canada and predicted that the Métis

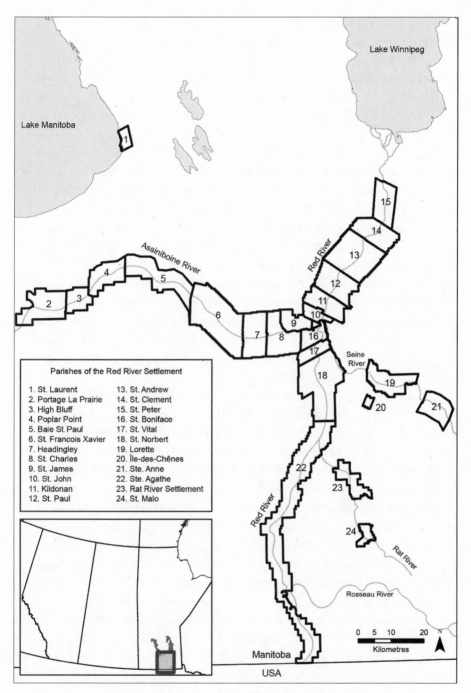

Parishes of the Red River Settlement

1. St. Laurent
2. Portage La Prairie
3. High Bluff
4. Poplar Point
5. Baie St. Paul
6. St. Francois Xavier
7. Headingley
8. St. Charles
9. St. James
10. St. John
11. Kildonan
12. St. Paul
13. St. Andrew
14. St. Clement
15. St. Peter
16. St. Boniface
17. St. Vital
18. St. Norbert
19. Lorette
20. Île-des-Chênes
21. Ste. Anne
22. Ste. Agathe
23. Rat River Settlement
24. St. Malo

FIGURE 1.1. Red River Settlement Parishes, Manitoba, 1870.

would be swept away with subsequent immigration.[52] Therefore, the news of Canada's acquisition of Rupert's Land made the Métis extremely apprehensive.

In 1869, a group of French Métis led by Louis Riel stopped the survey party, commissioned by the Canadian government to lay out agricultural lots along the Red River, and warned the incoming Lieutenant-Governor William McDougall not to enter the newly named North-West Territories without their consent.[53] Twenty representatives from English parishes and twenty from French parishes formed a provisional government, and Riel, initially as secretary and then as president, negotiated the terms of Manitoba's entry into Canada, including the recognition of Métis interests in land. In consequence, the Manitoba Act of 1870 set aside 1.4 million acres of land to be distributed among the children of Métis heads of families residing in the province. It also guaranteed all "old settlers" "peaceable possession" of the lots they occupied in the Red River Settlement prior to 15 July 1870.[54] On 12 May 1870, the Manitoba Act was passed by the Dominion Parliament, creating the new province of Manitoba. The 1870 census of the Red River Settlement shows the significance of the Métis population at the birth of Manitoba. Of 11,963 people, only 1,563, were Europeans, and about the same number, 1,553, were Cree and Saulteaux. The rest of the population, 9,848 people, were French and English Métis.[55]

The intent of the conditions negotiated by Riel's provisional government was to provide a viable land base so that Métis culture and economy could thrive despite the expected influx of non-Métis settlers. However, the government's implementation of the provisions for Métis lands in the Manitoba Act were, as the 1996 Royal Commission on Aboriginal Peoples (RCAP) concluded, characterized by irregularities, procrastination, and maladministration. RCAP describes a variety of factors affecting Métis lands in Manitoba after 1870. The confirmation of existing holdings and the distribution of new lands were commonly delayed for decades and, in the meantime, much of the choice land was distributed to non-Métis settlers. New land grants were dispersed, rather than concentrated near existing Métis settlements, frustrating Métis attempts to maintain their communities. In 1876, the federal government introduced scrip, a certificate allowing the bearer to claim 160 acres of land or obtain $160 as a process for extinguishing Métis land title. But facing long delays, many Métis sold their scrip at less than its value to a variety of land agents, speculators, and even government officials.[56]

As a result of institutionalized neglect, many Métis were dispossessed of their lands, and many others left Manitoba, migrating west and south.

Scholars have debated whether the dispossession of Métis lands represented federal and provincial government abdication of their fiduciary responsibilities, or whether Métis decisions to sell their land or scrip represented rational decisions to adapt to economic opportunities away from Manitoba and elsewhere.[57] In its investigation into the issue, the 1996 RCAP concluded that "the promises made to the Métis population in the creation of the new province in 1870 were violated or ignored (or their implementation delayed) on a massive scale." The commissioners argued that the problems with implementing Métis land claims drove the Métis to seek out other economic opportunities.[58] In 2013, the Supreme Court of Canada ruled that "the federal Crown failed to act with diligence in implementing the land grant provision set out in s. 3.1 of the Manitoba Act, in accordance with the honour of the Crown."[59]

While many Métis moved away from the Red River Settlement, many also stayed. Some Métis were economically successful in the changing Red River society, others were not.[60] The collapse of the buffalo herds, and therefore the trade in buffalo robes, meant that most Métis could no longer rely on the hunt to provide for their subsistence needs, and the development of the railway and steamboats meant that overland freighting jobs declined. However, transitioning to agriculture also created challenges. In addition to the delays in obtaining title to their lands, Métis faced a number of other hurdles. Historian Gerhard Ens wrote that the early 1870s were characterized by consecutive years of very poor farming conditions. Better crops returned in 1876 but, by then, many Métis who had taken out seed grain mortgages were unable to repay them and had to sell their river lots. The development of the railways in the late 1870s and 1880s made commercial grain farming possible, but successful farming required economies of scale not feasible on the small subdivided river lots. In addition, few Métis had the operating capital to buy modern equipment required for efficient farming practices.[61] Gradually, most small farmers, including the Métis, had been forced out of business by larger farm operations.[62] Similarly, Métis fishing families were gradually forced out by competition from large companies.[63]

Giraud revisited some of the Manitoba Métis settlements in the 1930s and described their economic conditions; he ignored structural explanations of Métis dispossession and concluded that their poverty resulted from an

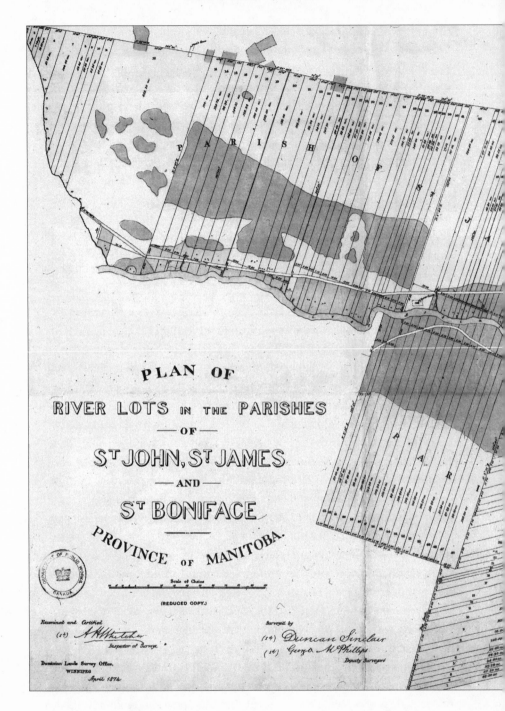

PLAN OF

RIVER LOTS IN THE PARISHES

— OF —

ST JOHN, ST JAMES

— AND —

ST BONIFACE

PROVINCE OF MANITOBA.

Scale of Chains

(REDUCED COPY.)

Examined and Certified

(sd) A.H.Whitcher
Inspector of Surveys.

Dominion Lands Survey Office,
WINNIPEG
April 1874

Surveyed by

(sd) Duncan Sinclair
(sd) George M Phillips
Deputy Surveyors

FIGURE 1.2. Plan of river lots in the parishes of St. John, St. James, and St. Boniface, 1874.

inability to adapt to the modern economy.[64] However, he did usefully depict the economic situation, which was similar to that of many families who eventually ended up in Rooster Town. Giraud wrote that these Métis were "dwelling beside families of strangers who have taken possession of a land where the Métis were once the only masters."[65] Large numbers lived at St. Vital, Fort Garry, St. Norbert, and at Ste. Anne-des-Chênes, often living on plots of land "two or three acres in extent."[66] He added, "many of these Métis are day laborers without any specialized occupation, who gain employment by chance whenever the occasion offers itself: some of them work in the fields as farm laborers, others in the towns, a few in the construction workshops of the CNR [Canadian National Railways]. Yet others, too, lacking in any kind of technical training to find an opening easily, or incapable of rearing their children with the produce of the land which they exploit are reduced to entering themselves on the relief rolls."[67] As Ens noted, "Metis leaders hoped that the Red River Settlement could remain a Metis homeland. This required political cooperation, the maintenance of the Metis land base, and a rapid adaptation to an agricultural economy."[68] Due to numerous obstacles, some discussed above, none of these conditions was fulfilled after 1870.

The growth of what would eventually be known as "Winnipeg" contributed to Métis dispossession. By 1869, a small settlement, focused on supplying the needs of the Red River population, had grown up around the HBC's store at Upper Fort Garry near the junction of the Red and Assiniboine Rivers. At that time, there were about a dozen business establishments scattered around the fort, but the population of the village was estimated at less than 100 people.[69]

With Manitoba's entry into Confederation, the Canadian government committed itself to the promotion of colonization and railway construction, and settlers began to pour into Winnipeg to take up homesteads in the new province. Winnipeg's population grew to 215 in 1871, 1,467 in 1872, and 3,700 by 1874.[70] When Winnipeg was incorporated in 1873, residents were contained within the area north and west of the junction of the Assiniboine and Red Rivers, now the Forks area near downtown Winnipeg.[71] By 1881, Winnipeg's population was 7,985 people, more than double what it had been in 1874.[72] After substantial lobbying from Winnipeg's City Council and Board of Trade, in 1881 the Canadian Pacific Railway (CPR) announced that the transcontinental railway would run through the city, making it the distribution point for the growing agricultural economy of the western prairies.

Expectations that the coming of the railway would increase land values for both commercial and residential sites created the real estate boom of 1881–82.[73] For a sixteen-month period, lot prices in Winnipeg and other prairie cities doubled and redoubled as speculators flooded in. The local property assessment of $4 million in 1880 doubled in 1881 and reached $30 million in 1882, as a result of the upsurge in valuations that characterized the boom. The boom collapsed in the spring of 1882 but not before its optimism led to sizeable extensions of the city's boundaries. In 1882, the city of Winnipeg expanded to incorporate a large area south of the Assiniboine River and west of the Red River, and speculators rushed to buy lands newly incorporated into the city.[74] The area that became the neighbourhood of Fort Rouge can be seen in Figure 1.2, where it is part of the Parish of St. Boniface.[75]

Few detailed histories of Fort Rouge and its neighbourhoods have been written. Before its incorporation into the city of Winnipeg, the area was known as St. Boniface West. Beginning in about 1835, the Hudson's Bay Company divided the area into river lots for fur trade employees released from service after the amalgamation of the North West and Hudson's Bay Companies. River lots extended two miles back from the river, with river frontage providing access to water, a necessary resource and the main avenue of transportation for the Red River Settlement. While the few existing explorations of the development of Fort Rouge development acknowledge the first long lot surveys, they do not identify this analysis as a part of Métis history and they also do not explore the mechanisms through which the Métis lost ownership of this land.

Local Manitoba historian Randolph (Randy) Rostecki's detailed exploration of the history of the ownership of what became Crescentwood, the area west of Armstrong's Point, untangles the complexity of early Winnipeg's ownership patterns, including sales by Métis (not identified as such) to Europeans.[76] His purpose, though, is to describe planning and urban residential development of the area, and he does not detail the relative socio-economic positions of buyers and sellers or the forces which prevented Métis people from capitalizing on their land titles. Another local historian, Joyce Solonecki, briefly mentions the early fort at the junction of the Red and Assiniboine Rivers that gave the area its name, but, in an understanding of the issue that was likely representative of the 1970s period in which she wrote, she notes only that "there was little settlement in the area, apart from the Metis squatters, who came and went at various times."[77] It is important to acknowledge that Fort Rouge was originally a largely Métis place, and to critically explore the processes through which it was changed from a Métis space to a predominantly European settlement. When the narrative shifts seamlessly from the rural Métis settlement of the past to the urban Euro-Canadian city, it obscures the unique processes of Métis dispossession and reinforces assumptions about the incompatibility of Indigenous cultures and urban space.

Before its incorporation, Fort Rouge was divided into river lots, and was occupied almost entirely by Métis people. In 1870, 312 residents lived in the area, and almost 99 percent of them were Métis.[78] There was only one three-person non-Métis family, and the other non-Métis men were married to Métis women. One individual listed as "Indian" seemed to be a boarder of a Métis family. Figure 1.2 shows Métis long lots in Fort Rouge (then called St. Boniface West) as they were laid out in 1874, along with cultivated areas and types of vegetation.

Ens has argued that the Winnipeg boom of 1881–82 made nearby river lots prime real estate and that "commonly the Metis used the cash stake acquired by these lot sales to re-establish themselves on land better suited to commercial farming."[79] Along with political scientist Thomas Flanagan, Ens proposes that between 1880 and 1882 "prices for land close to Winnipeg and to completed or projected railway lines skyrocketed. . . . Taking advantage of these prices, many Metis sold their river lots to re-establish themselves in the North-West Territories or in other parts of Manitoba."[80] A closer analysis suggests that this was not actually the case. While by 1881 almost all of the Métis land in Fort Rouge had been sold to speculators and most of the Métis householders had moved, Flanagan and Ens appear to take at face value the amounts recorded in Winnipeg's property assessments. However, there was no legal requirement to report the details of land transactions at that time, and further examination suggests that, especially during the boom years, purchases were defaulted and recorded prices did not represent what sellers actually received. Very few mortgages were listed as discharged, and the chain of buyers and sellers was frequently disrupted—suggesting defaults. A careful look at individual properties shows that most of the Métis in Fort Rouge sold their land at low prices (see Appendix A). Also, the subsequent socio-economic conditions of the few families that apparently received higher prices suggest that they did not actually collect the amounts listed in the existing property records.

Of all the Fort Rouge Métis families, the Berards' records are the most complete and, out of all the neighbourhood farmers, Jean Baptiste Berard received the highest price for his lot.[81] Therefore, the experiences of the extended Berard family demonstrate the kinds of challenges the Métis faced and similarly raise questions about estimated returns to the Métis on their river lot sales. The Berards' story also contradicts the views of the time—contending that the Métis were unable to cope with the modern urban economy—and it suggests that more structural explanations are necessary. Jean Baptiste Berard and his kin had for a long time farmed in the area annexed to the city of Winnipeg in 1882. His European father Louis was a carpenter for the HBC from 1831 to 1834 and in 1835 was listed on lot 31 in West St. Boniface.[82] Louis married Catherine Hughes, a Métis woman, and they had at least ten children.[83] In 1875, lot 31, which encompassed 149 acres, was patented to Louis's oldest son, Jean Baptiste. Jean Baptiste also wed a Métis wife, Helene Lavallee, and they had at least four sons and four daughters.[84] The 1876–79 Manitoba Directories list Jean Baptiste, his brother Francois, and Jean Baptiste's son Pierre as farmers in St. Boniface West. The property abstracts for lot 31 in the Winnipeg Property Registry Office show that in 1878 and 1879 Jean Baptiste sold two parcels of his land for $170 and $230 respectively.[85] In 1881, at the beginning of the Fort Rouge real estate boom, Jean Baptiste sold another parcel of land for $8,000 and later that year another parcel for $6,500. In 1883, Jean Baptiste made two more sales, one for $1,000 and one for $2,000. According to the assessment rolls for 1883, the Berards retained only about thirty acres of the original lot 31. At a time when an ordinary labourer in Winnipeg's building trade was reported to earn $1.75 a day, the recorded sales amounts for Baptiste Berard's property represented an astonishing fifty-three years of labourer's wages.[86]

The probability that the Berards did not receive the amounts recorded in the property abstracts is borne out by the family members' subsequent economic strategies. The 1891 census still lists Baptiste Berard as a farmer in the area and the ten-member Berard family occupying a small, two-room house.[87] The small size of the remaining land could not support Jean Baptiste's extended family. It included two grown sons, Alexandre Maxime and Pierre, and their families, and two of Jean Baptiste's daughters, Josephte and Silvia, married to Aime McDougall and Paul Blondin, respectively, and their families. The Manitoba Directories show that Jean Baptiste's brother Francois and his family had moved to Corydon Street in Winnipeg by 1884 and that Francois worked as a carpenter. The Jean Baptiste Berard family attempted to diversify their income base. All of the Berard men were periodically occupied as carpenters, training that had probably been passed down by their father Louis. In early 1883, the Manitoba Directories and the city of Winnipeg assessment rolls show that the Berards built a hotel on their land near Pembina Road. The 1883 city of Winnipeg assessment rolls valued the hotel and land at $8,500.[88] While the Berards clearly received some income from their property, which they used to build the hotel, the amount would have been much less than $8,500, for several reasons. First, that amount included thirty acres of land which the city at that time was evaluating at boom prices. Second, the Berards were carpenters, so the value of the hotel reflected labour as well as materials. In the mid-1800s, Pembina Road had become the main overland trading route with Fort Pembina, just across the U.S. border, and more importantly St. Paul, Minnesota. The Osborne Bridge, completed in 1883, connected the more developed northern Winnipeg to Fort Rouge, and the Berards likely hoped that this would improve access to the southern area and provide demand for accommodation on the Pembina trade route. Jean Baptise's son Pierre and son-in-law Aime McDougall are variously listed in the Manitoba and Henderson's Directories and the city of Winnipeg assessment rolls as proprietors of the Fort Rouge Hotel from 1883 to 1886.[89]

While Winnipeg's assessment of property values declined precipitously after the end of the boom, these amounts still remained relatively high. In 1884, Jean Baptiste paid $67.12 in taxes and Pierre, listed as a hotelkeeper that year, paid $100.68.[90] Taking into account the seasonal nature of most work in Canada, and especially of unskilled labour at the time, a labourer working six-day weeks for eight months would earn about $336.[91] This suggests that Pierre Berard could have paid back in property taxes about one-third of what he earned in wages. In fact, in 1885 the *Manitoba Free Press* reported that Jean Baptiste, Alexandre Maxime, and Pierre Bernard had challenged Winnipeg's assessment of their land and properties, including the hotel.[92] The case was decided in favour of the city regarding the land values, but the assessments of their residences and the hotel were slightly reduced. The appeal, which suggests that the Berards were having difficulty making ends meet, further suggests that the family did not receive the full amount listed in the property abstracts for their earlier sold properties. The Fort Rouge Hotel is listed in the Henderson's Directories for the last time in 1886, suggesting that, given the lack of development in Fort Rouge as well as high taxes, it did not remain profitable.

The Berards stayed on lot 31 for several more years, with Aime McDougall supplementing their income by farming on River Street (now Wellington Crescent), likely on what was formerly his grandfather Duncan's farm at the corner of the Red and Assiniboine Rivers. The Berard men may also have occasionally worked as carpenters in the city of Winnipeg. Despite the decline associated with the end of the boom, Winnipeg grew steadily and there must have been a demand for their labour.[93] By 1890, however, the city's assessment rolls show that Berards no longer owned part of lot 31; instead, it was owned by the Real Estate Loan Company. It seems likely that the Berards were not able to sell their remaining land at this time (no sale is listed in the property abstracts), and, given the lack of demand for land in Fort Rouge and the high taxes, they stopped paying taxes and the city transferred the land to the real estate company to sell. The above discussed records support our assertion that the Berards most likely did not receive the full amounts for their sold properties.[94] After 1891, the Henderson's Directories show that, unable to make a living off their land, Jean Baptiste, now widowed and in his sixties, his son Pierre, and son-in-law Aime did not leave Winnipeg. Instead, they moved to various neighbourhoods within it, including Wellington Crescent, Armstrong's Point, and the North End. With their carpenter skills in demand in the urban economy, they joined Francois Berard's family in the city's labour market in order to support their large households.

Prior to the autumn of 1881 there was very little settlement in Fort Rouge.[95] As properties within the 1873 city boundaries were snapped up in the 1881–82 real estate boom, speculators began to eye the forests and grassland south of the Assiniboine River. Large areas of Fort Rouge were surveyed and subdivided into lots, and plans were filed early in 1882. Speculators promoted the area as a place of luxury residential development, and spring sales of Fort Rouge property were brisk.[96] However, the boom collapsed in mid-April 1882 and the demand for Winnipeg properties, including Fort Rouge, fell precipitously. The bust ended dreams of the rapid development of Fort Rouge, and it would be decades before there was substantial population growth in the area. Social historian Alan Artibise offers a number of reasons for the relatively late development of Fort Rouge.[97] Lack of access was an important factor early on. The Osborne Street Bridge was only built in 1883, the Maryland Street Bridge in 1894, and a public Main Street Bridge in 1897. There was relatively little commercial or industrial development in the area and, as a result, residents of Fort Rouge travelled long distances to their place of employment. Finally, developers conceived of the Fort Rouge location as residentially desirable and marketed generously sized lots, building restrictions, and wide boulevards so only more affluent city residents could move into the area.[98] The 1913 recession, the First World War and the financial crisis following it, and the Great Depression of the 1930s held back residential and industrial development in Fort Rouge. In the 1920s and 1930s, the city seized large numbers of lots for tax arrears, and these sat empty until the decades of the 1940s and 1950s.[99] It was on these lots that the community that would subsequently be known as "Rooster Town" was established. In fact, much of the Rooster Town neighbourhood grew at the westernmost end of what was formerly Jean Baptiste Berard's long lot.

───────────

The growing literature on settler colonialism has documented some of the processes, attitudes, and practices that contained, expelled, and erased Indigenous peoples from urban spaces. However, that work has emphasized the experiences of First Nations people, registered under the Indian Act, to the exclusion of the Métis. That criticism has also paid relatively little attention to the way Indigenous people have challenged colonial mechanisms.

Métis cultures, communities, and identities emerged from a particular social and economic history of Red River. For some Métis families, their dispossession led to migration from the rural parishes to the southwest corner of Winnipeg and settlement in a community that would subsequently be known as Rooster Town. Such a settlement pattern allowed Métis to access Winnipeg's economy, and it challenged prevailing attitudes that saw Indigenous people, in general, and Métis people, specifically, as unable to cope with urban economies and cultures. Rooster Town residents were participating in a pattern replicated across the prairies and in British Columbia, where Métis people settled at the fringes of largely non-Métis urban settlements. This habitation was quite different from that of First Nations people, especially First Nations registered under the Indian Act. The following chapters turn to the formation and history of Rooster Town.

CHAPTER TWO

The Establishment
and Consolidation of
Rooster Town, 1901–1911

ON A COLD WINTER DAY IN 1901, nineteen-year-old Marie Julienne Henry married twenty-four-year-old Pierre Hogue in the small Manitoba town
of St. Boniface.[1] This was before St. Boniface, St. Norbert, and St. Charles
communities became a part of Winnipeg. After the wedding, the young
couple moved in with Pierre's widowed mother for a short period of time.[2]
Pierre's father, Amable, had died in 1892 and his mother had remarried and
been widowed again. Despite their poverty, Julienne and Pierre had found
enough money to have a wedding picture taken.[3] The 1901 census reported
that Pierre, the only wage earner in the household, was working as a farm labourer and earned $300 the previous year, about average for unskilled labour
at that time. Both Pierre and Julienne were listed as Roman Catholic. Neither could read nor write, both spoke French, and Pierre also spoke English.[4]

Julienne had been born in St. Norbert, the fifth of seven children, and
Pierre was born in St. Charles, one of ten children.[5] There is no record that
either the Henry or Hogue ancestors received title to land in their respective
parishes or towns.[6] As a result, they would have worked as seasonal farm
labourers. In 1901, Julienne's large family moved to what would subsequently be called Rooster Town and so did two of Pierre's married sisters, Marie
Adele, wife of German harness maker William Wendt, and Julia, wife of Métis
labourer Charles Logan.[7] Julienne and Pierre joined these families either
later in 1901 or early in 1902.[8] By 1906, according to the census, the couple

had two sons, two-year-old James and four-year-old Mab (likely named after Pierre's father, Amable). They lived on, what the census taker estimated to be, Mulvey Avenue, although streets had not yet been laid out in the area.[9] At the time, Pierre worked as a labourer. By 1911, Julienne and Pierre's name had been anglicized in many of the records, appearing as Julia and Peter, with "Hogue" being changed to "Hogg." The 1911 Winnipeg assessment rolls valued the house the Hoggs rented at $100; it was likely a small, self-built one- or two-room shanty, with no city services and an outside privy.[10]

Julia and Peter joined fifteen other Métis families who moved into southwest Winnipeg, onto land that had reverted to the city because of tax arrears. In 1901, these were the outskirts of the slowly developing, built-up area of Winnipeg. The Hoggs and their group joined eight Métis households that had moved into the area earlier, and in 1901 the community was comprised of 115 people. They lived in small self-built houses in the grass and bush of southwest Fort Rouge, as the area was known then. At least half of these families and their descendants would subsequently live in Rooster Town for the rest of their lives, although the location of the community shifted gradually farther south and west over the years.

The continued presence of Métis in Winnipeg, and the formation and growth of Rooster Town demonstrate a response to settler colonialism that differs from that of First Nations. A close examination of socio-economic and demographic characteristics of urban Métis people at the time also suggests that, challenging settler expectations of an inadaptability to urban circumstances, Métis used the urban environment to try and make a better life for themselves and their families.

Winnipeg, 1901–1911

Improved accessibility provided by the railway, and the Dominion government's ambitious program of colonization, resulted in a steady stream of land-seeking immigrants to Manitoba and the prairies. The Canadian prairie population grew from 419,512 in 1901 to 1,328,121 in 1911.[11] Although, in the first decade of the twentieth century, Winnipeg was affected by a few periods of economic decline associated with the changing national and world economy, as the main service centre for the burgeoning prairies, the city grew in population and wealth. Many immigrants stayed in Winnipeg to take advantage of expanding employment in industry, retail, and construction.

Manufacturing jobs grew from 3,155 in 1901 to 77,705 in 1911, and in those years Winnipeg's population alone grew from 7,985 to 136,035.[12] For impoverished Métis families struggling to survive by farming on small plots of land or working as agricultural labour, the city of Winnipeg must have presented a positive economic alternative.

That is not to say that simply moving to Winnipeg brought economic success or comfort. Also, finding employment did not always guarantee economic security. Thousands of families and individuals were malnourished, lived in overcrowded conditions without proper sanitation, and women and children worked in order to make ends meet. As documented by Artibise, a variety of private charities, individuals, the Trades and Labour Council, and various municipal agencies reported on income distribution inequity in the city and called for better health and building bylaws, municipal housing, fair wages, public works, and other measures.[13] The city's relief committee, formed in 1874, focused on individuals in desperate straits and could assist only relatively few. According to Artibise, Winnipeg's commercial elite was obsessed with the need for growth and discouraged investment in any measure that did not promote immediate economic returns.[14] After 1908, the private and municipal relief efforts were combined in the Associated Charities. This agglomeration coordinated the aid programs of various member organizations, established a wood yard for a work test, and distributed food and fuel (funded by the municipality) to the needy.[15] Government benefits were limited, though, with the assumption being that private individuals and organizations were responsible for the provision of social programs and material goods.

While the rate of housing construction rivalled or exceeded that of other North American cities throughout the decade, the high rate of population growth meant that Winnipeg experienced a chronic housing shortage.[16] Virtually every year between 1901 and 1911, the *Manitoba Free Press* published a major exposé on overcrowding and unsanitary housing conditions, primarily focusing on the area north of the CPR tracks. A lengthy May 1909 article, for example, asserted that "overcrowding is confined to a limited area of the city and almost altogether to those people who have come from certain European countries" in the district adjacent to the CPR tracks.[17] In contrast to other perspectives, which identified cultural preferences as the root cause of these conditions, this article recognized poverty. In a curious twist of logic, the writer was optimistic that the system of notices by health inspectors and the levying of fines would soon solve the

problem. Rooster Town does not feature in newspaper expressions of concern about poverty and inadequate housing during this period. Two possible reasons come to mind. First is Rooster Town's low population. The
1909 report identifies 20,000 individuals affected by overcrowding in all
of Winnipeg's North End—the 1911 Rooster Town population was only
183 people. The second reason has to do with location. Rooster Town, at
the edge of Fort Rouge, was spread out in the bush and prairie and did
not presumably pose the threat of disease as did the centrally located and
crowded residences north of the tracks. Instead, when Rooster Town came
into the media lens, it was for reasons having to do with its identity as the
exotic and violent "other."

Other Métis in Winnipeg, 1901

In 1901, not all the Winnipeg Métis lived on the fringes of the city. A substantial number also lived in the area north of the Assiniboine River—the most
developed part of the city. Métis and other prairie histories document settler racism and intense prejudice against Métis in many communities. Métis
families often experienced extreme discrimination in urban areas, and some
prairie towns in particular refused to provide them with basic services.[18]
However, Métis people were not systematically removed from urban spaces
the way the First Nations people were, nor were they confined, through legislation and administrative practices, to non-urban communities. Many Métis
appear to have continued to live in prairie cities, often using the strategy of
denying their heritage in order to fit in.[19]

While only seventy-two Métis lived in Winnipeg according to the 1870
Manitoba census, by 1901, the census identified more than 300 Métis living north of the Assiniboine River as well as in the developed area of Fort
Rouge.[20] It is likely that these individuals, dispossessed of their lands or finding it impossible to survive economically by farming, had moved within the
city limits to take advantage of employment in the growing Winnipeg economy. It is highly probable that there were more Métis that did not identify
themselves, or were not identified by census takers, as Métis.

Out of those Métis identified in the 1901 census, most individuals (56.6
percent) lived in Métis households where both the head and the spouse were
Métis. Slightly more than a quarter (25.9 percent) lived in families where
the head was non-Métis but both wife and children were identified as Métis

(Table 2.1). There were also Métis individuals working in non-Métis households as domestics, servants, or dressmakers. Finally, several (6 percent) lived in institutions, including fifteen in children's homes, five in jail, and one in the Deaf and Dumb Institute. The average wage of a Métis head of household working in Winnipeg was $396.67, considerably more than the average of $228 earned by a Métis head of household in Rooster Town (see below). Over half (58.8 percent) of the 1901 Métis residents in Winnipeg proper worked as labourers and earned on average $322 in 1900, further underscoring the economic marginality of Rooster Town residents.[21]

TABLE 2.1. Living Situation of Métis in Winnipeg, 1901.

	POPULATION	PERCENTAGE
In Métis families (n=42)	197	56.6
Head is non-Métis, wife and children are Métis (n=25)	90	25.9
Domestic, servants, live-in dressmaker	40	11.5
In institutions	21	6.0

Source: MS Census 1901, Manitoba, District 12 (Winnipeg).

Figure 2.1 shows that Métis families were clustered rather than evenly distributed across Winnipeg's neighbourhoods. The triangles represent domestics living in non-Métis households. The largest cluster is near the railroad yards where eight Métis families (thirty-two people) lived near each other, if not, in all cases, neighbouring each other. This cluster included four families whose members descended from families formerly living in St. Boniface West—including Francois Gendron (Genthon), Edward Carrier, Jean Baptiste Berard's brother Francois Berard, and the family of Alfred Berard, Francois's son. Three other families (eighteen people), including Jean Baptiste Berard's son Peter Berard, lived behind Broadway Street houses between the Northern Pacific Railway and Main Street on what the census called "The Terraces." Another three families (sixteen people) lived at the end of Portage Avenue, near the edge of the built-up area of city. Several other households were scattered in the North End. The residential patterns of Métis families suggest that they tended to live in more marginal areas of town and that the locations of their dwellings were clustered, possibly as a result of choice or lower costs, or a combination of the

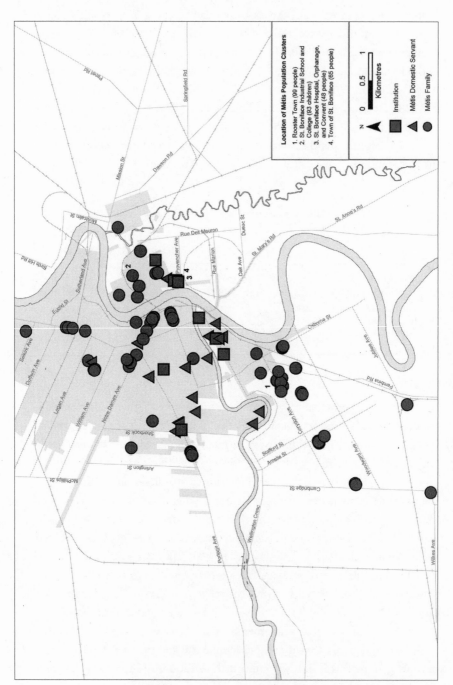

FIGURE 2.1. Living situation of Métis in Winnipeg, 1901.

two. The marginal, low-cost locations of these households support the argument that the Métis did not receive good prices for their land.

The presence of Métis individuals and households in Winnipeg also confirms that Métis were racialized differently in relation to the city than were the First Nations who were physically removed and conceptually erased from urban spaces. Clearly, Métis individuals and households were socio-economically marginalized, and many lived in poorer and more peripheral areas of the city. However, they were part of the city's workforce, and clearly some Métis from the parishes surrounding Red River, unable to lay claim to their land or unable to make a living from their river lots, joined Winnipeg's economy in order to make ends meet.

Rooster Town, 1901–1911

Rooster Town grew steadily during the first decade of the twentieth century, and the neighbourhood's characteristics indicate that Métis urbanization was an adaptive strategy, not a failure to cope with city life as settler attitudes suggest. A few Métis households had already moved to the fringes of the slowly developing suburb of Fort Rouge before 1901. Sometime around 1891, Scotch Métis James Septisen Omand moved his nine-children family from the Parish of St. Andrew's to a plot of land, about a block west of the more built-up area, which would subsequently become 669 Jessie Avenue.[22] By 1901, a small cluster of four houses sheltered members of the extended Omand family, including widowed daughter Charlotte Chipperfield.[23] In addition to the Omands, William Peppin, likely born in St. Boniface West, moved with his wife and three young children to Fleet Street outside of the developed area of Fort Rouge.[24] Nearby lived Isadore Fisher, his wife, and their two young children.[25] Aime McDougall, Jean Baptiste Berard's son-in-law, and his wife and three children rented land on River Avenue, just south of the Assiniboine River.[26]

In 1901, sixteen additional Métis households moved into southwest Fort Rouge.[27] Ten of the male heads of these households were originally from St. Norbert[28] and three others, Peter Hogg, James Starr, and William Smith, had married women from that parish. In other words, more than four-fifths (81.3 percent) of the families that moved into the area in 1901 had origins in the same parish. While there were some kin relationships between the sixteen households, most were not related. The number of households,

FIGURE 2.2. Map of Rooster Town, 1901.

1 Isadore and Adeline Fisher
2 Isadore and Marie Arcand
3 James Septisen and Jane Omand
4 Charlotte Chipperfield
5 Aime and Josephte McDougall
  John Baptiste and Rosalia Berard
6 Roger and Celine Henault
7 William and Virginia Peppin
  Marguerite Peppin
8 William and Victoria Curran
9 William and Marie Adele Wendt
10 Frances James and Sarah Omand
11 Alexander Septisen and Rachel Anne Omand

12 Alexander and Mary Minnie
13 Elice Minnie
14 Pierre and Elizabeth Comptois
  James White
15 John and Melanie Logan
  Charles and Julie Logan
16 Elice Marcellais
  Marie McDougall
17 James and Marie Louise Starr
18 John and Melanie Henry
19 Peter and Julia Hogg
20 William (Sr.) and Catherine Smith
21 Joseph and Rosalie Angelique Roy
22 Joseph and Nancy Poitras

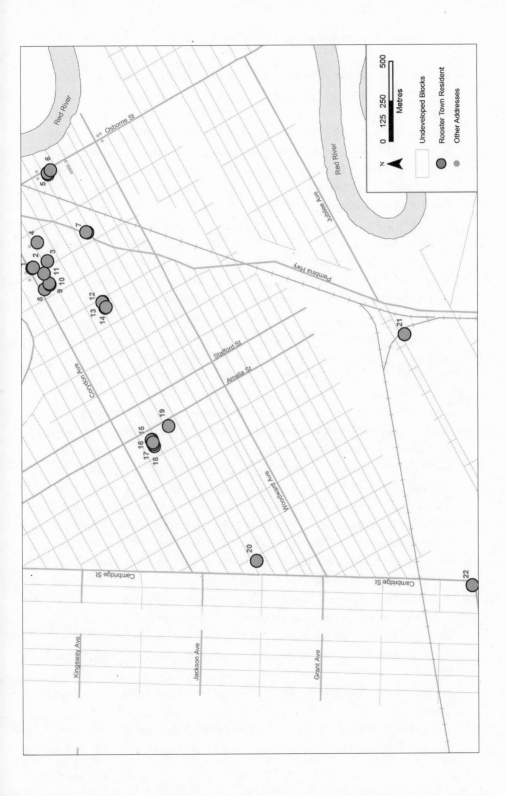

their relocation in the same year, and their origins strongly suggest that this was a coordinated move reflecting a preference to cohabit while pursuing city employment. This is further supported by the fact that six households, the Arcands, the Comptois, the Hoggs, the Smiths, the Wendts, and Elice Marcellais, had lived in other locations, either in Winnipeg or St. Boniface, just before moving to southwest Fort Rouge. Communication through social networks must have been at work in establishing the early nucleus of the Rooster Town community.

While there are no records that explicitly state the reasons for the choice of this location, the features of Fort Rouge lots as well as Métis people's history and their socio-economic characteristics at the time suggest some explanations. The 1881–82 speculative boom meant that many purchasers of lots in Fort Rouge found themselves owning land they had bought at inflated prices, with no prospect of immediate development and high property taxes. The prospect of renting land to Métis households, however minimal the rate, must have seemed like an attractive option for generating revenue. For the Métis, the lack of development in southwest Fort Rouge allowed households to engage in some subsistence farming to supplement their wage incomes. Unlike the rest of Winnipeg at that time, Fort Rouge was an area where Métis people had lived before. Many St. Norbert Métis, trading at HBC's Lower Fort Garry, would have travelled through this territory, so it may have appeared familiar. Finally, Winnipeg at the beginning of the twentieth century had an intense shortage of affordable housing. Métis households had a choice between finding scattered accommodation in various parts of the developed city, or building their own houses how they had in their particular parishes, organizing their settlement pattern in a way that allowed them to live near to other Métis people. It seems that the residents of what would become Rooster Town chose the latter. Rather than being incompatible with urbanity, Métis culture and community remained an important part of the city for these families.

There were very few other residents in Fort Rouge from 1901 to 1911, and most of them lived near the Assiniboine River, across from the earlier city boundary, or near the Red River, east of Pembina Road. As for the Métis in the area, one cluster of households, arriving in 1901, set up near the Omands, another cluster located further west, and others were strewn throughout the area (Figure 2.2).

The socio-economic characteristics of these Métis households suggest that a major objective of moving was related to the possibility of finding wage work in the growing Winnipeg economy. In most cases, neither heads of household nor their families had received the land promised to them by the Manitoba Act (Table 2.2). Some had ancestors who had been recognized as river lot occupants in 1870, but by then the land was patented to another person. In their 1998 study for the Department of Justice, Thomas Flanagan and Gerhard Ens found that thirty-four of 105 (32.4 percent) Métis families in their sample had no claims to river lots.[29] Flanagan and Ens misinterpreted the significance of this finding. They argued, on the basis of a few case studies, that these families were young and had been living with their parents at the time of the Manitoba Act and had purchased lots only later, or that they had already pursued opportunities and established residency outside of Manitoba. Our study, on the other hand, suggests Rooster Town Métis families whose ancestors were unable to establish a claim to a river lot were significantly impoverished and turned to urban wage economy to support themselves.

In 1900, most of the heads of Métis families who had moved to what would later become Rooster Town were working as general labourers, likely on a seasonal basis if they were farm labourers, and most had very low levels of income, even if they had worked for twelve months the previous year. A seasonal unskilled labourer at the time, working six-day weeks for eight months, would earn about $336, which was more than what most Rooster Town heads of household earned. According to the 1901 census, in Winnipeg's working-class North End area, individuals listed as labourers worked an average of nine months and earned on average $331 in 1900.[30] Rooster Town earnings were lower. Only three of the household heads moving into southwest Fort Rouge had made more than $300 in 1900, and the average individual income of household heads was $227.33. In some cases, the labour of adult children added to household income, but some families had young children and could not rely on the wages of sons and daughters. Life in the parishes was extremely difficult for these families. The varied ages of heads of household, which ranged from twenty-four to sixty-five (average 40.1 years), suggest a decision to move for economic reasons made by a wide social network, and not just the urbanization of a younger generation of households.

In Rooster Town, very few women were wage earners and women as heads of household fared very poorly. Elice Marcellais, widow of St. Norbert farmer Felix, who died in 1890, had moved with four young children to the village of St. Boniface by 1891.[31] In 1901, she was a washerwoman who lived in the bush near her daughter Marie, married to James Starr. Marie,

TABLE 2.2. Métis Families in Rooster Town in 1901.

HEAD	ORIGIN	LAND PATENT	OCCUPA- TION	MONTHS WORKED IN 1900	HEAD'S INCOME	HOUSEHOLD INCOME	SIZE OF HOUSEHOLD	AGE OF HEAD
Arriving Before 1901								
Charlotte Chipperfield	St. Andrew's	Yes	labourer	9	$350	$350	4	34
Isadore Fisher	St. Norbert	No	labourer	5	$150	$310	5	51
Aime McDougall	St. Boniface West	Yes	labourer				7	40
Francis Omand	St. Andrew's	Yes	labourer	8	$350	$350	2	24
James Omand	St. Andrew's	Yes	caretaker	12	$600	$1250	7	58
William Peppin	St. Boniface West	No	labourer	7	$300	29	6	29
Arriving in 1901								
Arcand, Isadore	St. Norbert	No	labourer	12	$200	$200	9	48
Comptois, Pierre	St. Norbert	No	labourer	7	$200	$200	4	58
Curran, William	St. Charles		shipper	12	$480	$480	5	28
Roger Henault	St. Anne	No	labourer	5	$150	$300	9	58
Henry, John	St. Norbert	No	labourer	12	$200	$320	10	49
Hogg, Peter	St. Charles	No	labourer	12	$300	$300	2	24
Logan, John	St. Norbert	Yes	labourer	5	$100	$100	2	69
Logan, Charles	St. Norbert	No	labourer	5	$100	$100	2	26
Marcellais, Elice	St. Norbert	No	washer woman	12	$100	$150	3	53
Minnie, Alexander	St. Norbert	No	labourer				3	25
Minnie, Elice	St. Norbert	No	none	0	0	$300	3	50
Poitras, Joseph	St. Norbert	No	farmer	12	$300	$575	6	65
Roy, Joseph	St. Norbert	Yes	section man	12	$480	$480	6	32
Smith, William	St. James	Yes	labourer	7	$300	$300	7	47
Starr, James	Reserve	Not Métis	labourer	12	$100	$150	2	31
Wendt, William	Germany		teamster	8	$400	$400	5	27

NOTE: BLANK CELLS MEANS THAT INFORMATION IS MISSING.

Sources: MS Census 1901, Manitoba, District 12 (Winnipeg), Subdistrict a-3 (Ward 1), Sprague and Frye, 1883.

who also worked as a washerwoman, earned $50 in 1900 to supplement her husband's very low earnings of $100.[32] Living with Elice was the widowed seventy-three-year-old Maria McDougall (née Irvine), who also worked as a washerwoman in 1900, earning only $50. While another neighbour, Elice Minnie, was listed as a head of the household, her twenty-year-old son Henry worked for twelve months as a labourer in 1900, and had earned $300.[33] Elice and the members of her household lived next to her brother Pierre Comptois's family. Living next door to relatives must have provided some security for women without living husbands.

The housing conditions of the Métis families at the fringes of Fort Rouge underscore their extreme economic marginality (see Table 2.3). Of the households for which information is available, a combination of census information and assessment roll data shows that most (eight out of nine households) owned their dwelling unit but leased their land. The details of arrangements with landowners are not available, but given the extreme poverty of these households, any rent would have had to be minimal. Only three households were able to purchase the land they lived on. However, even owning one's land could be precarious. In 1901, James Omand's recently widowed daughter Charlotte owned a three-room house and two lots on which the Chipperfield family lived. In 1903, the Chipperfield house and land was sold in a tax sale.[34] Charlotte was likely unable to earn enough to support herself and her small children, and the extended Omand family did not make enough to subsidize her and her offspring. As a result, she was unable to pay the taxes on her property and lost it.

The small houses that the Métis lived in must have been built by heads of household or moved there from another property. Most of the houses were small, with an average of two rooms per house. Five households lived in one-room houses, and the Logan dwelling was a two-room unit, which housed two families, John and his wife, and son Charles and his wife. Some indication of the size of the buildings can be obtained from the very few building permits available for this period. In 1902, Jean Baptiste Fountaine took out a building permit to build a wood frame cottage, one story, with a size of 14 x 20 feet, valued at $250 by the city.[35] This was somewhat higher than that of most Rooster Town dwellings, since the average assessed value was less than $200, and almost half of the houses were assessed at the extremely low rate of $50. Even William Smith's six-room house was assessed at only $100.[36] In 1905, Fred Savage, who had moved into the area, built a dwelling the city of Winnipeg called a "shanty."[37] It was a one-story wood shelter with dimensions of 14 x 14 feet, valued at $50. According to the building permit, the inhabitants would share the privy with the house at the front of the lot. Henry George Paquin, who also moved to Rooster Town by 1905, took out a building permit for a one-story, 16 x 18–foot wooden house with a shanty roof, without basement, sewer, or water, valued at $250. The permit indicates that the plan of a privy was provided with the application.[38]

TABLE 2.3. Characteristics of Métis Housing in Southwest Fort Rouge, 1901.

HEAD	TENURE	ROOMS IN HOUSE	VALUE OF HOUSE	LOTS	BARN	HORSES	OTHER
Arcand, Isadore	Tenant	4		1	1		
Charlotte Chipperfield	Owner	3		2	1		
Comptois, Pierre	Tenant	2	$50	2	0	0	0
Curran, William	Tenant	4	$200	6	0	0	0
Fisher, Isadore	Tenant		$50	2	0	0	0
Henault, Roger	Tenant	2	$100	4	0	0	0
Henry, John	Tenant	2	$50	3	1	2	2
Hogg, Peter	Tenant		$200	2	0	0	0
Logan, John	Tenant	1	$50	3	0	0	0
Marcellais, Elice	Tenant	1		2			
McDougall, Aime	Tenant	3	$100	2	1	6	1 cow, 6 sheep
Minnie, Alexander	Tenant		$50	2	0	0	0
Minnie, Elice		1		2			
Omand, Alexander	Tenant	2	$100	2	1	0	0
Omand, Frank	Tenant		$50	2			
Omand, James	Owner	2	$200	2	1		
Peppin, William	Tenant	4	$100	3	1	0	2
Poitras, Joseph	Tenant	2	$50	2	1	0	2
Roy, Joseph	Tenant	1	$50	6	1	2	1
Smith, William	Owner	6	$100	9	1	4	1
Starr, James	Tenant	1	$50	2	0	0	0
Wendt, William	Tenant	2	$100	2	0	0	0

NOTE: BLANK CELLS MEANS THAT INFORMATION IS MISSING.

Sources: MS Census 1906, Manitoba, Winnipeg District, Subdistrict 1-b; City of Winnipeg Assessment Rolls, 1906, Ward 1, City of Winnipeg Archives and Record Centre (CWARC).

Richard Harris's research on self-building in the Toronto suburbs in the 1901–1907 period found that only 5.5 percent of the dwellings built were assessed for less than $150.[39] According to Harris, values of less than $150 represented basic one-room shacks.[40] Harris quotes from economist James Mavor's autobiography where he writes that in Toronto "workmen bought ... small lots [for about $100], and for $40 or $50 they bought enough lumber to enable them to build houses by means of their own labour."[41] Very few Rooster Town households owned the land their houses stood on, and given their low incomes, it seems unlikely that many were able to purchase many building materials. The small amount of information available about building practices in subsequent years suggests that many Rooster Town householders might have purchased small structures from elsewhere, moved them, and then made the necessary modifications.

A random search through 1901 advertisements of houses for sale in Winnipeg provides some additional context for these values.[42] The lowest-priced dwelling advertised for sale in Fort Rouge was a five-room house near the CPR shops, listed at a value of $800. There is an even more striking contrast with 1902–1903 advertisements for buildings on the elite street of Wellington Crescent, indicating that large lots were only for houses costing over $10,000, that all houses on the Crescent must cost at least $6,000, and that no house in the entire area could cost less than $3,500.[43]

Although streets are shown on the map to provide a sense of location, none had been paved in this area in 1901. Most households were located in the forested area of Fort Rouge, which may account for the fact that almost none of these households were listed in the Henderson's Winnipeg Directories at the time. The small houses were probably hidden along paths in the bush. Although their listing in the city's assessment rolls indicates that they were known to municipal officials and to non-resident lot owners, Rooster Town inhabitants received no city services.

According to the 1901 census, households owned or rented, on average, 2.9 city lots, and only Isadore Arcand lived on one lot. The largest holdings were those of English Métis William Smith, who also had a stable, four horses, and one "head of cattle," likely a dairy cow. Of the nineteen households that information is available for, over half (52.6 percent) had barns, and five households, in addition to the Smiths, had some livestock. Métis families must have engaged in some subsistence gardening and farming to support their large families on low incomes, reproducing aspects of Métis life before urbanization.

By 1906, the Rooster Town community had grown. Of the twenty-two households listed in 1901, most (90.9 percent) remained until 1906. Between 1901 and 1906, Rooster Town lost four families, and two heads of household died (Table 2.4). At the same time, it gained fourteen families and two individuals. The two widows remarried: William Smith's widow Catherine married St. Norbert widower Henry Parisien, who had previously been working for the family; and widowed Charlotte Chipperfield (née Omand) married non-Métis plasterer Henry Griffiths (see Table B.1).[44] Three Rooster Town residents established their own families, and one non-Métis family, that of Henry Parker, moved into the community.[45]

TABLE 2.4. Changes between 1901 and 1906.

GONE FROM ROOSTER TOWN	
Deaths	2 individuals, 1 family
Not listed or moved	2 families
ADDED TO ROOSTER TOWN	
Without obvious kin links to Rooster Town	1 family
With kin links to Rooster Town	2 individuals 10 families
Married widow or formed with previous families or descendants	2 individuals, 3 families

Sources: MS Census 1901, Manitoba, District 12 (Winnipeg), Subdistrict a-3 (Ward 1); MS Census 1906, Manitoba, Winnipeg District, Subdistrict 1-b; 1901 to 1906 Henderson's Directories; City of Winnipeg, City Clerk's Department, Election Rolls, 1901–1906, City of Winnipeg Archives and Record Centre (CWARC). The City of Winnipeg voters lists complemented the city directories as a source for location of Rooster Town residents as well as tenancy information. Like the directories, citing every use of the resource would multiply references extensively. Instead we note in the text when voters lists were consulted for information.

The inclusion of Henry Parker and his family in the list of Rooster Town residents, and the fact that there were a few non-Métis households nearby, requires an explanation of how Rooster Town households were identified. We used several interlocking characteristics. One had to do with origins. Residents were primarily Métis in origin, and they were perceived as such by the general public, as shown by representations in the media and some official correspondence. The first newspaper reference to the community occurred in 1906 in relation to lobbying for the provincial election and demonstrates public perceptions of the inhabitants. Several members of the extended Morrissette family went to the police to report that Thomas Smith, attempting to generate support for his candidate, was using alcohol to canvass for votes.[46] The tactic of offering alcohol and the reporter's use of the words "the natives of Fort Rouge" indicated that this was a community that was known to Winnipeg citizens and that it was distinguished from other Fort Rouge residents by its Indigenous origins.

A second criterion reflected stability. Most Rooster Town inhabitants stayed in the community for many years while the non-Métis residents located near Métis households were almost always gone by the next census period. The non-Métis Parker family, however, lived on Cambridge Street for the entire life of Rooster Town. The location outside the built-up and serviced area of Fort Rouge and position near other Métis households in the community were other criteria. The lifestyle of the dwellers was also connected to this characteristic: residents of what would become Rooster Town mostly lived in basic housing without access to plumbing, electricity, or street transportation. Clearly this characteristic was not permanent: in 1907 James Omand's dwelling was connected to the city's sewage system.[47] However, our analysis continues to follow the Omand household because it was a part of the original settlement and because the dwelling's overall valuation was modest compared to that of nearby houses. The city of Winnipeg assessment rolls valued Rooster Town houses much lower than other dwellings, even when these other dwellings were found near Métis households, helping to confirm the marginal economic status of Métis households.

Finally, social interactions and family relationships suggest the strong ties that characterized the community. Families seemed to coordinate the decision to move to the area. The descendants of the non-Métis Parker family married into Métis families, and Métis residents' sons and daughters married within the community. The Smiths also employed other Métis. While newspapers articles primarily document problems, these reports also point to joint activities and greater social interaction. In 1912, for example, James Starr and Alexander Morrissette, not connected through kinship ties, were fined for stealing wood from the Tuxedo Park together.[48]

Most of Rooster Town's growth until 1906 was created by the addition of fourteen families. The substantial incoming number of households suggests that, by 1906, Rooster Town was known among Métis in the province and recognized as a settlement option for households and families who sought urbanization as an economic strategy for survival. Most of the new families were members of two extended family groups, the Berards (six households) and the

FIGURE 2.3. Map of Rooster Town, 1906.

1 Henry and Charlotte Griffiths
2 Thomas and Suzette Atkinson
3 Aime and Josephte McDougall
4 William and Marie Adele Wendt
5 James Septisen and Jane Omand
6 William and Victoria Curran
7 Alexander and Rachel Anne Omand
8 Frederick and Eleanor Gertrude Chassie
9 Peter and Sarah Berard
  Pierre and Harriet Berard
  Frank Berard
10 Frederick Joseph Berard
11 Henry George and Madeline Paquin
12 William and Virginia Peppin
13 Francois and Marguerite Berard
14 Florent and Mary Louise Berard
15 Alfred and Georgeline Berard
16 James and Marie Louise Victoria Starr
17 Frederick W.J. and Isabella Savage
18 William Morrissette
19 John James and Florence Mulvaney

20 John Baptiste and Mary Rose Fountaine
21 Isadore and Marie Lousie Fisher
22 Isadore and Marie Arcand
23 John and Melanie Logan
   Charles and Julie Logan
24 Isadore (Jr.) and Adeline Fisher
25 Elice Marcellais
26 Abraham and Mary Christine Morrissette
27 John and Melanie Henry
28 Alexander and Mary Minnie
   Elice Minnie
29 Pierre and Elizabeth Comptois
   Patrick and Mathilde Conway
30 Peter and Julia Hogg
31 Elie and Euphrosinna Morrissette
32 Henry and Catherine Parisien
   Alexander and Agnes Smith
33 Henry Edward Lafrance and Amelia Grace Parker
34 Joachim and Josephte Poitras
   Nancy Poitras

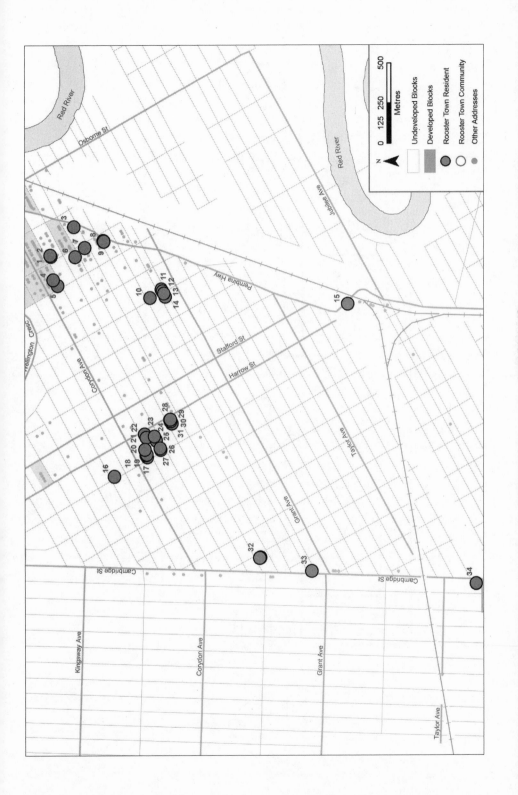

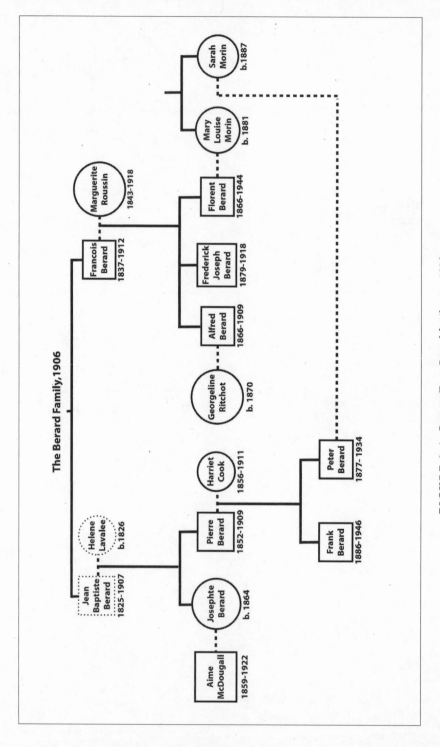

FIGURE 2.4. Rooster Town Berard family tree, 1906.

Note that John Baptiste Berard and Helene Lavalee, depicted with dashed lines, never lived in Rooster Town, but they are included to allow a depiction of relationships.

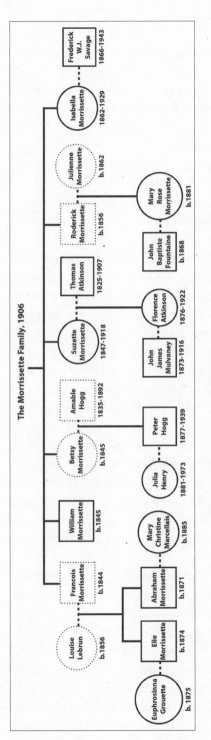

FIGURE 2.5. Rooster Town Morrissette family Tree, 1906.

Note that the individuals depicted with dashed lines did not live in Rooster Town, but are included so that relationships can be identified.

Morrisettes (eight households). As noted in the previous chapter, members of Jean Baptiste Berard's family, who had formerly owned a river lot and farmed in St. Boniface West, had left what remained of their lot by 1901 and joined the urban labour force. By 1906, six related Berard households had moved southwest and lived within a six-block radius of each other in Rooster Town. This put them in proximity to Aime McDougall and his wife Josephte Berard, who had lived in Fort Rouge since their 1882 marriage. The relationships between Berard families living in Rooster Town are shown in Figure 2.3. Having formerly lived north of the Assiniboine River, in Francois Berard's case for more than a decade, the Berards must have viewed this as a chance to live near each other and other Métis households.

The extended Morrissette family (eight households), descended from Métis Francois Morrissette and Philomene Favel, on the other hand, were White Horse Plain Métis who had origins in the parish of St. François Xavier and had moved to St. Eustache in the 1870s and 1880s.[49] According to St-Onge, this group was the most impoverished of the White Horse Plain Métis.[50] While Francois obtained a patent to a river lot in 1878, the lot could not provide for the large Morrissette family.[51] By 1906, the Morrissette siblings Francois, Suzette, Isabella and their families and five other related Morrissette families had moved to the outskirts of Fort Rouge and lived within eight blocks of each other (Figure 2.4).

The 1906 map shows the 1901 families who remained in the area, the location of the Berard and Morrissette families moving into the area by 1906, and the non-Métis family of Henry Parker that moved to Cambridge Street in 1902, establishing a farm near the Smith family operation (Figure 2.3). Some of the built-up area of Fort Rouge was approaching the extended Omand family households, but Rooster Town households, in general, were still located at the fringes.

By 1911, several newspaper articles demonstrate the nature of the public opinion in regards to the settlement. The first appearance of the name "Rooster Town" occurred in a 1909 piece in the *Manitoba Free Press*, which reported that John Fountaine (Jean Baptiste Fountaine) had been charged with running a raffle and had been allowed to go with a warning.[52] The reporter went on to give a description of the residents, their location, and the presumed disorderly nature of their community: "This settlement, which consists mainly of halfbreeds, lies on the south side of Fort Rouge and is frequently the scene of wild orgies, which have been the subject of reports to the police from time to time.

A raffle is one of the most fruitful sources of trouble and an effort will be made to break them up."[53] Likely reflecting attitudes of other Winnipeg residents, the reporter depicted Rooster Town as a strange, separate community populated by Métis people—he eroticized it (as the scene of wild orgies) and found it so disorderly that a simple raffle could create trouble requiring police intervention. An article about the 1911 domestic assault of Jessie Villebrun, by her husband, provides some additional information.[54] In describing the assault, the reporter reflected his understanding that most of the residents spoke French (likely Michif) and also mentioned the community's separation from the rest of the city: "The shack where the tragedy occurred is about a mile to the west of Portage crossing and is isolated in the bush. It is at the extreme west of the French settlement, the nearest neighbour being about a mile away." Figure 2.5 shows that, by 1911, most Rooster Town residents were living outside of the developed area of Fort Rouge. The built-up area had surrounded the extended Omand family, but other households were set in the bush and grasslands of Fort Rouge, with only a few non-Métis households nearby.

Rooster Town in 1911 contained thirty-nine households (forty-two families). Three households, belonging to Jane and James Omand, Frederick and Eleanor Chassie, and Frederick and Isabella Savage, were surrounded by the developed area of Fort Rouge, and are therefore differentiated from the rest of the settlement.[55] The rest of the community was spread south and west of the developed area, with very few non-Métis households among them.

TABLE 2.5. Changes between 1906 and 1911.

GONE FROM ROOSTER TOWN	
Deaths	2 individuals, 1 couple
Not listed or moved	3 families, 3 individuals
ADDED TO ROOSTER TOWN	
Without obvious kin links to Rooster Town	4 families
With kin links to Rooster Town	4 families
Married widow or formed with previous families or descendants	6 families

Sources: MS Census 1906, Manitoba, Winnipeg District; MS Census 1911, Manitoba, Winnipeg, Districts 3, 4, 5, 7; 1906 to 1911 City of Winnipeg Henderson's Directories; City of Winnipeg, City Clerk's Department, Election Rolls, 1906–1911, City of Winnipeg Archives and Record Centre (CWARC). Details about these changes are found in Appendix B.

FIGURE 2.6. Map of Rooster Town, 1911.

1   *Frederic W.J. and Isabella Savage*
2   *Frederick and Eleanor Gertrude Chassie*
3   *James Septisen and Jane Omand*
4   William and Victoria Curran
    David Butchart
5   Peter and Sarah Berard
6   James Albert and Florence Smith
7   Bruno and Ernestine Ritchot
8   Henry George and Madeline Paquin
    Angelique Rosalie Paquin
9   Alexander and Cecile Parisien
10 Florent and Mary Louise Berard
11 Alfred and Nathalie Cyr
12 John James and Florence Mulvaney
13 Alexander and Adelaide Morrissette
14 Francois and Marguerite Berard
    Frederick Joseph Berard
15 Edward and Jessie Villebrun
16 George and Hilda Grace Land

17 John William and Catherine Omand
18 John Baptiste and Mary Rose Fountaine
    John Baptiste and Marguerite St. Arnaud
19 Alexander Septisen and
    Rachel Anne Omand
20 Alexander and Mary Minnie
    James Charles and Marie Louise Parisien
    Elice Minnie
21 Aime and Josephte McDougall
    William McDougall
22 William Morrissette
23 Isadore and Adeline Fisher
    Isadore (Jr.) and Marie Louise Fisher
24 Suzette Atkinson
25 Nola and Susan Jane Souchereau
26 Charles and Julie Logan
27 Peter and Julia Hogg
28 James and Marie Louise Victoria Starr
29 John Henry and Melanie Henry

30 Isadore and Marie Arcand
31 Frank Berard
32 William and Virginia Peppin
33 Pierre and Elizabeth Comptois
34 Patrick and Mathilde Conway
35 William and Marie Smith
    Henry and Catherine Parisien
36 Alexander and Agnes Smith
37 William Exavier and Mary Jane Dunnick
38 Henry Edward Lafrance and
    Amelia Grace Parker
39 Joachim and Josephte Poitras
    Nancy Poitras

Note: Names in italics represent householders who no longer reside within the perimeters of Rooster Town but contiue to be a part of Rooster Town community.

Only four families and five individuals left the settlement between 1906 and 1911 (Table 2.5).[56] Fourteen new families moved in or formed by marrying Rooster Town members. Most of the new families (71.4 percent) had kin ties with existing Rooster Town inhabitants. Four other Métis families—without obvious kin relationships to other Rooster Town residents—settled outside the built-up area near other longer-term Rooster Town dwellers. The pattern and place of origin for the new families varied slightly from that of earlier years. More households were composed of previous Rooster Town residents, marrying each other or outsiders. While nine individuals came from St. Norbert and St. François Xavier, the main sources of previous incomers, five other parishes were included in the origins of those migrating in, suggesting that Rooster Town was becoming known to the broader Manitoba Métis population. In 1911, there were 183 people in Rooster Town and the average family size was 4.4 people.

TABLE 2.6. Characteristics of the 1911 Rooster Town Population.

GONE FROM ROOSTER TOWN	
Deaths	2 individuals, 1 couple
Not listed or moved	3 families, 3 individuals
ADDED TO ROOSTER TOWN	
Without obvious kin links to Rooster Town	4 families
With kin links to Rooster Town	4 families
Married widow or formed with previous families or descendants	6 families

Sources: MS Census 1911, Manitoba, Winnipeg, District 5; City of Winnipeg Assessment Rolls, 1911, Ward 1, City of Winnipeg Archives and Record Centre (CWARC).

Table 2.6 describes the characteristics of the Rooster Town population in 1911. The average age was 40.3, very similar to the 1901 age profile; older and younger families both lived in and moved into the settlement. Most household heads were labourers, and a few filled the transportation niche of teamster, managing a team of horses to deliver goods. Only a few held more skilled and high-paying positions such as switchman, tram driver, and carpenter. Wage rates had more than doubled, increasing from an average of

$283 for all 1901 heads of household to an average of $677 in 1911. According to Leacy's *Historical Statistics of Canada,* hourly wage rates for labourers in Winnipeg did increase from $0.20 in 1901 to $0.28 in 1911, a 40 percent increase, but Rooster Town residents' average wages increased by 139 percent.[57] Information for the few residents, for whom data are available for both 1901 and 1911 census years, suggests that families did find opportunities to increase their income with movement to the city. William Peppin, who in 1901 reported a $300 income, earned by working for seven months (twenty-eight weeks) the previous year, reported fifty weeks of work and earnings of $750 in the 1911 census. Similarly, Charles Logan, who reported five months (twenty weeks) of work and $100 earnings in 1901, reported fifty weeks of city street work and $600 earnings in 1911. In 1911, Alexander Omand disclosed working fifty-two weeks as a carpenter and earning $1,200 the previous year, in contrast to the $500 he reported working as a gardener in 1901. In contrast to the $300 William Smith Sr. earned in 1901, the Smith estate, engaged in the teamster business, by 1911 supported four households (the two Smith brothers now married, William Smith's widow now married to hired labourer Henry Parisien, and hired labourer William Dunnick, married to one of the Smith daughters). At the time, Smith Sr. had houses and stables valued at $1,000. The move to the outskirts of growing Winnipeg may have provided partial relief from the intensity of the poverty in the parishes.

Nevertheless, wage rates were available for fewer than half of household heads, and families like those of Isadore Fisher and his son continued to report extremely low incomes, of $270 and $300 respectively, on the 1911 census. In 1910, official estimates of basic food, fuel, lighting, and rent costs in Canadian cities came to $665, close to the average that Métis households reported earning that year.[58] Many Métis families were large, though, and reformers complained that the basic diets comprising official estimates led to malnutrition. In 1911, Winnipeg social reformer James S. Woodsworth quoted a New York study of "working-men's families" to suggest that "an income under $800 is not enough to permit the maintenance of a normal standard" for a family, but that an income of $900 "probably permits the maintenance of a normal standard at least so far as the physical man is concerned."[59] Woodsworth argued, however, that this amount did not support cultural needs or the ability to create a comfortable home. Rooster Town residents, for whom information was available in 1911, did appear to have bettered their economic situation, but they were still in the low-income portion of the city population.

Rooster Town's poverty is demonstrated by the dwelling values. Of the twenty house values available, over half (55 percent) were recorded at $200 or less; this was at a time when sheds were being gauged at $50 and garages were assigned a value of $150. In addition, according to Artibise, the average cost of a modern frame house with concrete foundation and plumbing in 1908 was $3,000, a price vastly greater than even the most "expensive" housing occupied by Rooster Town residents.[60] The description of the house where the Villebrun assault took place, as a two-room, board structure with a shed, surrounded by the bush, probably applied to others in the community. William Peppin's 1909 building permit, for example, was for a 14 x 18–foot one-story dwelling with the slanted roof the city called a "shanty roof," wherein there was no basement, no electricity, and no sewer or running water. The house also had no road access, and was assessed by the city as being worth $200.[61] In 1910, John Henry applied to construct a 13 x 12–foot building on sills and blocks, with a shanty roof and no amenities, valued at $150.[62] Frank Berard's permit the same year described an only slightly larger one-story wooden dwelling of 14 x 16 feet on sills, also with a shanty roof and no amenities. Still, attached to the building permit was a plan for a privy.[63]

Overall, by 1910, a few households had managed to find the means to improve their dwelling units. Long-time resident James Omand's house, valued at $200 around 1901, was now valued at $830, considerably more than the poorest Rooster Town resident dwelling, but nowhere near the cost, according to Artibise, of a modest, modern dwelling unit.[64] Part of the cost increase of the Omand house may have come about because the house now had plumbing. A 1907 *Manitoba Free Press* article noted that the city proposed to connect 669 Jessie Street to plumbing lines, but that the owner could not afford it. As a result, the city would charge an annual levy to cover the costs.[65] Building permits show that William Wendt raised the roof of the dwelling he had erected in 1905, finished the attic, and repaired the stable for two horses.[66] These repairs likely allowed him and his family to sell the house and move into the more developed area of Fort Rouge.

Richard Harris's study documents the strategy Toronto households employed of investing their own labour to increase the value of housing on the fringes.[67] While the continued low housing values of most Rooster Town residents suggest that they were not able to access the capital and use this approach, William Curran's case provides an exception and an illustration of the kinds of circumstances necessary for households to make this type of investment. In October of 1906, the *Winnipeg Tribune* reported that William Curran was suing the city of Winnipeg for $10,000 because his seven-year-old daughter, Grace, was injured when she fell into an uncovered sewer hole at the corner of John and Jessie Streets.[68] Grace fell twenty feet and had a number of serious injuries. The city offered Curran $1,000, but he refused to settle for an amount under $2,235 (the calculation necessary to reach this amount was not described in the newspaper). The final settlement was $1,500, and by 1907 Curran had built a one-and-one-half-story house with four rooms, valued at $600 in the assessment rolls.[69] It seems very likely that the lawsuit provided Curran with enough capital to build a house for himself and his family.

In contrast to settler assumptions that this poor community was disorderly and maladapted, the formation of Rooster Town around 1901 was almost certainly an adaptive strategy by Métis households to access the urban labour market, address rural poverty, and keep housing costs down. The steady growth of the community over the decade suggests that other Métis living in poverty in the rural parishes saw this as a potential way to build better lives for themselves and their families.

In her interviews with Métis women born between 1911 and 1924 and living in St. Eustache, historian Nicole St-Onge found that they viewed cities as threatening. She reported: "Certainly for the Fort Rouge [nickname for Métis neighbourhood in St. Eustache] families, linguistic and educational barriers along with an awareness of latent racism kept them away from urban areas where the possibility of better jobs existed. Several times in the interviews, Fort Rouge narrators expressed their fear and distrust at the idea of having abandoned or sold their plots and moved to Winnipeg or even a smaller city such as Portage La Prairie to look for better working conditions."[70] For Rooster Town residents, the possibility of living near other Métis neighbours, some of whom were kin, and others who were former neighbours, must have been a defence against racism from the majority of Winnipeg's growing white population. Rather than being incompatible with urban life, Métis culture and community helped to support it.

The lack of scholarly attention to the unique patterns of Métis urbanization and their experiences of settler colonialism led us to explore the details of the Rooster Town residents' labour force participation, kin and community relationships, and housing and tenure strategies. Métis households moved to the Rooster Town community as a group with social ties and as extended families. They built or moved, and then repaired their small houses, often squatting on city land, but purchasing land when they could afford to. Heads of household worked primarily as labourers and a few appeared to experience some economic mobility over the decade. These settlement patterns are very different from those of First Nations people who, registered under the Indian Act, were almost entirely settled on distant reserves by this time. In 1909, the settlement gained its name, and it would be subsequently remembered as Rooster Town. In the coming decades, its residents would participate in the First World War and develop innovative strategies to try and gain economic and housing security.

Devising New Economic and Housing Strategies: Rooster Town During the First World War and After, 1916–1926

PETER AND JULIA HOGG AND THEIR EXTENDED FAMILIES experienced some major life changes between 1916 and 1926. Julia's sister Marie Cora (sometimes listed as Clara) had married Rooster Town resident Joseph Arcand in 1915 and they continued to live in the community. Julia's sisters Mathilda and Marie had married Rooster Town residents, Patrick Conway and William Smith (Jr.), respectively, and also continued to live in Rooster Town.[1] Julia's father, John Henry, died in 1914 and her mother, Melanie, married widower Phidme Gagnon, who had emigrated from France in 1881. Finally, Julia and Peter's son James, probably born in 1904, is no longer listed in official documents, suggesting that he may have died between 1916 and 1926.[2]

In addition to the stress these deaths must have caused, the couple seems to have had a serious disagreement about Peter's decision to join Canada's war effort in Europe. In his 1915 attestation papers, Peter indicated that he was not married and gave his aunt Isabella Savage's address as his next of kin.[3] Until August 1915, married volunteers had to provide written permission from their wives to enlist.[4] Thirty-eight-year-old Peter had been working for Winnipeg's Sewer Department at $2.50 per day.[5] This would likely have been seasonal relief work, and with six-day weeks for eight months, he would have earned less than $500 a year. Like several other Rooster Town servicemen, he was illiterate, which would also have affected his ability to find well-paying work.[6] Nevertheless, Peter's departure would have thrown Julia into even greater poverty. It seems entirely plausible that Julia refused to give permission for Peter to enlist, and so he, like other volunteers, misrepresented his marital situation.[7] Unfortunately, this also meant that Julia did not receive a separation allowance. After Peter left, Julia worked as a domestic, earning $300 a year, and their sixteen-year-old son, Mab, worked as a labourer earning $400, bringing the total household income to only $700.[8]

Peter would go on to fight on the Western Front as part of the 9th Regiment, Canadian Mounted Rifles. He was reported as wounded in the 17 May 1916 *Winnipeg Tribune*.[9] He was shot through the left shoulder and spent eight and a half months in a hospital in England, and three months in a convalescent home in Winnipeg. Subsequently, he was unable to lift his arm or carry any weight, and suffered pain at night and during damp weather.[10] Upon discharge he made the statement: "I am unable to do any manual labour as I am unable to raise my left arm. The gratuity of $75.00 is not in my opinion a fair compensation for loss of the use of my arm."[11] Peter asked the vocational counsellor, who interviewed him prior to his discharge, if he could have some further education, since he had received virtually none. His military forms are all signed with a mark, so he could not even sign his name. There is no evidence this request was honoured.[12]

Peter eventually returned to Rooster Town, but Winnipeg's voters lists and the Henderson's Directories show that his living patterns were erratic: sometimes he stayed with Julia, sometimes with other Rooster Town residents, and sometimes he failed to be recorded in the official record. The 1921 census, for example, does not list Peter as a resident with Julia or anywhere else.[13] His occasional presence living with his wife suggests that they continued to have some kind of relationship, but his erratic living arrangements also imply that he suffered from the trauma of his military experience. Peter's army records show that he was recommended for a military pension.[14] It seems likely that this was granted, because in 1926 Julia was present on Winnipeg's voters list as the owner of a small house at 1141 Lorette Avenue, which was not connected to city amenities. Given Julia's very low earnings and the likelihood that Peter would have had difficulty finding employment, some form of military compensation appears as the most probable source for the sum required to purchase both land and a dwelling. If Peter received a pension, it may also have helped the couple to keep up with municipal taxes. On Winnipeg's 1926 voters lists, Peter is described as a "tenant" at 1141 Lorette Avenue, indicating that the house was in Julia's name.

Peter and Julia's experiences during these years demonstrate many similarities to those of other Rooster Town residents—the military service as an alternative to poor wages, the impoverishment of women and families left behind, the legacy of injuries and trauma for returning veterans and their families, and the varied strategies Rooster Towners used to attempt to create some economic and housing security—all displaying persistence and innovation in their urban adaptation.

Winnipeg's Economy, 1916–26

This period saw the end to Winnipeg's frantic economic and population growth. The real estate market collapsed in 1913. The outbreak of the First World War, in 1914, disrupted European wheat production, and Canadian wheat prices soared. The devastation associated with the war meant that the demand for Canadian agricultural products remained high, even after the war ended in 1918. According to economic historian Ruben Bellan, "The profitability of agriculture induced large numbers of Canadian city men to take up farms during the war years."[15] Winnipeg, however, faced a decline in economic activity and the population decreased, both because of individuals serving overseas and because of people leaving for farms. Construction virtually stopped during the war, and, according to Artibise, 1914 marked the end of an era for Winnipeg.[16] By 1915, Winnipeg faced a serious unemployment problem. The city's economy improved somewhat because of purchases associated with farming expansion, the manufacturing of materials required for the war, and the stationing of troops in the city. Winnipeg's role as a transshipment point was eroded after the war and the city never regained its pre-wartime growth rate.

Inflation was a significant issue facing low-income families in Winnipeg throughout and after the First World War. The national and international demand for raw materials during the war and the reconstruction afterwards drove up prices, and a massive six-week general strike paralyzed the Winnipeg economy in 1919.[17] Commissioner Hugh A. Robson, appointed to investigate the strike, restated the causes offered by the president of the Trades and Labour Council, James Winning: "Labour was very much dissatisfied—dissatisfied with conditions as they existed. The cause of the dissatisfaction in my opinion—or at least one of the causes—was unemployment. Another cause was the high cost of living; lack of the

Government to give relief; long hours of employment; inadequate wages, undesirable working conditions, profiteering, the growing intelligence of the working class of inequality in modern society; the refusal on the part of some employers to recognize the right of the employee to organize labour."[18] The Commission agreed with Winning that the high cost of living in relation to wages was a major cause of the strike.

The year 1920 ushered in a postwar depression that lasted until 1925. Decreasing wheat prices and agricultural incomes contributed to a drop in demand for Winnipeg goods and services. The decline of wartime production led to increasing unemployment. The opening of the Panama Canal meant that Vancouver now competed with Winnipeg as a transshipment point for prairie grain, and other prairie cities took on greater roles in the merchandise distribution trade. Winnipeg experienced very little growth from 1920 to 1925. According to Bellan, "the depression experienced by Winnipeg in the years after 1920 reflected the disastrous metamorphosis in the fortunes and prospects of the Wheat Economy, together with the reverses suffered in the ceaseless rivalry with other cities for the trade of the hinterland."[19]

Concern with overcrowding continued during this period. A 1913 *Manitoba Free Press* article described severe congestion in Winnipeg's largely immigrant North End.[20] Winnipeg's Committee on Public Health and Welfare appointed a tenement inspector and the city attempted to address the issue of overcrowding through regulation and inspections.[21] Construction had virtually stopped during the war, and rising prices associated with the subsequent inflation discouraged builders from erecting affordable housing. The 1919 Health Department Tenement Report indicated that "the cost of building . . . increased 60 percent, perhaps more, within the past four years, and as rents have not increased proportionately, it is not to be wondered at that builders hesitate to build."[22] The tenement inspector quickly recognized that the shortage of affordable houses meant that closing units that did not meet the city's housing standards "would be a hardship on a number of occupants who were not in good circumstances financially." As a result, his policy was to "take no action in the meantime."[23]

The inspector's annual reports demonstrate that this policy was in effect from 1916 to 1926. The report for 1917, for example, indicated that the city's policy was to "carry on" and that "only flagrant cases of overcrowding" would be directly addressed.[24] The housing reports of the Committee on Public Health and Welfare become repetitive, decrying the lack of adequate space and reporting on overcrowded houses—cleared by inspectors—reverting to their previous conditions.[25] The 1919 federal government loans to fund municipal building focused on homeownership and failed to address the needs of low-income families.[26] Just as before 1916, there are no records of inspections in the Rooster Town area, and there are no references to the community in the media. Like the working-class, self-built fringe communities in Toronto, the economic and housing conditions of Rooster Town residents were mostly hidden from public consciousness.[27]

Low-income families faced serious challenges maintaining a basic standard of living during this period. The *Labour Gazette* estimated that in 1915 a family of five in Manitoba required $697.44 per year for food, fuel, and rent.[28] However, a 1913 study by the well-known social reformer James S. Woodsworth argued that "a normal standard of living" in Winnipeg required an income of at least $1,200 per year. Woodsworth sensibly added costs of clothing, transportation, house furnishings, health expenditures, recreation, education, insurance (not then available from employers), and savings to his budget. Yet, according to Woodsworth "large number of workmen are receiving under $600 per year, many under $500, half of what is necessary."[29] According to Artibise, the overriding commitment of Winnipeg's elite to growth meant that there were few public resources left over to guarantee a satisfactory standard of living for all. He wrote that "the poor of Winnipeg lacked steady, well-paid work, adequate housing and decent medical care."[30] As mentioned before, the civic relief committee, established in 1874, aided only a small number of people in desperate straits.[31] The attitude of civic authorities toward the economically distressed was illustrated by the 1912 report of the Associated Charities Bureau, which was created to prevent overlap and fraud in the provision of relief: "Unfortunately, the large majority of applications for relief are caused by thriftlessness, mismanagement, unemployment due to incompetence, immorality, desertion of the family and domestic quarrels. In such cases the mere giving of relief tends rather to induce pauperism than to reduce poverty, and it is upon such cases that the five visiting agents of the department spend most of their time."[32]

In the context of these attitudes, needy families relied on what Artibise termed a "host of voluntary associations."[33] He describes, in detail, the work and extensive activities of two major organizations, the Margaret Scott Nursing Mission and the All Peoples' Mission.[34] However, these organizations focused mainly on immigrants, and their geographical emphasis was north of the railway yards. In his well-known book *Strangers Within Our Gates*, J.S. Woodsworth, who was heavily involved with the All Peoples' Mission, listed the perceived characteristics of different ethnic groups in the city and outlined the challenges associated with their social and economic integration. One chapter focuses on "Negros and Indians," but the material on First Nations describes only conditions on reserves. There is no acknowledgement of issues facing urban First Nations and Métis. Presumably Métis people in Rooster Town could rely on assistance from local churches, but it is likely that they also relied on other community members during this period.

Along with the rest of the Canadian economy, the prairie provinces experienced an improvement in economic conditions beginning in 1925. According to Bellan, "employment and output rose sharply in 1925 above levels which prevailed during the post-war slump and each year attained new peaks."[35] While Winnipeg prospered after 1924, it failed to match the growth of other cities and "while the index of employment rose by 37 percent in the three prairie provinces between 1925 and 1929, the increase in Winnipeg was only 27 percent."[36]

Rooster Town, 1916–1926

The 1916 population of Rooster Town was similar to its 1911 population, with thirty-four households and an estimated 190 people.[37] Table 3.1 describes the nature of changes in the community between 1911 and 1916. A slight difference from earlier years was due to a greater number of deaths of several early Rooster Town settlers. Some of the original inhabitants had been born in the mid-seventeenth century and the community had existed for over a decade. Widows and widowers sometimes moved or left the community to live with children or relatives. Like other Winnipeg city dwellers, several families, the Chassies, Cyrs, and Omands bought farms and relocated to rural areas, likely taking advantage of the profitability of farming during and after the First World War.

Modeste and Sarah Cardinal and their daughter and son-in-law, Marie Francoise and Alfred Richard, had no kin relations among the other Rooster Town residents when they moved to the area. They had previously lived in the parish of St. Laurent. Neither Modeste's nor Alfred's father had been recognized as river lot occupants. At its formation, St. Laurent was a semi-permanent settlement based on winter fishing and the production of salt on the shores of Lake Manitoba.[38] By 1870 the Métis in the parish had made the transition to commercial fishing combined with other activities, including some farming. Modeste was listed as a farmer; he probably was a farm labourer before he moved.[39] Alfred and his father, on the other hand, had been fishermen but increasing competition, along with cyclical slumps in prices, must have made Winnipeg seem like a good economic prospect.[40] The two Cardinal families were the first of what would become a large extended family group to live in Rooster Town and stay until the neighbourhood's destruction. Other families moving into Rooster Town were related to families who already lived there—the Omands, the Morrissettes, the Parisiens, the Currans, and the McDougalls. Four households were also formed with Rooster Town descendants marrying each other.

TABLE 3.1. Changes between 1911 and 1916.

GONE FROM ROOSTER TOWN	
Deaths	7 individuals
Not listed or moved	7 families
ADDED TO ROOSTER TOWN	
Without obvious kin links to Rooster Town	2 families
With kin links to Rooster Town	4 families
Married widow or formed with previous families or descendants	4 families

Sources: MS Census 1911, Manitoba, Winnipeg, Districts 3, 4, 5, 7; MS Census 1916, Manitoba, District 15 (Winnipeg South), Subdistrict 14, 17, 23; City of Winnipeg, City Clerk's Department, Election Rolls, 1911–1916, City of Winnipeg Archives and Record Centre (CWARC); 1911 to 1916 City of Winnipeg Henderson's Directories. Details about these changes are found in Appendix B.

The map shows that the developed area of Fort Rouge had increased but only one Rooster Town house, the Omands' at 669 Jessie Avenue, was in the middle of a developed block (Figure 3.1). The residents of three families, George Albert Smith and Blanche Curran, James Albert Smith and Florence Atkinson, and Henry George Paquin and Mary Lund, appear to be located within the developed area of Fort Rouge on Lorette Avenue. However, the 1927 aerial photograph shows that, although houses were built on both sides of these families, the land they actually were living on

FIGURE 3.1. Map of Rooster Town, 1916.

1 *Henry and Charlotte Griffiths*
  James Septisan Omand
2 William and Victoria Curran
  Albin Zecheriah David and
  Marie Grace Henderson
3 Peter and Sarah Berard
4 Henry George and Madeline Paquin
  Angelique Rosalie Morrissette
5 James Albert and Florence Smith
  George Albert and Blanche Rose Smith
6 Florent and Mary Louise Berard
7 Isadore (Jr.) and Marie Louise Fisher
8 Frank Berard
9 Frederick Joseph Berard
10 Adeline Fisher
  Joseph and Mary Cora Arcand
  Marie Arcand
11 Modeste and Sarah Cardinal
12 John and Naomi Peppin
13 Edward and Jessie Villebrun

14 Frederick W.J. and Isabella Savage
  Andrew Dinning
15 Nola and Susan Jane Souchereau
  John James and Florence Mulvaney
  Suzette Atkinson
16 John William and Catherine Omand
17 Alexander and Adelaide Morrissette
18 Alexander and Elizabeth Orivs
19 Aime and Josephte McDougall
  Duncan Archibald and Mary Alice
  McDougall
  William McDougall
  Daniel Berard
20 Peter and Julia Hogg
21 James Charles and Marie Louise Parisien
  Elice Minnie
22 Alexander and Mary Minnie
23 James Phidme and Melanie Gagnon
24 Alexander and Cecile Parisien
25 Alfred and Marie Francoise Richard

26 Pascal and Veronique Parisien
  Dolphes Parisien
27 William and Virginia Peppin
  Marguerite Peppin
28 Patrick and Mathilde Conway
  Elizabeth Comptois
29 William Exavier and Mary Jane Dunnick
30 Alexander and Agnes Smith
  William and Marie Smith
31 Henry and Catherine Parisien
32 Louis Raphael and Ida Parisian
33 Henry Edward Lafrance and
  Amelia Grace Parker
34 Joachim and Josephte Poitras
  Nancy Poitras

Note: Names in italics represent householders who no longer reside within the perimeters of Rooster Town but continue to be a part of Rooster Town community.

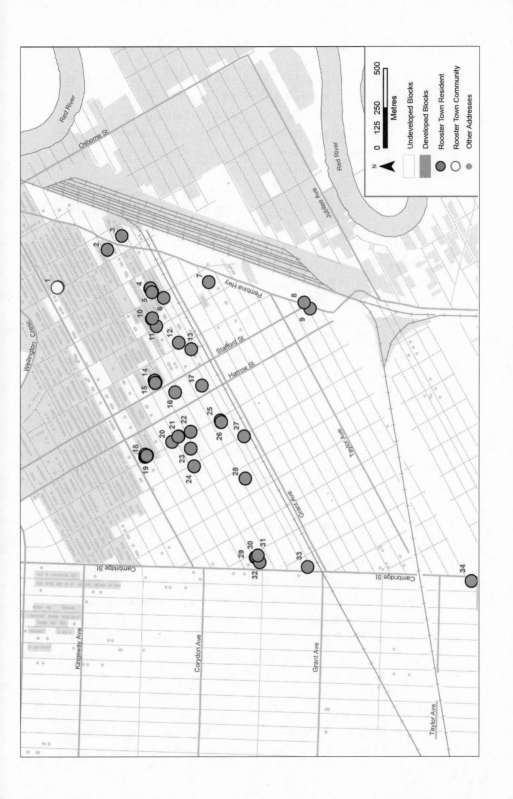

was grass and bush and occupied by just two small shacks.[41] According to the assessment rolls, the Paquin's dwelling was worth only $200 in 1916.[42] The other Métis households simply lived in Fort Rouge's bush or prairie, with a few houses north and east at the developed ends of streets. Rooster Town Métis continued to draw on the community of kin and friends to help them deal with the racist urban environment.

The First World War, which began on 28 July 1914 and lasted until 11 November 1918, also affected Rooster Town's history. Métis military historian Bryn Cyr writes that "when World War One was declared, volunteers from all areas of the Métis nation came forward to join the Canadian Army. They had to forget the inhumane treatment which other Canadian soldiers had recently inflicted on their fathers and mothers during the dark days of 1870 and 1885."[43] In Rooster Town the proportion of eligible men enlisting was virtually identical to that of the Manitoba as a whole, standing at 59.3 percent compared to the Manitoba statistic of 61.1 percent.[44] Fewer than half (47 percent) of Manitoba men who served had volunteered, rather than having been drafted. In contrast, 90 percent of the Rooster Town servicemen volunteered. The proportion of Rooster Town men who actually participated in the war effort may even be higher. By ploughing and irrigating a field near his house, teamster Alexander Morrissette broke or trained horses for the Canadian military, but there are no attestation or conscription records for him.[45] The Rooster Town rate of service is somewhat surprising. Unlike many immigrants, Métis had no pre-existing loyalty to the European countries involved in the war. Yet they volunteered in record numbers. According to war historian Desmond Morton, the 1914 depression in Canada encouraged unemployed men to volunteer because it meant that their families had at least some income and Rooster Town wage earners probably were susceptible to a similar logic.[46] Scattered information in the military records gives hints about the precarious socio-economic status of some of the Rooster Town servicemen that may have encouraged them to serve. Several Rooster Town residents volunteered, but years of poverty and hard work meant that their health conditions prevented them from making it past a gruelling training regime and they were released before they went overseas.

Available documents describe the ongoing legacy of the First World War conditions on soldiers and their families, even after the war was over. Forty-year-old Peter Berard, who served in the 101st and 43rd Battalions, was struck with pleurisy, an inflammation of the lungs caused by pneumonia.

His medical board record of 17 August 1917 reads: "In France 9 months. Invalided with pleurisy left 30-4-17 complains of general weakness and pain in left during deep respiration and when lying down. He looks about 45 years."[47] Berard was hospitalized for two months and given three months' pay and allowance after his discharge. The medical board's estimate of the illness's impact on him earning a full livelihood was one out of five on discharge and one out of ten at the end of three months. However, according to his obituary, Peter's death in 1934, when he was only fifty-seven, was caused by "toxic coitre and pneumonia. Death was due to service."[48]

Peter's brother Frank Berard was wounded in duty on 5 October 1918, with a gunshot to the face, chest, and shoulders.[49] He lost his left eye and consequently had scars on his face, chest, and shoulders. Forty-eight-year-old Jean Baptiste Fountaine was reported to have "pains in shoulders and hip and especially in region of right groin; marching causes severe pain.... Cold and damp weather also aggravated his condition." He was discharged on 11 November 1918, being "medically unfit for further war service."[50] Jean Baptiste had moved out of Rooster Town by 1921 and he and his wife and four children lived in the North End. He worked as a labourer and earned only $500 in 1920, less than the $710 he had earned a decade earlier.[51] John Baptiste Peppin had both feet injured by a hand grenade, less than five months after he had arrived in France. While his right foot was initially saved, it was amputated twenty days later due to gangrene and the lack of sanitary conditions of the medical facilities at the time. Peppin spent seven months in hospitals and convalescent homes in France and England before returning to Winnipeg.[52] Frederick Savage was kicked in the knee by a horse and, while he was recovering, he developed pleurisy and a severe ear infection that resulted in deafness in his left ear.[53]

Other Rooster Town Métis were actually killed in battle. William Curran was "killed in action 3 June 1917 while serving with the 44th Battalion."[54] Albin Henderson, serving as a private with the 28th Battalion, was killed in action 18 July 1918.[55] The *Manitoba Free Press* report about his death mentioned that he was survived by a wife (Grace Curran) and three children, one of whom he had not seen.[56] John James Mulvaney was killed in action on 4 October 1916.[57]

Notably, incomes from service could not support families, especially not the generally large families of Rooster Town residents. Rates of support for families—even when they received assistance from the Canadian

Patriotic Fund (CPF) created in 1914—were lower than official living estimates, which, as noted above, left out essential items such as clothing
and health expenditures.[58] According to Morton, "for soldiers' wives the
pain of separation was all the greater once they realized that, without their
breadwinner, their abandoned families faced destitution."[59] Moreover, the
CPF reportedly behaved like charities of the day, with invasive inspections
and requirements. As a result, many families refused to seek aid.[60] John
James Mulvaney's wife Florence came under CPF's scrutiny. Mulvaney had
identified Florence as his wife, and she received a separation allowance
and was awarded a widow's pension upon his death. About a month after
Mulvaney's death, the War Service Gratuity forms show the entry "pension
cancelled, immorality."[61] Florence had been married to Aime McDougall's
brother, Joseph, in 1888, but had been living with Mulvaney since at least
1907.[62] Various city administrative records occasionally refer to her as Florence McDougall, suggesting that she had not obtained a formal divorce.
Mulvaney's military documents show that she was reinstated due to a letter
from the "Patriotic Society" and that she received his military medals.[63]

The hardships imposed by the war are underlined by strategies,
to survive economically, of the families left behind. Morton writes
that "many soldiers' wives had taken in boarders or their neighbour's
laundry, or they sewed or cleaned houses for better-off women of the
community."[64] Rooster Town soldiers' wives were no exception. Albin
Henderson's wife Grace Curran and their three children moved in with
Grace's mother, Victoria, and lived in a four-room house at 616 Garwood Street.[65] Rose Curran, wife of George Albert Smith, lived with
her father and mother-in-law.[66] Jean Baptiste Fountaine's wife Marie
Rose and their six children relocated to Ste-Anne-des-Chênes, likely
to live with or near relatives.[67] Modeste Cardinal's wife Sarah and their
children came back to St. Laurent, also probably to be near kin.[68] Florence Paquin, wife of James John Mulvaney, moved in with her sister's
family, the Souchereaus.[69] Isabella Morrissette, married to Fred Savage,
returned to Rooster Town, from the developed area of Fort Rouge, and
took in a boarder.[70] In the context of economic hardship, Métis families
continued to rely on kin and family.

The Rooster Town population declined from 1916 to 1921, but
then stabilized and began to grow. Between 1916 and 1921, six Rooster
Town residents died, including three who died in battle (Table 3.2).[71]

This period saw the largest migration out of Rooster Town since it was formed in 1901 and the community dropped to the smallest size it would be, until the late 1950s. Only thirty households remained, containing about 144 people. It seems likely that the postwar depression in Winnipeg, combined with rising prices, made it difficult for Métis households to survive in the city.

TABLE 3.2. Changes between 1916 and 1921.

GONE FROM ROOSTER TOWN	
Deaths	6 individuals
Not listed or moved	11 families, 5 individuals
ADDED TO ROOSTER TOWN	
Without obvious kin links to Rooster Town	1 individual
With kin links to Rooster Town	4 families
Married widow or formed with previous families or descendants	1 individual

Sources: MS Census 1916, Manitoba, District 15 (Winnipeg South), Subdistrict 14, 17, 23; MS Census 1921, Manitoba, Winnipeg South District; City of Winnipeg, City Clerk's Department, Election Rolls, 1911–1921, City of Winnipeg Archives and Record Centre (CWARC); 1916 to 1921 City of Winnipeg Henderson's Directories. Details about these changes are found in Appendix B.

Philius Laramee, whose extended family would soon represent a significant presence in Rooster Town, moved into the city to work for the teamster and ranching operation of William Dunnick. Philius had moved from Quebec with his father, who married a Métis woman from St. Norbert, and the Laramee family, including Philius, his brothers, and his father, farmed there. At some point between 1916 and 1921, William Dunnick purchased a property on Ash Street and by 1921 Dunnick's wife, Mary Jane, lived there with Philius and her and William's children. William, on the other hand, lived at the Cambridge Street location, near Alexander Smith and his teamster and ranching enterprise. Official statistics do not offer much insight into the details of everyday life in the Rooster Town community, but scattered media details suggest that Dunnick was facing some personal challenges at the time he become estranged from his family. On 24 December 1919 he was arrested and charged with drunkenness, having consumed two quarts of liquor prescribed for his [four] horses by a veterinary surgeon. He explained to the magistrate: "I couldn't help it, the temptation in a dry town was too great."[72] Dunnick was arrested for drunk driving several years later.[73] His 1939 obituary mentioned only his wife and son, and not his daughters.[74] The impression that Dunnick was estranged from his family is supported by the fact that in 1962, many years after Mary Jane's death, her children posted memorial poems for their mother, but never for their father.[75]

Two Parisien families also moved into Rooster Town between 1916 and 1921, bringing the number of Parisien households in the community to six. The European and Canadian ancestors of these families were born in the late 1700s and early 1800s, and, because none were listed as HBC employees, they may have been associated with the NWC.[76] Bonaventure Parisien was listed in the 1835 HBC survey of Red River as living in St. Norbert. He owned one horse and four cattle but no farm implements and no land, suggesting that, like other parish residents, his main source of income came from the buffalo hunt.[77] Although the Parisiens were listed as living in St. Norbert in the 1870 census, none received patent to their land.[78] Before they moved to the city, most of the Parisien heads of household had been working as farm labourers, and the urban economy must have represented better opportunities for them, similarly to the Métis families that had moved to Winnipeg earlier.[79] Three other families became a part of Rooster Town between 1916 and 1921: Francois and Marie Sais came from St. Norbert, and Francois died in 1921, so perhaps they moved because of health reasons;[80] boarder David Butchart married Victoria Curran; and no additional information is available about the Vandal family.[81]

Rooster Town continued to grow south and west of the developed area of Fort Rouge, with a few dwelling units in the more populated area but at the edges of housing clusters (see Figure 3.2). The Smith/Paquin cluster on Lorette occupied land that had not yet been developed, but was becoming surrounded by rows of larger houses. The cluster of dwellings that would develop between the two railway tracks west of Cambridge Street, along Ash and Oak Streets, began around this time. Other Rooster Town households were scattered throughout the area, with very few non-Métis households between them. A group of homes near to the Rooster Town houses immediately south of the developed area (at Lorette and Scotland Avenues) was probably the source of the comments by census taker Thomas Erskine, who noted that "a considerable number of the residents in South Ward 40 sub district 42 are foreigners, many of them have squatted in the bush where there are no streets laid out, the location is given as nearly correct as it is possible to [illegible] but in many cases no number can be given as none exists."[82] There were no media references to Rooster Town between 1916 and 1921, and the spread-out nature of the settlement may have contributed to its general invisibility to the rest of the city.

TABLE 3.3. Characteristics of the 1921 Rooster Town population.

AGE OF HOUSEHOLD HEAD	Average: 43.8; Range: 27–64 years old
OCCUPATIONS	50.0 percent labourer, 33.3 percent teamsters
HOUSEHOLD SIZE	Average: 4.8; Range: 1–15
WAGES	Average: $812; Range: $300–$1440

Source: MS Census 1921, Manitoba, Winnipeg South District, Subdistrict 42.

Data from the 1921 census make it possible to describe some of the social and economic conditions of these families. The demographics of the community were very similar to those of earlier years, and so were the occupations. According to a 1974 souvenir booklet on Fort Rouge, Frank Pound, a florist whose greenhouses opened on Mulvey Avenue near Rooster Town in 1924, employed some Rooster Town residents. He stated that the area "where Grant Park Shopping Centre is now was known as Rooster Town, quite a number of his help came from those people and good workers they were when they were available for working."[83] In an interview, Pound's daughter Doreen confirmed that a number of Métis men from Rooster Town, including Mab Hogg and Louis Laramee, were permanent employees of the business.[84] The average Rooster Town wages had increased from $677 in 1911 to $812 in 1921. However, almost half of the income data are missing, and inflation during the war years meant that the real value of earnings had diminished. Also, the average hourly wage rates for labourers in Winnipeg had increased from $0.28 in 1911 to $0.53 in 1921, wherein an individual working the sixty-hour work week for eight months should have earned $1,018—this was more than the Rooster Town heads of household averaged and almost certainly an insufficient amount to meet the needs of large families.[85] Official cost-of-living estimates for urban areas in 1926 indicated that a family needed $1,334.84 to afford basic needs.[86] It is unsurprising that as

FIGURE 3.2. Map of Rooster Town, 1921.

1 David and Victoria Butchart
2 Pascal and Veronique Parisien
3 *Aime McDougall*
  Archibald McDougall
4 *Joseph Roderick Patrick*
  and Agnes Morrissette
5 Henry George and Madeline Paquin
  Anqelique Rosalie Morrissette
6 James Albert and Florence Smith
  George Albert and Blanche Rose Smith
  Andrew Dinning
7 Florent and Mary Louise Berard
8 *Daniel Berard*
9 Jessie Villebrun
10 Frank Berard
11 John William and Catherine Omand

12 Alexander and Adelaide Morrissette
13 Florence McDougall
14 Peter and Julia Hogg
15 James Phidme and Melanie Gagnon
   Arthur Henry
16 James Charles and Marie Louise Parisien
17 William and Virginia Peppin
18 Louis Raphael and Ida Parisian
19 Alexander Minnie
   Elice Minnie
20 Patrick and Mathilde Conway
21 Eduard and Marie Julienne Parisien
22 Joseph Adolphes and
   Marie Adele Vandal
23 William Exavier Dunnick

24 Alexander and Agnes Smith
   William and Marie Smith
25 Ovide Phillip and Marie Louise Parisien
26 Henry Edward Lafrance and
   Amelia Grace Parker
27 Francois and Marie Sais
28 Philius and Mary Jane Laramee
29 Henry and Catherine Parisien
30 Joachim and Josephte Poitras
   Nancy Poitras

Note: Names in italics represent householders who no longer reside within the perimeters of Rooster Town but contiue to be a part of Rooster Town community.

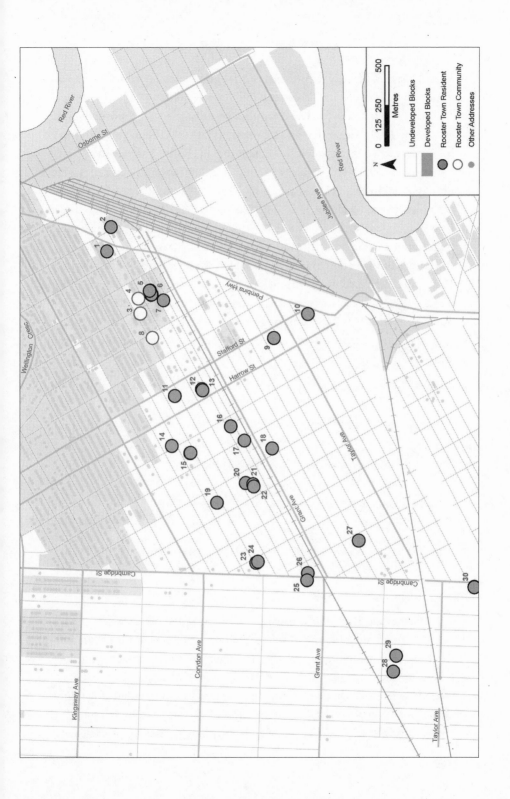

a result of this poverty, two-thirds of the households for which there was information available had more than one wage earner.

Still, several Rooster Town families had experienced some economic success by 1921. Alexander Smith owned his father William's property and his success as a contract teamster meant that his house was valued at $800, his land at $720, and his stables at $300.[87] While Alexander's earnings were not reported in the 1921 census, his seventeen-year-old son, who worked with him, earned $420 in 1920, his sixteen-year-old son, who worked as a labourer at a sawmill, earned $530 in 1920, also contributing to the household budget.[88] Apparently, even more successful was William Dunnick, Alexander's former employee and possibly estranged husband of his sister Mary Jane. While William Dunnick was not listed in the 1921 census, Winnipeg's 1920 and 1921 assessment rolls indicate that Dunnick purchased both the property at 713 Cambridge Street, where he lived, and the property at 958 Ash Street, where his wife Mary Jane lived with their children and employee Philius Laramee.[89]

TABLE 3.4. Characteristics of the 1921 Rooster Town Housing.

TENURE	75 percent own; 25 percent rent
DWELLING VALUE	Average: $399; Range: $100–$1,200
RENT	Average: $12.6; Range: $3–$18
NUMBER OF ROOMS	Average: 3.2; Range: 1–7

Sources: MS Census 1921, Manitoba, Winnipeg South District, Subdistrict 42; 1916–1921 City of Winnipeg Assessment Rolls, Ward 1, City of Winnipeg Archives and Record Centre (CWARC); 1916–1921 City of Winnipeg Building Permits, Ward 1, City of Winnipeg Archives and Record Centre (CWARC).

Information from the census, building permits, and assessment rolls helps to round out a picture of the varied forms of tenure and the relationships of the inhabitants to property in this community. The data indicate that residents' strategies were considerably more complex than the later depictions of homogeneous squatting, tax evasion, and shanty-dwelling imply. The evidence supports the idea that, along with other practices, self-building and squatting were prudent ways of coping with marginality and exclusion.

According to the 1921 census, three-quarters of Rooster Town households indicated that they owned, and only one-quarter that they rented their dwelling unit. Even so, the assessment rolls reveal that most of these households did not own the land on which their dwelling stood. By 1921 most of the speculators, who had purchased vast quantities of Fort Rouge land during the 1881–82 Winnipeg land boom, had long tired of paying taxes on the properties, which held no promise of quick profit, and large swaths of land had reverted to the city of Winnipeg. Some Rooster Town residents lived on city-owned land while others occupied land purchased by a variety of real estate companies, for very little money, from the original owners or from the city. Dwelling unit values were low, with only 958 Ash Street—where Philius Laramee and Mary Jane Dunnick lived—coming in at over $1,000.[90] The assessment of their property likely also included stables associated with Philius Laramee's and William Dunnick's teamster operations. The few individuals who rented were in small shanties of one to three rooms and their rents were low, compared to city averages. In 1925 the average monthly rent for a six-room house with modern conveniences in Winnipeg was $35, and a similar house with no conveniences rented at an average of $24.50.[91] Rooster Town dwellings averaged three rooms, and the largest was teamster Alexander Smith's house, with seven rooms for his fifteen-member family.

Winnipeg's building permits provide a partial record of the nature of housing in Rooster Town, and the assessment rolls provide some additional details.[92] In 1922, Phidme Gagnon obtained a building permit to move a dwelling onto a lot on Fleet Street and to add a cement basement valued at $300.[93] The lack of property markers in the area meant that the building was located across the boundary of two lots of land in 1926, at which time it included a shed and was valued at $500.[94] Just like with other Rooster Town residents, it is impossible to piece together the arrangements Phidme had with the land owner because the category for tenure was labelled "Tenant/ Occupant." As a result, we do not know whether he paid rent for his land, paid property taxes, or simply squatted on land that had little other value at the time. In 1918, Nola Souchereau obtained a building permit for a tiny 8 x 19–foot house valued at $100, for his wife and five children.[95] However, as already established, building a house did not indicate economic security. Something must have happened to Nola, because the 1921 census has no record of him or his wife Susan Atkinson. But, using a strategy that other financially strapped Rooster Town residents employed in desperate times, their daughter went to

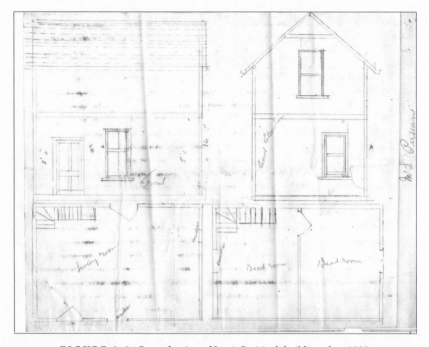

FIGURE 3.3. Reproduction of Louis Parisien's building plan, 1920.

live with Susan's sister Florence at 937 Lorette, and their two sons were placed in St. Joseph's orphanage.[96] Unfortunately, Nola died in 1927.[97]

Marginal notations in Winnipeg's assessment and collector's records provide a clue to another practice that Rooster Town residents might have utilized to gain some security and to protect investments they made in their dwelling units. In 1920, Louis Parisien obtained a building permit to build a two-story house on sills, with dimensions of 12 x 18 feet, at 1065 Weatherdon Avenue.[98] The building permit indicated that the house had no amenities and was valued at $300 (Figure 3.3). Louis had completed only part of his building in 1921 and the census describes the dwelling as a one-story house with three rooms.[99] He must have completed his building some time later in 1921, and the 1926 collector's rolls value the house at $600. They also provide some details about property arrangements that are missing for most of the Rooster Town records.[100] Six lots on Weatherdon, including the land Louis built on, were owned by the Interior Trust Company, with three dwelling units being situated next door to each other. Louis Parisien was sent the tax bill for all three addresses, and the record indicates that he refused to pay it. Instead, Louis subsequently paid the tax bill of $30.75 for two of the lots, which, besides his house, also contained a stable. Clearly, Louis had an arrangement with the Interior Trust Company to pay the taxes on the land he occupied.[101] The ability to pay or withhold the tax payments gave him leverage with the company and helped him to protect his building investment. No information is available about the arrangements for the other households.

Despite their intense poverty, a number of Rooster Town households attempted to create some security for their families by buying the land on which their dwellings stood. Although there are no records of sale prices in the public records, it is conceivable that the city of Winnipeg and other land owners in the area—mostly real estate organizations—were willing to sell parcels of land to Rooster Town residents at relatively low prices because the land was not bringing them any revenue. For the city, Métis ownership generated property taxes and no immediate additional expenses since, almost without exception, Rooster Town properties were not connected to sewer lines and did not have roads, electricity, or water. In 1929, Joseph Conway, son of Patrick Conway and Mathilda Henry, bought two lots with the address of 1075 Dudley.[102] Each lot had a small building valued at $200 where Patrick and Mathilda, and Joseph and his wife, Dorilda, lived. As described above, Mathilda's sister, Julia, married to Peter Hogg, also owned property. William Roussin and his family, who moved into Rooster Town in 1926, purchased a Carter Avenue lot from the city for $130.[103] In 1927 he took out a building permit for a 12 x 15–foot, one-story wooden "shack" valued at $200.[104] Similarly, Joseph Adolphes Vandal and his family relocated to the area around 1923 and acquired 1143 Lorette, next door to the Hoggs.[105] Vandal received a permit to add a room to an "existing shack" and line it up with lot boundaries.

For these low-income and economically vulnerable families, purchasing created an additional source of uncertainty. In his work on self-building in Toronto's fringe communities, Richard Harris documents the risks involved: "in the long run, owning their own home gave [families] some security; in the short run, however, they had run down their small savings to zero. Even the slightest setback made them destitute."[106] In a story familiar to those of Métis households, ownership meant property taxes that created challenges when Rooster Town heads of household became unemployed or faced other misfortunes. For example, veteran John Mulvaney and

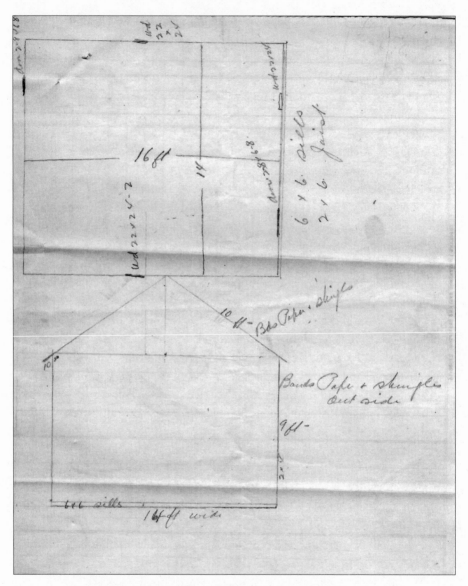

FIGURE 3.4. Reproduction of James (Jim) Parisien's building plan, 1921.

Florence Atkinson owned their lot at 937 Lorette, and in 1913 John took out a building permit to move a small dwelling, valued at only $50, onto their lot and make repairs to it.[107] John was killed in war service in 1916, and by 1921 Florence was in arrears for the house, now valued at $100.[108] Similarly, James Charles (Jim) Parisien had purchased 1019 Scotland Street by 1921, and he secured a permit to construct a one-story "dwelling (shack)" with dimensions of 14 x 16 feet, estimated at $400.[109] The sketch accompanying the building permit shows a simple four-room house (Figure 3.4). By 1926, the assessment rolls showed that he was in arrears with his property taxes.[110] Parisien managed to pay his taxes and arrears off for a few years, but from 1929 to 1931 he was in debt again, although he attempted to make partial payments.[111] Still, by 1932 the property was owned by a real estate agent, and although the Parisiens continued to rent there, they lost their equity in the building, which now belonged to the agency.[112] In another instance, around 1923, George Land purchased a lot at 1023 Scotland Street and obtained a building permit to build a 22 x 20–foot one-story wood house without a cellar, electricity, water, or a sewer.[113] The sketch with the building permit showed a four-room house with a slanted roof that, at the time, was called a "shanty roof" (Figure 3.5). George also built a stable for two horses to support his occupation as a teamster. The assessment rolls of 1926 show that there were nine people in the Land household, that George worked as a teamster, and that the land and buildings (stable included) were valued at $400 and $500 respectively.[114] By then, according to the collector's rolls, George's property taxes were in arrears.[115]

Facing slightly different circumstances, in 1927 John Peppin, married to Irishwoman Agnes Muir, built a relatively large house (by Rooster Town standards) at 952 Scotland: the building permit valued it at $2,000.[116] Peppin's wife Agnes might have been attempting to supplement her family's income in 1928 when she was convicted for keeping liquor for sale.[117] The judge fined her instead of sending her to jail, recognizing that she had two small children at home and that her husband was ill. By 1929 Peppin was in arrears with his tax payments, owing $99, and by 1930 a real estate company, McDiarmid Brothers Limited, owned the property.[118]

Similarly to the strategies Richard Harris documented for Toronto's fringe residents in the early decades of the 1900s, a few of Rooster Town's inhabitants were able to use their self-building to create some economic equity in their properties.[119] Around 1915, John William Omand, the only

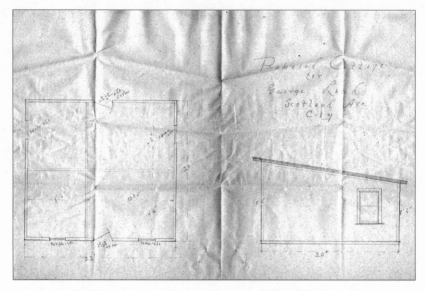

FIGURE 3.5. Reproduction of George Land's building plan, 1923.

remaining descendant in the area of the extended Omand family that had lived in Fort Rouge since the 1890s, purchased a lot at 915 Garwood Avenue.[120] In 1921 William Omand obtained a permit for a $100 addition to their house, which was described as a small, 10 x 14–foot one-story house with a peaked roof, valued at $500.[121] William continued to make improvements to the dwelling, by putting in a dormer window and beginning to excavate for a basement in 1924.[122] By 1926 the assessment rolls appraised his house at $1,400, considerably higher than most Rooster Town buildings.[123]

Two Morrissette brothers, Alexander and Roderick, comparably gained some equity through self-building. In 1913, Alexander moved a small dwelling onto the family lot rented from the First National Investment Cr. at 935 Lorette, and took out a building permit to make repairs.[124] The house was classified as a "shanty," valued at only $100. By 1921 Alexander owned a three-room wooden house at the same address and the city of Winnipeg assessment rolls valued the land at $400 and the house and stables at $200.[125] In 1926, Winnipeg's collector's rolls indicated that Alexander was in arrears with his property taxes. However, he eventually must have cobbled together enough money to pay them,[126] because while the value of his property remained modest, city directories and voters lists show that Alexander's family and his son's family continued to live on the same

FIGURE 3.6. Alexander Morrissette's house, 2016.

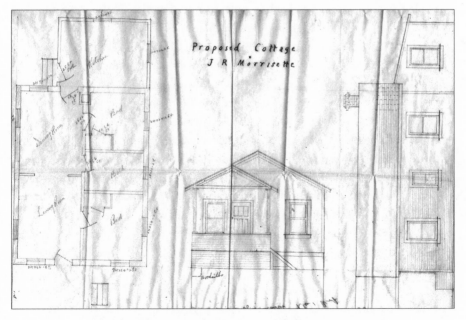

FIGURE 3.7. Roderick Morrissette's building plan, 1922.

lot into the 1960s. The house at 935 Lorette is still intact today (Figure 3.6). In 1921, Alexander's brother, veteran Roderick Morrissette, and his Scottish bride, Agnes Forbes, rented a four-room house at 713 Dudley.[127] Roderick then purchased land at 787 Carter Street and in 1922 he took out a building permit to construct a one-story house on wood sills, with no basement and a peaked roof.[128] The plans, however, show that this dwelling was considerably more elaborate than most of the Rooster Town shanties (Figure 3.7). Also, this house was connected to all amenities and valued at $1,500. Like William Omand, Roderick continued to make improvements; in 1928, for example, he received a permit to put in a cement basement.[129] Today the house at 787 Carter Street is a one-story, five-room house currently valued at $195,000.[130]

Finally, some Rooster Town residents built or repaired dwelling units that they subsequently rented out to other members of the community. There are very few records that document this occurrence, but the 1911 assessment rolls indicate that the house Aime McDougall rented at 1019 Jessie was owned by Fred Savage, who had moved out of Rooster Town by then.[131] Philius Laramee's property ownership pattern documents an extended period of a rental dwelling unit. As noted earlier, Philius Laramee relocated to Rooster Town between 1916 and 1921, to work for William Dunnick. In 1921, he purchased 937 Lorette, either from Florence Atkinson, who owned it and was in arrears following the death of her husband in the Great War, or from the real estate company the property was sold to for taxes owing.[132] In 1922 Philius obtained a building permit to add a $1,000 addition to the house Florence's husband had originally moved onto the lot and made repairs to in 1913.[133] The diagram accompanying Philius's plan for the addition show that the original was a small 14 x 16–foot house with a slanted roof, and was much like the shanties built by many other Rooster Town residents. Philius constructed another story and an addition (Figure 3.8). At the same time, Philius lived on Ash Street with William Dunnick's wife Mary Jane, and, over the years the community was in existence, he rented out the house at 937 Lorette to a variety of Métis families. The house still stands today (Figure 3.9).

These varied relationships to dwelling, property, and ownership provide a lens into the strategies that Rooster Town residents used to wrest some security for their families in the context of poverty and exclusion. These practices show resilience and innovation, not an inability to adapt, as

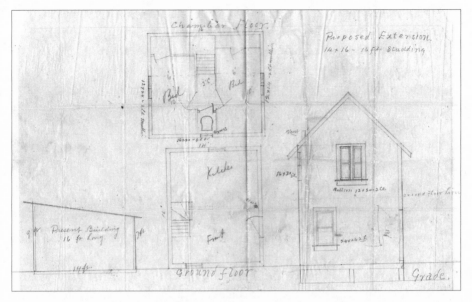

FIGURE 3.8. Reproduction of Philius Laramee's building plan, 1922.

FIGURE 3.9. Philius Laramee's house, 2016.

settler prejudices continue to suggest. While relatively few Rooster Town household heads could afford to use self-building and unit upgrades to generate wealth, they nevertheless used self-building to provide their families with shelter. Dwelling units were small, and commonly a family would move a building onto a property and live in it while the head of household and likely older sons, if there were any, made improvements. Although relationships with land owners are impossible to unravel for all households, the Louis Parisien example described above shows that self-building and paying property taxes on land could be a strategy to protect a housing investment. When they were able to save enough money, Rooster Town families bought modest lots and, for the most part, built small shanties on them. Property ownership was a two-edged sword, though, and during periods of unemployment or other economic hardships, unpaid taxes could lead to the loss of the homeowner's full equity. According to Canadian historian James Struthers, even during times of economic prosperity in the "roaring" twenties, 30 percent of workers lost some time to unemployment each year, and the average spell of joblessness lasted eighteen weeks.[134] For unskilled labourers working at low wages, it was difficult to set aside money for property taxes or rent during periods of unemployment.

Building their own dwelling units helped many Rooster Town residents to avoid the major expense of rent incurred by other poor households, living, at the time, in the extremely overcrowded and unsanitary conditions of Winnipeg's North End. While Rooster Town inhabitants relied on privies and hauled water, often from several kilometres away, they avoided the unsanitary conditions north of Winnipeg's downtown, wherein dwellers also depended on privies but in much more crowded conditions. Importantly, Rooster Town residents had the freedom to make changes to their housing in response to their household needs, recognizing, of course, that the income to make these changes was often limited. We do not mean to celebrate Rooster Town housing conditions, which were characterized by overcrowding and lack of water and sewer lines, and often provided inadequate shelter. However, in the context of discrimination and exclusion and a desire to live in a Métis community, we propose that self-building and squatting represented viable economic and social strategies. The growing and varied Winnipeg economy must have attracted Métis to the city, and Rooster Town grew from thirty households in 1921 to thirty-five in 1926. If household size, on average, remained what it was in 1921, then Rooster Town in 1926 had a population of 168, compared to 144 people in 1921. At its twenty-fifth anniversary, one-third of the families in Rooster Town had lived there since 1901 or earlier (Table 3.5). The second-largest contingent of families, 29.7 percent, had moved into the neighbourhood between 1921 and 1926. The year 1926 marked the last addition of larger family groups (the Parisiens and Cardinals) to Rooster Town; they would comprise the mainstays of the community into the 1950s. Subsequent growth in Rooster Town came from descendants forming new families or relatives moving in. After 1926, only the occasional non-kin household moved into the area, usually staying for only a short period of time.

TABLE 3.5. Changes between 1921 and 1926.

GONE FROM ROOSTER TOWN	
Deaths	1 individuals
Not listed or moved	4 families, 1 individuals
ADDED TO ROOSTER TOWN	
Without obvious kin links to Rooster Town	1 individual
With kin links to Rooster Town	10 families
Married widow or formed with previous families or descendants	1 family, 3 individuals

Sources: MS Census 1921, Manitoba, Winnipeg South District, Subdistrict 42; 1916–1921 City of Winnipeg Assessment Rolls, Ward 1, City of Winnipeg Archives and Record Centre (CWARC); 1916–1921 City of Winnipeg Building Permits, Ward 1, City of Winnipeg Archives and Record Centre (CWARC).

TABLE 3.6. Year of Arrival of 1926 Rooster Town Households.

YEAR	PERCENT
1901	35.1 percent
1906	13.5 percent
1911	10.8 percent
1916	5.4 percent
1921	5.4 percent
1926	29.7 percent

Sources: MS Census 1926, Manitoba, Winnipeg South District, Subdistrict 42; 1916–1926 City of Winnipeg Assessment Rolls, Ward 1, City of Winnipeg Archives and Record Centre (CWARC); 1916–1926 City of Winnipeg Building Permits, Ward 1, City of Winnipeg Archives and Record Centre (CWARC).

The Parisien and Cardinal families that moved into the Rooster Town community at the time (Figure 3.10) included household heads Marcien and Maxime Cardinal, Joseph Andre Berard, and Adolph Joseph Pilon. They had been rural farm labourers before they were recruited for war service, and once they were discharged in 1918 or 1919, they married in 1921, and moved to Winnipeg.[135] They joined other rural veterans who moved to cities after they were discharged. By 1926, there were no members of Jean Baptiste Berard's extended family remaining in Rooster Town, and most of the Morrissettes and the Omands were gone as well.[136] Joseph Andre Berard, who was living on Bond Street, was not related to the earlier Berard family. The other new household, containing individuals not related to earlier Rooster Town families, was that of Kenrick (Kenny) Peter Campbell, nephew of Douglas Campbell, who would later become premier of Manitoba. Campbell's mother had purchased land in the area of Oak and Ash Streets much earlier, and he would live there for the rest of Rooster Town's existence.[137] Two of Premier Campbell's daughters, Sonya and Dwili, remembered visiting Kenny with their father and seeing the row of small Métis houses that matched the dwelling in which Campbell lived.[138] Sonya read to Dr. Evelyn Peters from a family history, which described Kenny Campbell as "living in a trash built shack near the railway in Winnipeg."[139]

Fort Rouge grew very slowly between 1921 and 1926. The undeveloped section on Lorette where the Paquins and Smiths had lived was filled in. There is no record of where the two Smith households moved, but Henry George Paquin and his family ended up renting 937 Lorette from Philius Laramee. The house William Omand purchased and improved at 915 Garwood Avenue was now within the developed area of Fort Rouge, and Roderick Morrissette's house at 787 Carter Avenue would soon be swallowed by development. The cluster on Ash, Oak, and Waterloo Streets expanded the most between 1921 and 1926. While this group included families that matched the socio-economic characteristics of Rooster Town residents, there were also exceptions. Four households of the extended Laramee family represented about half of the population in this part of Rooster Town, and most of these householders appear to have owned their lots.

The 1927 aerial photos suggest that, in contrast to assumptions about the socio-economic homogeneity of Rooster Town residents, there were considerable variations. The cluster of houses where the Grant Park Mall would be built decades later appeared to be mostly small shacks with paths

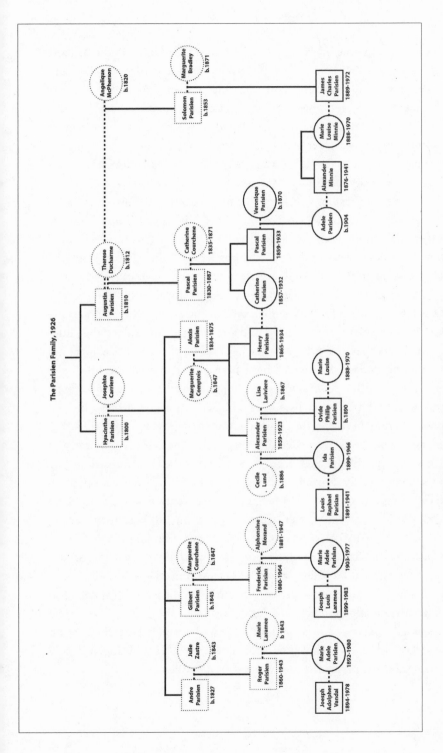

FIGURE 3.10. Rooster Town Parisien family tree, 1926.

Note: Individuals in dashed lines did not live in Rooster Town but are shown to illustrate relationships.

winding between the houses. There were also small shanties in the Ash and Oak Street area, but here more residents appeared to garden, possibly supplementing family incomes by growing some of their own food.[140] The area around 958 Ash Street, where Philius Laramee and Mary Dunnick lived, appeared to be the most extensively developed. The 1927 aerial photos suggest that their house was larger than most of the nearby dwellings and there are two outbuildings and four large cultivated areas, being either gardens or pasture. The 1926 city of Winnipeg tax assessment rolls valued the buildings at $1,200, and the property was registered under Mary Jane Dunnick's name. She was still married to William Dunnick but was living with Philius Laramee by then. There were seven people living in the house, most likely including the Dunnick children, and probably some hired hands.[141] The Dunnick and Parker residences similarly showed several buildings and some cultivated spaces.

The Smiths also seem to have been doing relatively well economically at the time. William Smith's son Alexander now owned the Smith estate; Winnipeg's assessment rolls listed him as a teamster and valued the buildings on his property at $1,100.[142] The 1927 aerial photo shows a house, an outbuilding, and what must have been a garden and a pasture. While larger than other Rooster Town houses, the house nevertheless must have been crowded: the 1921 census listed Alex, his wife Agnes, and their thirteen children living there, and the family continued to grow after that time.[143] A rare family photo of Alexander, his wife, Agnes, their fifteen children and Agnes's mother, likely taken around 1926, shows the family posed outside in the winter, likely in front of one of the outbuildings on the property.[144] The older children are posed by height, the men wear suits, ties, and pocket handkerchiefs, and the women are also dressed up, likely in their Sunday best. The photo also gives a few clues about the Smith family life. Clearly the fact that the Smiths chose to commission a family photo demonstrates their pride in their large family, and Agnes positions the smallest infant to face toward the camera in a desire to record even the baby. The photo also shows obvious affection between Alexander and his children in the way he cradles a daughter on his lap and the way another small daughter leans on her father's knee. As a whole, the photo communicates pride in family and in being able to provide for family in the urban milieu.

FIGURE 3.11. Alexander Smith and his family, c. 1926.

Even though Rooster Town and its residents flew under the radar of the media during this period, several administrative databases allow us to access
and draw conclusions on some aspects of the Métis inhabitants' community
life. Population numbers remained relatively steady, with a decrease in 1921,
which probably related to hardships for veterans' families during the war and
the postwar depression that led some families back to the rural parishes. By
1926, Rooster Town population had rebounded as rural veterans married
and moved to the city to take advantage of the improving urban economy,
and Rooster Town descendants formed their own households. The relative
stability of the community shows that this settlement pattern was not a tem-
porary response to bewildering urban life. Instead, this was a unique Métis
adaptation to poverty, dispossession, and rural and urban racism.

The First World War affected Rooster Town families the way it affected
other low-income populations, with hardships for women and children left
behind during the fighting, and the effects of war service in terms of injuries, trauma, and an inadequate health care and social safety net, which meant
that families and communities bore the brunt of dealing with returning veterans. Census data show that Rooster Town residents remained very poor,
although the level of poverty seemed to be less grave, for some, by 1921. Also

some households, particularly those belonging to the Smiths, William Dunnick, and Philius Laramee—whose heads worked as teamsters and whose families seemed to be engaged in some ranching operations—appeared to be modestly successful. Rather than failing to adapt to urban life, Rooster Town residents' participation in wage labour—and the modest success of some— shows a strong adaptability in the context of the low levels of education they received and the high levels of discrimination they experienced.

Winnipeg's assessment and collector's rolls and its building permits provide glimpses into the variety of tenure and housing strategies Rooster Town residents employed to try to cobble together some comfort and security by squatting, renting, paying taxes on lots they occupied, and purchasing land. While purchasing land and self-building could lead to increased wealth and security, for the inhabitants the need to pay property taxes also made them vulnerable. When hardship struck, residents could lose their investments as the city foreclosed on their property. Squatting, therefore, can be interpreted as a resourceful response to poverty rather than evidence of an inability to cope with the urban economy. By 1926 the patterns of residency and the socio-economic characteristics of the Métis families that would remain in the neighbourhood had been established, and subsequent configurations of Rooster Town built on these foundations.

Persistence, Growth, and Community: Rooster Town During and After the Great Depression, 1931–1946

WHILE THE ABSENCE OF CENSUS DATA MEANS that there is less socio-economic information about Peter and Julia Hogg between 1931 and 1946, there are still scattered clues about their situation. Winnipeg's assessment rolls list Julia as the owner of 1141 Lorette Avenue during this period, and she manages to pay the taxes on the house. It was a small house, but the city valued it at $250, higher than many other Rooster Town dwelling units.[1] However both Julia's and Peter's residency patterns are changeable. They move between Lorette Avenue and other Rooster Town households, sometime living together and sometimes living apart. For example, in 1931 the city's assessment rolls list them both as living at 1141 Lorette Avenue, but in 1935 Winnipeg's voters lists show that they lived with their son Mab and his wife, Alice, who was the daughter of Rooster Town residents Joseph Eduard and Marie Julienne Parisien. They lived at 1145 Weatherdon Avenue along with three other Rooster Town families.[2] While the house at 1145 Weatherdon Avenue did appear to have a second story, it was nevertheless small, and must have been severely crowded that year (Figure 4.1). Many other low-income households in Winnipeg doubled up as they attempted to cope with widespread unemployment, throughout the Great Depression, and inadequate relief provisions. Possibly Peter and Julia rented 1141 Lorette Avenue to other families in order to generate an income; the Henderson's Directories and Winnipeg's voters lists occasionally show other Rooster Town residents living there during this period.

FIGURE 4.1. *Winnipeg Free Press* photo of Weatherdon houses, 1959.

Peter's extended family had moved out of Rooster Town by the 1930s, but the city of Winnipeg voters lists show that Julia had extensive kin networks in the community. Although their mother, Melanie, had died in 1932, Julia's siblings remained there.[3] Occasional references provide some insights into Julia's family's relationships and circumstances. The 1935 city of Winnipeg voters lists show Julia's widowed sister, Mary Cora, living with sister Mathilda and her husband Patrick Conway, perhaps as a result of hardship during the Great Depression.[4] The Conways had been able to purchase their property in 1929.[5] This doubling up, as well as that of Julia and Peter described earlier, demonstrates how Rooster Town families helped to support each other when times were difficult. In another example, 1935 voters lists show that Julia's sister Marie, seemingly estranged from husband William Smith, stayed with her brother Arthur Henry and his wife Esther for a short while during these years.[6]

Lack of available details about two other Henry siblings demonstrates the extreme marginality of some Rooster Town residents. In 1923, Julia's sister Marie Josephine had married Joseph Arthur Eugene (Archie) Parisien.

Despite the fact that Josephine and Archie had three sons, they were never listed in any administrative records—this may have been due to Archie's infrequent employment and that his family lived with other Rooster Town households.[7] By 1936, Josephine had moved in with non-Métis John Paddison, with whom she stayed for the rest of her life.[8] Winnipeg's voters lists show that John Paddison worked as a brakeman for the CNR, but the couple still lived in poverty. In 1958, the *Winnipeg Free Press* listed their residence at 819 Ebby for sale at only $1,500, and described the property as "a corner lot with a three-room shanty, with water and toilet."[9] In comparison, in 1961, the average cost of single detached dwelling unit was $13,615.[10]

Patrick Henry's circumstances were even more economically tenuous. The Henderson's Directories and voters lists rarely provide an occupation for Patrick, and there is no evidence that he married. He is frequently not listed, and when he is, he is living with members of his extended family. A particularly bigoted article in the 1947 *Winnipeg Tribune* nevertheless sheds some light on both Patrick's situation and the continuing attitudes toward, and assumptions about, Rooster Town and its residents.[11] In the article "Before the Magistrate," reporter Ron Poulton gave his perspective on the case of Patrick, almost certainly Patrick Henry from Rooster Town. He wrote, "There, now and then, the sun coaxes Patrick out of his dingy cocoon. He emerges somewhat frowzily from his tax-free domain to seek the city." Patrick was arrested while begging for money to fix his car, and according to Poulton, "The police, who have known this bald-headed little grafter since the dawn of the service, say that Patrick's car always costs 75 cents to fix, no more, no less." The available information suggests that Patrick was developmentally challenged, so the article not only insults individuals with disabilities but also reinforces views of Rooster Town as being "dingy" and a "tax-free domain" that is not a part of the city.

In early April 1939, tragedy struck the Hogg family when Peter was struck by a train as he was walking home (then 1003 Weatherdon Avenue) and killed.[12] Subsequently, Julia moved back to 1141 Lorette Avenue, and the voters lists show that she was soon joined there by Frank Gosselin, a Rooster Town resident whose wife Adeline had died in 1938.[13] Frank, originally from St. Norbert, rented out the property he had lived on with Adeline and that income, plus the wages he earned as a truck driver, likely allowed Julia to move back to her 1141 Lorette Avenue residence.[14] Winnipeg's voters lists often list her brother, Patrick, as living with her and Frank.

Julia and Peter's extended family's circumstances probably represented the experiences of other families in Rooster Town. Clearly Patrick and Josephine Henry were more marginalized, while the Conways, and Julia and Peter Hogg, were able to gain some housing security by purchasing their lot and building a dwelling unit on it. However, like most of their neighbours, they were still extremely poor. Reliance on family, close-knit networks, marriage within the community, and varied housing strategies to cope with poverty and economic insecurity were practices that characterized other Rooster Town families and households as well. Despite persistent views that Indigenous cultural institutions are incompatible with urban life, Métis community ties helped many Rooster Town residents survive the years of the Great Depression. Furthermore, the steady growth of the settlement between 1931 and 1946 challenged views that the place of Métis people is in rural communities away from urban centres.

Winnipeg, 1931–1946

The year 1929 saw the end of the short post-1925 period of economic growth in the prairie economy and brought in the Great Depression. Wheat prices fell precipitously in response to the decrease in European demand and the 1929 Wall Street stock market crash. Disastrous crops in 1931 and 1933 and the introduction of U.S. tariffs in 1930 dealt additional blows to economic well-being on the Canadian prairies. Resource development, construction, and hydro-electric plants came to a virtual standstill. Accompanied by mechanization which decreased the need for farm labour, the numbers of unemployed individuals soared. Although Canada did not have a consistent measure of unemployment during the depression of the 1930s, the Dominion Bureau of Statistics estimated that unemployment had climbed to 17.4 percent in 1931, from a rate of 4.6 percent in 1926. By 1933, unemployment rates were estimated to be 16.6 percent.[15] Unskilled labourers were hit even harder: in 1930–31, 58 percent of all male unskilled workers were unemployed for more than six months of the year.[16] The 1931 census showed that the average annual earnings of an unskilled male worker were less than $500, or under $10 a week, at a time when $1,040 was considered the minimum yearly income to provide a family with bare essentials.[17] Overall, Manitoba's per capita salary decreased by 49 percent between 1928 and 1933.[18]

Governments were not prepared to offer adequate social assistance to the victims of the brutal economic downturn. Assuming that the Depression would be short-lived, the federal government was reluctant to increase its debt in order to provide assistance. Municipalities, of which main sources of revenue were property taxes and charitable organizations, were soon overwhelmed by the extent of the destitution and turned to provincial governments, which eventually turned to the federal government. In 1930, the federal government agreed to provide $20 million for relief to the provinces and municipalities, with matching funding from lower levels of government.[19] Initially, the relief took the form of a variety of public works initiatives, at a subsistence wage. In Winnipeg, recipients of work relief were expected to repay their debt by working at the rate of 42.5 cents per hour for the number of hours necessary to pay it off.[20] Struthers notes that: "Although irregular and inadequate, relief work provided the unemployed with a means of preserving pride and self-respect. The wages were low but not humiliating and useful labour was performed in return."[21] However, even in Winnipeg, one of the few Canadian cities to possess a public welfare department, overworked city staff reported that they were "unable to give what they considered adequate relief, owing to political interference from a city council anxious to keep property taxes down."[22] Often "relief" men worked only two or three days a week.[23]

In order to reduce administrative costs, the federal government shifted to direct relief in 1932, and most provincial and municipal governments followed suit.[24] Federal expenditures climbed to $175 million in 1935, matched by the provinces and municipalities. In Winnipeg, unemployment soared. While 405 people had registered for relief in the winter of 1928–29, 2,094 persons registered in the winter of 1929–30, and by February 1931 the Relief Department had 2,555 cases on its rolls.[25] Inadequate relief allowances created serious hardships for families. In Winnipeg, monthly amounts for a family of five in 1935 were $24.98 for food, $7.32 for fuel, and $12 for rent. This came to a total of $49.50, or $594 per year, lower than the $697.44 that the *Labour Gazette* estimated a family of five in 1915 Manitoba required yearly for food, fuel, and rent.[26] As a result of families' strained economic circumstances, overcrowding increased. Winnipeg's Committee on Health and Welfare painted a vivid picture of children "penned up in one small room used for living, cooking and sleeping during the winter when storm sashes are in position . . . ," and of old and leaky gas stoves serving as the only sources of heat."[27] Also, with the cessation of construction, fire and demolition led to a net loss of housing stock over the course of the decade.

In 1933 the downward drift of economic activity on the prairies began to show signs of halting, and in 1934 there were some signs of improvement. Wheat prices began to rise and the federal government invested heavily in public relief projects across the country. The reduction of tariff barriers with the United States and Great Britain increased the value of agricultural exports and various resource-development projects opened up in the northern parts of the central provinces.[28] However, in August 1937, there were still 4,334 families receiving relief in Winnipeg. The city also continued to face serious housing challenges. In 1936, the prairie provinces' censuses showed that some 55 to 70 percent of relief families were inhabiting less than one room per person, with rentals (particularly in Winnipeg) often falling into the generally "unaffordable" $15 to $24 monthly range.[29] Poverty and unemployment meant that very few families could afford rents that would cover landlords' costs, and construction failed to increase.[30] During this period, the Health Department did not appear to pay attention to Rooster Town accommodations, and there were no specific references to the community in the department's minutes.

The prairie economy improved after Britain and France declared war on Germany in September 1939.[31] The demand for wheat multiplied as imports to Britain grew, and the farmers' increased purchasing power improved the economy of urban centres like Winnipeg, which served rural populations. Ottawa's investments, in relation to Second World War activity, also contributed to economic development in Winnipeg as the federal government located a cordite plant, built air-training facilities, and contracted local firms to produce equipment, clothing, and food for overseas. The unemployment of the 1930s virtually disappeared and by the end of 1941, the number of male heads of household on city relief rolls in Winnipeg was down to fifty.[32] The end of the war in 1945 did not bring about the renewed depression of the 1930s. Europe's desperate need for food continued, and the general public snapped up material goods they had not been able to buy during war years.

The vast number of workers, flowing into centres of wartime industry, were housed mainly through further overcrowding. Meanwhile, private housing construction almost entirely halted as a result of rationing policies.[33] By 1941, Alexander Officer, Winnipeg's long time Tenement and Housing chief working with the Health Department, was a frustrated man. He reported that:

"The shortage of accommodation for the low-income group has been acute for years and I have referred to this over and over again in these reports. The present plight of the average working man to find moderate but satisfactory living quarters for his family is lamentable. The health and physical being of his children are endangered by the unnatural surroundings in which they are compelled to exist. And all because our various governing bodies shirk the responsibility of providing healthy dwellings suitable for family life."[34]

In later years, Alexander Officer's replacement, Fred Austin, worked to identify and remedy many of the same problems that had long plagued the Health and Housing Departments. In 1946, Winnipeg's Committee on Health and Welfare reported that families were occupying churches, unfinished dwellings, garages, stores, former barracks, immigration sheds, and even cellars.[35] This occurred while a large number of people were also living in official emergency shelters—in 1947, this included a staggering 1,413 people. Additionally, 4,818 families were waiting to get into these shelters as of June of that year.[36] For the low-income population of Winnipeg, housing shortage was a defining characteristic of the age, the conditions were poor both in absolute terms and in comparison with the national average.[37] Even in 1951, there were 0.8 people living per room in Winnipeg, only a slight reduction from the rate of approximately 0.83 people per room rate that had prevailed in 1941.[38] By the time emergency shelter and soldiers' rental housing construction were halted, in 1948 and 1949 respectively, there remained a dire need for low-income housing that the various levels of government were only beginning to address.[39]

The challenging state of housing throughout Winnipeg meant that Rooster Town received no Winnipeg media attention from 1931 to 1946, other than the two *Winnipeg Tribune* reports of arrests associated with homebrew.[40] Neither did the minutes of the Health Committee mention Rooster Town at this time. The extreme shortage of housing meant that others were also poorly housed, and attempts to move Rooster Town residents would have simply exacerbated the situation. Difficult dwelling conditions in the community were, however, public knowledge. In February 1944, the city papers reported that Winnipeg's health officer argued to council that the widespread use of outhouses, especially in Fort Rouge, presented a "serious menace to the health and welfare of the city."[41] Alderman William Scraba asked, "Is it in Rooster Town?" and was told that many of the Fort Rouge properties that had reverted to the city for non-payment of taxes and were now being sold were not connected to the sewer system. The exchange was picked up by journalists outside of Winnipeg, and the

22 April 1944 issue of Eatons' national *Flash* magazine contended that "Winnipeg can lay claim to the dubious distinction of being the most backward city in Canada in regard to housing and sanitary conditions." The magazine gave Rooster Town as its worst example.[42]

Rooster Town, 1931–1946

While the number of Rooster Town households increased to forty-six (including three that had been overtaken by the growing Fort Rouge suburb) from 1931 to 1936, there was very little change to the family groups who lived there.[43] The only adult listed in 1926 but not in 1931 voters lists was Marie Smith (née Henry). Her former husband, William Smith, now lived with Frances Cardinal, daughter of Charles and Marie Josephine Cardinal. Since Marie was listed as living with her brother, Archie Henry, in 1936, it is possible that she remained in Rooster Town but was missed in the written records. Only one family without kin linkages to Rooster Town residents joined the community at the time. The Butcharts, David and Victoria (née Mignault) were non-Métis, and they moved a small building onto a lot on Weatherdon and made repairs to it.[44] Victoria had earlier been married to Métis William Curran and they had previously lived in Rooster Town. For the first time in the neighbourhood's history, most of the household increase during this period came from former Rooster Town residents returning, or descendants of current inhabitants forming their own families.

Settlement patterns also remained very similar to those of 1926. Two households managed to improve their situations and, while they lived near other Rooster Town residents, they were able to generate enough savings to invest in their homes. John Omand continued to build up his house, and both his and Joseph Patrick Morrissette's house were now part of the developed area of Fort Rouge (see Figure 4.2).[45] The Morrissettes seemed integrated into the non-Métis community by this time. Born in Edinburgh, Agnes Morrissette had likely met Joseph Patrick during the war. The *Winnipeg Free Press* reported that in 1931 Winnipeg's mayor helped an Englishwoman, who wrote to him, find a husband in Winnipeg. The Morrissettes hosted a dinner party for the couple, at which the major presented them with a wedding present.[46] The Morrissettes' dinner parties and showers were featured on the *Winnipeg Free Press* society page several times before Agnes Morrissette's death in 1940.[47]

TABLE 4.1. Changes between 1926 and 1931.

GONE FROM ROOSTER TOWN	
Deaths	1 individual
Not listed or moved	1 individual
ADDED TO ROOSTER TOWN	
Without obvious kin links to Rooster Town	1
With kin links to Rooster Town	2 families
Married widow or formed with previous families or descendants	7 families

Sources: 1926 to 1931 City of Winnipeg Henderson's Directories; City of Winnipeg, City Clerk's Department, Election Rolls, 1926–1931, City of Winnipeg Archives and Record Centre (CWARC). Details about these changes are found in Appendix B.

Some people's dwelling situations may have improved but for others this is more difficult to ascertain. According to Winnipeg's voters lists, after the death of his wife Hilda Grace, George Land rented a house on Lorette in the more developed area of Fort Rouge. But the 1929 aerial photo of the area shows that the block of Lorette Street, where he lived, was not built up.[48] The area west of Cambridge, on Ash and Oak Streets, now had eleven households, an increase of two since 1926. Other households were scattered west of the populated area of Fort Rouge, with very few non-Métis neighbours. The only non-Métis who were relatively long-term residents of the community were the extended Parker family, with two Parker sons marrying Rooster Town daughters, and Kenny Campbell, who lived in the Ash and Oak Street cluster. Herman Larsen, a painter, and his wife Lydia also resided among the Ash and Oak Street group for about a decade.

Despite the migration out of the neighbourhood and the death of several Rooster Town "old-timers," Rooster Town grew again, by 1936 reaching a total of fifty-one families living in forty-six households, with three of the households now being located within the developed portion of the city. A number of the families moving to Rooster Town were elderly: Charles and Marie Josephine Cardinal, Modeste and Sarah Cardinal, and Francois and Marie Larocque. They likely moved from rural parishes to retire in a more urban community.[49] Charles and Modeste were members of the extended Cardinal family that would continue to be an important part of Rooster Town

FIGURE 4.2 Map of Rooster Town, 1931.

1 George Land
2 *Joseph Roderick Patrick and Agnes Morrisette*
3 *John William and Catherine Omand*
4 Maurice and Winona Louise Peppin
George Allan Peppin
5 Alexander and Adelaide Morrisette
6 John and Agnes Peppin
7 Florent and Marie Louise Berard
8 Edward Scott and Mary Grace Smith
9 Jessie Villebrun
10 James Charles and Marie Louise Parisien
11 Emile Ernest and Marie Juile Ann Lepine
12 Alexander and Adele Minnie Elice Minnie
13 William Peppin
14 William and Frances Malvina Smith
15 David and Victoria Butchart

16 Arthur and Esther Catherine Henry James Phidme and Melanie Gagnon
17 Joseph and Mary Cora Arcand
18 Patrick and Mathilde Conway
19 Joseph Amadee and Dorilda Conway
20 Peter and Julia Hogg
21 Joseph Adolphes and Marie Adele Vandal
22 Pascal and Veronique Parisien
23 Louis Raphael and Ida Parisian
24 Joseph Andre and Alexandrina Evangeline Berard
25 Thomas and Grace Adele Jenkins
26 Alexander and Agnes Smith
27 William Exavier Dunnick
28 David and Violet May Parker
29 Henry Edward Lafrance and Amelia Grace Parker
30 William and Rachel Ogidile Anne Roussin

31 Joseph Alexandre and Aurelia Pilon
32 Frederick and Alphonsine Parisian
33 Joseph Noel and Marie Marguerite Laramee
34 Adolph Joseph and Marie Josephine Pilon
35 Paul and Marie Julie Laramee
36 Philias and Alice Laramee
37 Philius and Mary Jane Laramee
38 Herman and Lydia Larson
39 Kenrick Peter Campbell
40 Joseph Louis and Marie Adele Laramee
41 Henry and Catherine Parisien
42 Marcien Peter and Marguerite Cardinal
43 Joachim and Josephine Poitras

Note: *Names in italics represent householders who no longer reside within the perimeters of Rooster Town but contiue to be a part of Rooster Town community.*

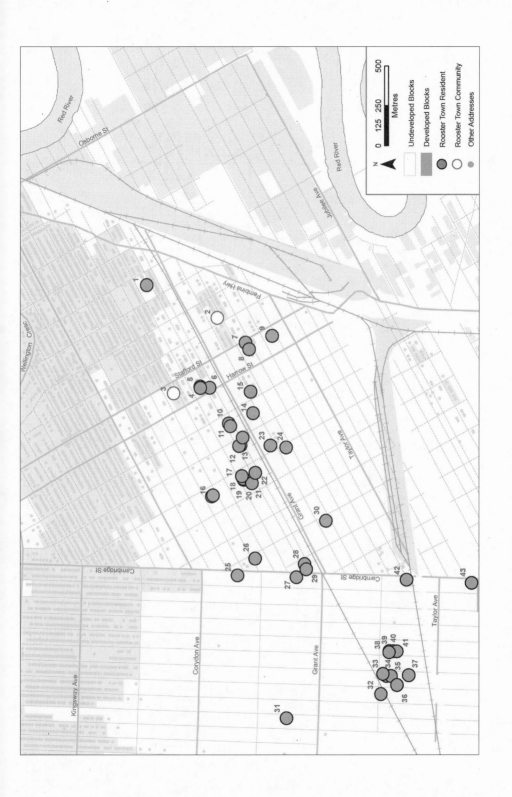

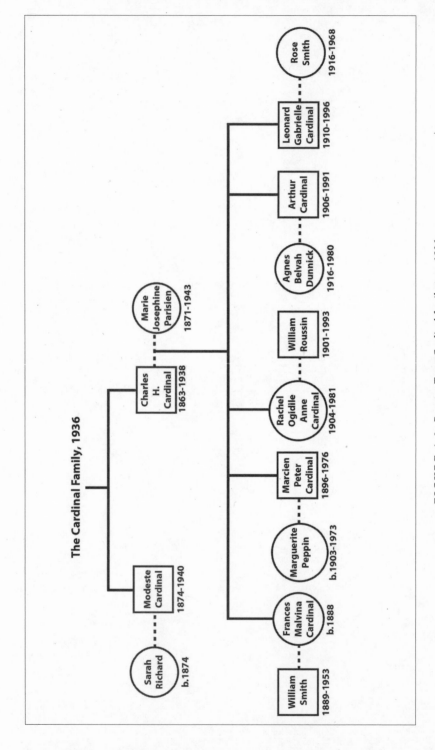

FIGURE 4.3: Rooster Town Cardinal family tree, 1936.

Note that the individuals depicted with dashed lines did not live in Rooster Town, but are included so that relationships can be identified.

until the community was destroyed in the late 1950s (Figure 4.3).[50] Eleven couples formed by one or two Rooster Town residents marrying. Settlement patterns of 1936 remained similar to those of 1931, but the developed area of the city was creeping closer to the community (Figure 4.4).

Many of the individuals marrying Rooster Town residents came from rural Métis areas. For example, brothers Joseph Leon and Alphonse Peter Courchene and John Nolin, who married Smith and Dunnick daughters, came from St. Norbert and Ste. Anne respectively.[51] Like many non-Métis, they may have moved to Winnipeg because small communities could not afford relief, or because chances for employment were better in a large city. Ethnologist Marcel Giraud, who attributed Métis poverty to a failure to adapt to the modern economy, nevertheless gave a good description of the intense destitution many rural Métis experienced in the 1930s:

> One encounters such people scattered among the various parishes of the Red River and dwelling beside families of strangers who have taken possession of a land where the Métis were once the only masters. . . . Living on inconsiderable plots of land, two or three acres in extent or sometimes even an acre or less, whose poverty contrasts with the comfortable circumstances which here and there are manifested in the establishment of some rich landowner. Many of the Métis are day laborers without any specialized occupation, who gain employment by chance whenever the occasion offers itself: some of them work in the fields as farm laborers, others in the towns, a few in the construction workshops of the CNR. Yet others, too lacking in any kind of technical training to find an opening easily, or incapable of rearing their children with the produce of the piece of land which they exploit, are reduced to entering themselves on the relief rolls.[52]

The 1935 federal voters list provides a description of the occupations of male household heads of Rooster Town (Table 4.3). Almost without exception, Métis men in the neighbourhood were unskilled, and most worked as labourers. Many of the teamsters and gardeners were likely self-employed and their incomes were probably precarious. More than a quarter of Rooster Town residents were listed as unemployed, but this number was probably even greater, in line with the 1930–31 estimates that over half of all unskilled labourers in Canada were unemployed for more than six months of the year.[53]

FIGURE 4.4. Map of Rooster Town, 1936.

1 Maurice and Winona Louise Peppin
2 *Joseph Patrick and Agnes Morrissette*
3 *Josephine Poitras*
4 *John William and Catherine Omand*
5 Edward Scott and Mary Grace Smith
6 Alexander and Adelaide Morrisette
7 John and Agnes Peppin
  Allan Alexander Peppin
8 David and Victoria Butchart
  Blanche Rose Smith
9 Charles and Lucy Villebrun
10 James Charles and Marie Louise Parisien
11 Marcien Peter and Marguerite Cardinal
12 Arthur and Esther Catherine Henry
   Patrick Henry
   Marie Smith
13 Remauld Frank Xavier
   and Adeline Gosselin
14 Alexander and Adele Minnie
   Elice Minnie
15 John and Marie Josephine Paddison
16 Louis Raphael and Ida Parisian
   Modeste and Sarah Cardinal

17 Michael and Ellen Slemko
18 Joseph and Mary Cora Arcand
19 Patrick and Mathilde Conway
20 Joseph Amadee and Dorilda Conway
21 Joseph Adolphes and
   Marie Adele Vandal
22 William and Frances Malvina Smith
23 Joseph Arthur and Marion Parisien
   Veronique Parisien
24 Thomas and Grace Adele Jenkins
25 Alexander Smith
26 Adritch and Florida Smith
27 Arthur and Agnes Belvah Cardinal
28 Leonard Gabrielle and Rose Cardinal
29 Amable and Alice Hogg
   Peter and Julia Hogg
   Charles H and Marie Josephine Cardinal
   Orlando Alem and Marie Adele Weaver
30 William and Rachel Ogidile
   Anne Roussin
31 Joseph Edgar and Genevieve Weaver
32 Francois and Marie Larocque
33 William Exavier Dunnick

34 Joseph Francois and Marie
   Adele Parisien
35 Henry Edward Lafrance and
   Amelia Grace Parker
36 Frederick and Alphonsine Parisian
37 Philias and Alice Laramee
38 Herman and Lydia Larson
39 Joseph Noel and Marie
   Marguerite Laramee
40 Adolph Joseph and Marie
   Josephine Pilon
41 Paul and Marie Julie Laramee
42 Joseph Leon and Florence Courchene
43 Philius and Mary Jane Laramee
   John and Alice Nolin
44 Alphonse Peter and Caroline Courchene
45 *Kenrick Peter Campbell*
46 Joseph Louis and Marie Adele Laramee

Note: Names in italics represent householders who no longer reside within the perimeters of Rooster Town but contiue to be a part of Rooster Town community.

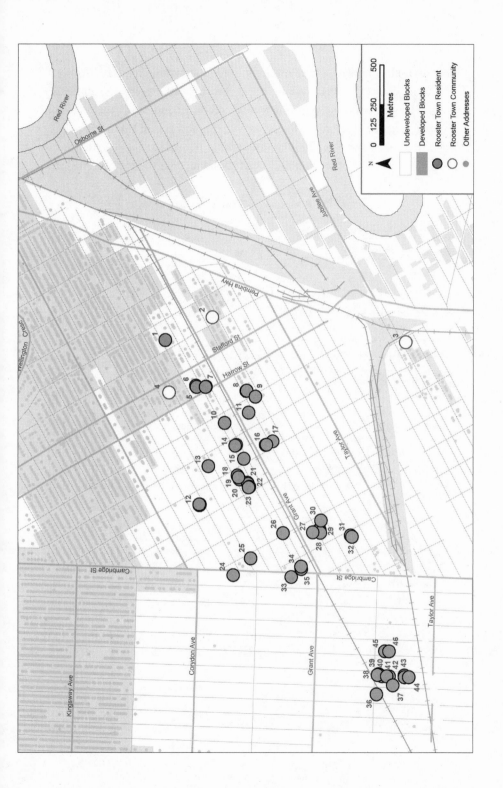

For example, Louis Raphael Parisian is listed as a labourer in the 1935 federal voters lists, but the notes in Winnipeg collector's rolls between 1931 and 1936 warned collectors to keep off the family's premises, indicating that Parisian was on relief and paying off his property taxes at a rate of three dollars per month. Louis Raphael and his family, in their attempt to survive and protect their investment in their building, had likely become tired of interference

TABLE 4.2. Changes between 1931 and 1936.

GONE FROM ROOSTER TOWN	
Deaths	6 individuals
Not listed or moved	1 individual, 5 families
ADDED TO ROOSTER TOWN	
Without obvious kin links to Rooster Town	0
With kin links to Rooster Town	5 families
Married widow or formed with previous families or descendants	2 individuals, 11 families

Sources: 1931 to 1936 City of Winnipeg Henderson's Directories; City of Winnipeg, City Clerk's Department, Election Rolls, 1931–1936, City of Winnipeg Archives and Record Centre (CWARC). Details about these changes are found in Appendix B.

TABLE 4.3. Rooster Town Employment, 1935.

OCCUPATION	PERCENT
Unemployed	28.6
Labourer	38.7
Teamster or truck driver	16.3
Gardener	8.2
Other	8.2

Source: 1935 Voters Lists, Federal Elections, 1935–1980. R1003-6-3-E (RG113-B). Library and Archives Canada, Ottawa, Ontario, Canada.

from both tax collectors and relief officers and had clearly communicated this to a variety of officials.[54]

There are other small insights into Rooster Town residents' strategies to persevere during these years, which may have been even more difficult than some of the previous ones. In 1936, for example, Josephine Henry, living with non-Métis John Paddison at 1097 Scotland Avenue, was sent to jail for three months for "having liquor in her possession not bought from a government liquor commission."[55] She was likely bootlegging in order to generate an income. In 1937, William Dunnick, his son, and Raymond Smith, neighbour Alexander Smith's son, were arrested and charged with theft of one ton of old iron from CN yards at Paddington Junction. They were caught loading "old railway spikes, 'fish' plates from old locomotives and other scrap iron" into a truck, hoping to sell them on the scrap metal market.[56] Finally, while Rooster Town residences were overcrowded throughout the community's history, this time period may have been the most severe. Although in earlier years most families and couples lived in separate households, in 1936, six families were living with other families, reflecting the intense poverty of this decade.

Stephen Casey, writing about his years with the Jesuits, described Rooster Town poverty and living conditions. He recounted a Rooster Town schoolmate in the mid-1930s: "Joe lived in what everybody then called Rooster Town, beyond Waugh's grocery store on what was then open prairie, rough grass punctuated by a few willows and scrub oaks. . . . These Metis spoke French and were separate from the Scottish Metis who lived north of Winnipeg. They were desperately poor in those days and most lived in tar paper shacks. Joe was bow-legged, a victim of rickets, like his three sisters; you could drive a barrel through his short legs."[57] The 1935 federal voters list refer most likely to Joe's father, Joe Gosselin, and his wife as dwelling at 995 Lorette Avenue. Joe is listed as being unemployed.[58]

A few dispersed references to housing in this decade provide additional insights about housing structures, tenure arrangements, and location choices of Rooster Town residents. Winnipeg's building permits indicate that, in 1933, Ukrainian immigrant Wasyl Uhryn, a stationary fireman or boiler operator who lived nearby, purchased the lot at 1003 Weatherdon Avenue and moved a building onto it. The inspector noted that the dwelling was damaged and needed repairs. On 11 April, he described the structure in a note attached to the building permit: "old building moved on to site and set on wood blocks resting on concrete blocks laid on the sod. It has been shingled on outside and relined on the inside with V joints on draft paper. Ceilings are also V joint."[59] By 31 May, a summer kitchen with a smoke pipe had been added, and Uhryn was instructed to build a chimney. In August 1933, the inspector again voiced his concern that the stovepipe stuck out through the side wall of the summer kitchen, clearly constituting a fire hazard, and that the stovepipe in the upstairs room was only three inches from the ceiling. The stovepipe conditions must have been resolved, because there were no further inspector's reports on the structure. The current property description indicates that the building has six rooms, but the 1948 aerial photo suggests that it originally was a four-room structure like many of the other houses currently in the area, with an attached summer kitchen.[60] The house is a single story today, so the attic "room" that the inspector mentioned probably was not finished. Six different Rooster Town families were subsequently listed as living at 1003 Weatherdon Avenue. The limited information available in the records does not allow us to unravel ownership patterns, but it may be that other non-Métis residents, living nearby, saw the possibility of building modest units for rent to Métis inhabitants.

In 1938, Thomas Alexander Parisien demonstrated self-building, the strategy that had been largely out of reach for most Rooster Town residents in previous years but now, as economic conditions improved, was increasingly possible for some. Although Thomas's parents had not lived in Rooster Town, his sister, Marie Adele Vandal, did. Thomas likely moved from his father's farm in St. Adolphe. His father's obituary in 1943 indicated that Thomas had seven siblings, two of whom remained in St. Adolphe, possibly farming. The family homestead could probably not support the large family and Thomas chose to look for work in the city.[61] He bought some land at 1046 Garwood Avenue, and in early spring of 1938, according to Winnipeg's building permits, he disassembled an old house on the property and used the lumber to build a 21 x 26–foot frame dwelling on stone pads.[62] Parisien also planned that the house would be connected to sewer and water when they became available. By the end of April, the house was roofed and shingled, and in mid-May the family moved in. At that time, the inspector noted that the house had no chimney, but by the beginning of August, a chimney had been constructed in compliance with Winnipeg's building codes.

These examples undermine the stereotype that Rooster Town was composed entirely of tar paper shacks, scattered randomly throughout the grass and brush of the Fort Rouge prairie. Both of the structures described above

still stand, although 1003 Weatherdon Avenue has been extensively reno-
vated. Nevertheless, both line up with the street plan and both were hooked
up with city sewer and water lines eventually. While these houses were extremely modest, they must have been reasonably well-built to last eighty
years, until now. An examination of the current streetscape near the houses
indicates that both would have looked very much like the standard housing
subsequently erected nearby. Even though Thomas Parisien improved his
house through self-building, he still chose to buy and build within a couple
of blocks of a cluster of long-term residents (Arcands, Conways, and Julia
Hogg), away from the developed area of Fort Rouge. The Parisiens' ability
to purchase the lot and the building materials for a house suggests that they
would have had some choice in where they relocated. Like other Rooster
Town dwellers in the 1930s and earlier, their choice of Weatherdon indicates
that they saw the advantages of living near a Métis community.

While reporter John Dafoe wrote in 1959 that Rooster Town reached its
peak in the 1930s, the year 1941 actually had the largest number of households, likely reflecting the influx associated with the Great Depression.[63] The
map of Rooster Town in 1941 was largely unchanged from its map in 1936—
the households were constructed at the edge of the developed area and sprin-
kled in the bush and grasslands east and west of Cambridge Street (Figure
4.5). A rare photo of Rooster Town resident Elise Sais (née Arcand) and her
daughter Mary taken circa 1940, shows what the Rooster Town grasslands and
brush must have looked like. Elise had married Charles Sais, who had moved
into Rooster Town by 1935, and the family owned the house at 1501 Hector
Avenue. Elise's grandson Darrell indicated that in the photo she was pregnant
with his Aunt Ruth, born in 1940, and the small child was his Aunt Mary, born
in 1938. The clean clothes and careful dress demonstrate the selective nature
of the later portraits printed by the newspaper that depicted all residents as
ragged and dirty.

By 1941, Rooster Town included one more family than it had in 1936,
reaching a total of fifty households. While the same number of deaths of older Rooster Town residents was registered by 1941 as by 1936, it is also likely
that Modeste and Sarah Cardinal, not listed in 1941, Francois Laracque, and
Adele and Elice Minnie had died by then. Elice had been living with her son
Alexander Minnie and his wife Adele previously, and in 1941, Alexander was
living with his sister Marie Louise and her husband James Charles (Jim) Parisien. A 1937 *Winnipeg Tribune* interview with Elice Minnie reported that

FIGURE 4.7. Map of Rooster Town, 1941.

1 *Roderick Patrick Morrissette*
2 Alphonse Peter and Caroline Courchene
3 Alexander and Adelaide Morrisette
   Patrick and Elsie Morrisette
   Charles Parisien
4 Philius and Mary Jane Laramee
   William Dunnick (Jr.) and Agnes Birston
   Alice Nolin
5 Marie Josephine Cardinal
6 James Charles and Marie Louise Parisien
   Alexander Minnie
7 William (Jr.) and Frances Malvina Smith
   Adrich and Florida Smith
8 David Butchart
   Blanche Rose Smith
9 Charles and Lucy Villebrun
10 Remauld Frank Exavier Gosselin
11 Arthur and Esther Catherine Henry
12 Joseph Edgar and Genevieve Weaver
13 Gavin and Elianna Ann Smith
14 Archie and Marion Parisian
15 Thomas Alexander and
   Beatrice Mary Parisien
   Veronique Parisien

16 Joseph and Mary Cardinal
17 John and Marie Josephine Paddison
18 Edward and Marion V. Parisian
19 Joseph George and Josephine
   St. Germaine
20 Michael and Ellen Slemko
21 Joseph and Mary Cora Arcand
22 Emile Ernest and Marie Julie Ann Lepine
23 Patrick and Mathilde Conway
24 Joseph Amadee and Dorilda Conway
25 Julia Hogg
26 Joseph Adolphes and Marie Adele Vandal
27 Thomas and Grace Adele Jenkins
28 Raymond Smith
29 Marcien Peter and Marguerite Cardinal
   Horamidos and Angeline Laramee
30 Gordon and Delia Margaret Parker
31 Joseph Francois and Marie Adele Parisien
32 Henry Edward Lafrance and
   Amelia Grace Parker
33 Stanley and Julia Therese Parker
34 Herbert Edwin and Clara Parker
35 Arthur and Agnes Belvah Cardinal

36 Leonard Gabrielle and Rose Cardinal
37 William and Rachel Ogidile
   Anne Roussin
38 Amable and Alice Hogg
39 Laurel and Anne Jean St. Germain
40 Charles Maxime and Elise Sais
41 Frederick and Alphonsine Parisian
42 Joseph and Marie Rose Marcoux
43 Herman and Lydia Larson
44 Joseph Noel and Marie
   Marguerite Laramee
45 Adolph Joseph and Marie Josephine Pilon
46 Paul and Marie Julie Laramee
47 Alphonse and Frances Cora
   Theresa Laramee
48 Philias and Alice Laramee
49 Kenrick Peter Campbell
50 Edward Scott and Mary Grace Smith
51 Joseph Louis and Marie Adele Laramee
52 Joseph Leon and Florence Courchene

Note: Names in italics represent householders who no longer reside within the perimeters of Rooster Town but continue to be a part of Rooster Town community.

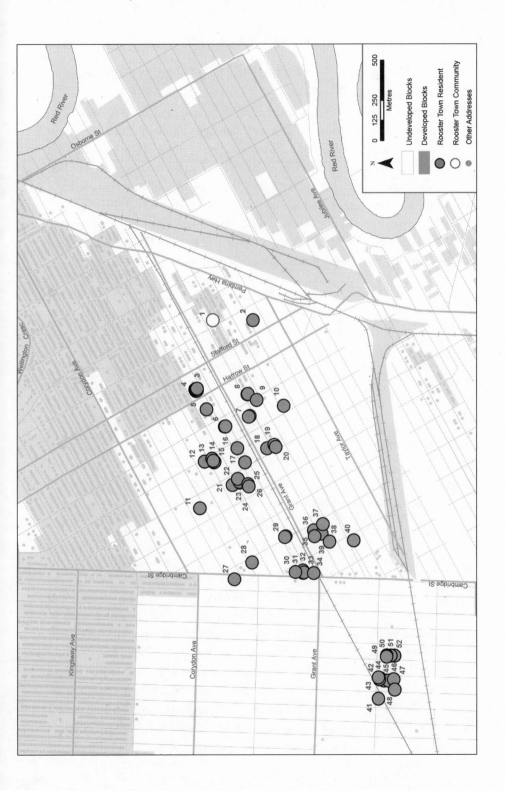

she was an Indian, 102 years old, and had lived in Winnipeg all of her life.[64] Historical records, though, show that she was born in 1851, had previously lived in St. Norbert, where she had applied for scrip, and as a widow, in 1901, she had moved to Rooster Town with her two children.[65] The reporter remarked that Elice had trouble communicating in English. He wrote that she lived with her son in a house that was tinier than most garages; the blurred image in the newspaper shows a very small house with the one door and window almost taking up a whole wall. Patrick Henry, Peter Hogg, and Ida Parisian were probably still living in Rooster Town but were not reported in official documents. Although their family had lived in Rooster Town since before 1901, the Peppin descendants moved away by 1941.

TABLE 4.4. Changes between 1936 and 1941.

GONE FROM ROOSTER TOWN	
Deaths	7 individuals
Not listed or moved	7 individuals, 3 families
ADDED TO ROOSTER TOWN	
Without obvious kin links to Rooster Town	1 family
With kin links to Rooster Town	7 families
Married widow or formed with previous families or descendants	1 individual, 8 families

Sources: 1936 to 1941 City of Winnipeg Henderson's Directories; City of Winnipeg, City Clerk's Department, Election Rolls, 1936–1941, City of Winnipeg Archives and Record Centre (CWARC). Details about these changes are found in Appendix B.

Only one new, non-Métis family moved into the area between 1936 and 1941. Quebec-born Joseph Marcoux, his wife Marie Rose L'Heareaux, and their family joined the cluster of small residences on Oak and Ash Streets. In those five years, seven Métis families with kin living in Rooster Town relocated there, and eight families and one one-person household formed from Rooster Town descendants. As had been the case between 1931 and 1936, Rooster Town grew more through natural increase, rather than outsiders migrating in.

Rooster Town had very similar demographic characteristics in 1946 as it had in 1941. It dropped slightly to forty-nine households (this count leaves out the households that had moved to the nearby but developed area of Fort

FIGURE 4.6. Elise Sais and her daughter Mary in Rooster Town, c. 1940.

Rouge). In addition to Adrich Smith, who was killed during the Second World War, a number of Rooster Town's older residents died between 1941 and 1945. Very few families without kin connections moved into the community, and most of the increase was from the descendants of Rooster Town families forming families of their own. By 1941, the extended Laramee family made up a large component of the Rooster Town population (Figure 4.7).

However, the Rooster Town of the late 1940s showed an interesting development in terms of housing and choice of location, raising new challenges in how, as researchers, we would define the community. Throughout its existence, Rooster Town households occasionally became surrounded by suburban development that was connected to city services. This pattern became more pronounced during the second half of the 1940s. Some Rooster Town residents, probably benefitting from the general economic upturn of Winnipeg in that decade, were also able to purchase property at the edge of the developing suburb of Fort Rouge, and move out of what the general public perceived as Rooster Town. Even so, their residences still kept them relatively near family and friends. While these dwellings were small, so were many of the houses built around them, and they would have been indistinguishable from those of their neighbours.

These moves, to the edges of Fort Rouge development, raise questions about how to define the location and composition of Rooster Town. A few clues assist us in defining what the general public considered to be the settlement's geographical boundaries. From Casey's description in the 1930s, the tar-paper dwellings, their location in the brush and prairie grasses at a distance from the rest of Fort Rouge, and their lack of access to city services clearly differentiated them from the rest of the growing suburb. In addition, two sources suggest that the residents who purchased houses on Weatherdon around Wilton did not consider themselves, and were not considered by others, to be part of Rooster Town. The first source is from a short profile of Métis Ron Nunn, who worked for British Columbia's Ministry of Natural Resources, which states that he grew up "near Rooster Town."[66] The Henderson's Directories show that the Nunns lived at 1038 Weatherdon, just west of the early 1950s cluster of Rooster Town shanties on Weatherdon. The other source is Donald Laramee, Joseph Noel's grandson, who explained that his grandfather was able to buy 1023 Weatherdon and "move out" of Rooster Town in the 1940s.[67] This indicates that Rooster Town residents themselves considered the houses further west, as well as those at Oak and Ash Streets (where Joseph Noel Laramee had

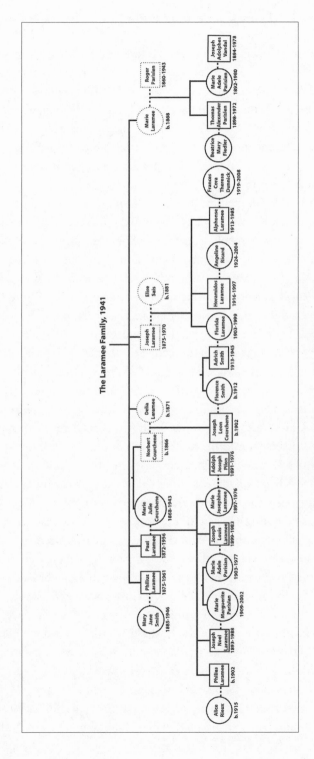

FIGURE 4.7. Rooster Town Laramee family tree, 1941.
Note the individuals in dashed lines did not live in Rooster Town but are included to show relationships.

lived previously), to represent Rooster Town. Figure 4.10, therefore, differentiates between the homes of Rooster Town residents and the dwellings of former residents who moved into or were surrounded by Fort Rouge development. Similarly, the four houses east of Paul Parisien, at 1065 Weatherdon, were not identified as Rooster Town houses. These buildings were occupied by non-Métis inhabitants, and an examination of the 1948 aerial photo of the area shows that these dwellings look like the suburban development in Fort Rouge and they are in alignment with the street.[68]

While there is little information about where Métis worked during these decades, there is evidence that a few businesses in the area provided employment to Rooster Town household heads throughout the years. The Winnipeg Henderson's Directories record that Frank Pound lived at 1044 Mulvey Avenue in 1919, and by 1920, he had established a nursery and landscape gardening business at that location, which survived into the 1960s. Figure 4.8 shows the house and the greenhouses behind it. The operation took up the entire city block.[69] In the photograph, at the front of the house is an unpaved road. Doreen Pound, Frank's daughter, recalled that her father regularly had about half a dozen Métis men working for him.[70] She remembered that Louis Laramee (likely Joseph Louis, son of Paul Laramee) was a teamster and delivered soil for her father. Figure 4.9 shows the Pound delivery truck that Louis may have used. Doreen also remembered writing out paycheques for Mab Hogg, Julia and Peter's son. Another name she recollected was Pete Roussin, William Roussin's son, who also made deliveries for them. As soon as she received her driver's licence, Doreen's father had her drive to Rooster Town to pick up employees in the morning. Frank Pound also employed Métis to clear snow for neighbouring households in Fort Rouge in winter, as well as to pack soil in the plant established at Waverley Street and Bison Drive.

Métis labourers also worked at the nearby Cambridge Riding Club. The 1936 Henderson's Directories provide the first listing of the Cambridge Riding Club at 650 Cambridge Street. Walter J. Kane, also owner and manager of Kane Tractor and Equipment—a large implement dealership in Winnipeg—established and managed the club until at least 1953, the last time it was mentioned in the Directories. The club was large; it hosted yearly competitions featuring many different activities and age groups. Kane bought, broke, and bred horses, and stabled horses owned by others. He employed local Métis labourers for every aspect of his operation, from exercising the horses, breaking them, and cleaning their stables, to feeding and grooming them.[71] The

FIGURE 4.8. Photo of Frank Pound's greenhouse at 1044 Mulvey Avenue, 1930s.

FIGURE 4.9. Pound delivery truck, early 1920s.

TABLE 4.5. Changes between 1941 and 1946.

GONE FROM ROOSTER TOWN	
Deaths	7 individuals
Not listed or moved	2 individuals, 5 families
Integrated	1 individual, 6 families
ADDED TO ROOSTER TOWN	
Without obvious kin links to Rooster Town	2 families
With kin links to Rooster Town	1 individual, 4 families
Married widow or formed with previous families or descendants	1 individual, 5 families

Sources: 1941 to 1946 City of Winnipeg Henderson's Directories; City of Winnipeg, City Clerk's Department, Election Rolls, 1941–1946, City of Winnipeg Archives and Record Centre (CWARC). Details about these changes are found in Appendix B.

Royal Dairy at the south end of Cambridge, established by Adolph Van Walleghem in the early 1900s and sold in 1965, also employed local Métis labour to make deliveries as well as to work in their barns.[72]

City of Winnipeg records provide some information about the developments on the block of Weatherdon Avenue east of Wilton Avenue, where the members of the extended Laramee family bought land and constructed houses in 1943 and 1944. In 1943, Joseph Noel Laramee, Paul Laramee's son, moved his house from its Ash Street location to a lot he had purchased at 1023 Weatherdon Avenue.[73] The "cottage" was valued by the city at $200. Joseph began to build a stable and was notified by the housing department that he had not obtained a permit. In his renovations, he put a metal chimney smokestack through the roof and was reminded that he also needed to build a brick chimney. Joseph built the chimney, obtained a permit to build a stable for three horses, and in 1944 he obtained a permit to construct a basement "to take care of water and sewer which is being put in this street."[74] By 1949 the assessment rolls valued Joseph's home at $950, substantially more than its 1943 estimate of $200.[75] Arthur Edmond Laramee, another of Paul Laramee's sons, similarly moved his four-room cottage from Ash Street to 1022 Weatherdon Avenue, across the street from his brother, and made improvements. In 1944, Arthur's house was valued at $600.[76]

Louis Raphael and Ida Parisian's son Edward and his wife Marion had lived in the house Louis had constructed at 1065 Weatherdon, but by 1942 Edward had bought 1004 Weatherdon Avenue and began to construct a house and garage on the lot. Winnipeg's current property assessment of the house at 1004 Weatherdon Avenue describes it as containing four rooms built in 1943. Although its price today is not available, the 1948 assessment rolls valued Edward's house at $1,800.[77] Joseph Laramee also built a home on the same block for his daughter Florida married to Adrich Smith, who was serving in the army overseas. The house was tiny—the current property assessment website indicates it is less than 500 square feet. The building in-spector indicated that some of Joseph's framing was not up to code, but he eventually allowed it. Florida Smith and her three children lived there in the small four-room, one-story house, assessed at $600 in 1948.[78] In 1943, Métis Joseph Hamel, born in St. Norbert, and his wife bought and moved to 1918 Weatherdon Avenue, a house neighbouring the Laramees. The Hamels did not have any relatives living in Rooster Town, but it is possible that they relo-cated to be near other Métis in the area.[79]

Side by side, Alexander and Adelaide Morrissette's and Philius and Mary Jane Laramee's houses were now within the developed section of Lorette Av-enue and as a result (see Figure 4.10). Philius had made improvements to the house in the 1920s, changing it from a one-story shanty to a one and one and half story house.[80] The house was likely connected up to the sewer lines in the 1920s. However, it was counted as part of Rooster Town in earlier years because it was at the edge of the developed area, slightly separated from other houses on Lorette, and had been rented to a succession of different Rooster Town families—Henry George Paquin and his wife, several Peppin families, and Edward Scott Smith. The Morrissette house next door was also at the edge of the city until 1946. In 1948, Alexander built an addition to the house. Since the house is currently listed as having four rooms, it must have had only two or three rooms before then, and was relatively small, even by Rooster Town standards, for the Morrissette family of four.[81]

The 1948 aerial photo clearly shows the relationship between the devel-oping urban landscapes in Fort Rouge and the Rooster Town homes and also provides some tantalizing bits of information about neighbourhood's resi-dents.[82] Orlando Weaver's household at 1019 Scotland Avenue, living in what was formerly James Charles (Jim) Parisien's house, is located among a cluster of dwellings south of the much more developed north side of Lorette Avenue. Scotland Avenue has been laid out to Cambridge, but clearly not paved yet. Julia Hogg's and Joseph Vandal's houses on Lorette Avenue are not serviced by a street yet; they sit just south of Dudley Avenue, which has been built up

FIGURE 4.10. Map of Rooster Town, 1946.

1 Roderick Patrick Morrissette
2 Alphonse Peter and Caroline Courchene
3 Alexander and Adelaide Morrisette
   Patrick and Elsie Morrisette
4 Philius and Mary Jane Laramee
5 Marcien Peter and Marguerite Cardinal
6 Orlando Alem and Marie Adele Weaver
7 Joseph Noel and Marie Marguerite Laramee
8 Arthur Edmond and Marguerite Laramee
9 Joseph Alphonse and Mary Louise Hamel
10 Edward and Marion V. Parisian
11 Florida Smith
12 Charles and Lucy Villebrun
13 Josephine St. Germaine
14 Arthur and Esther Catherine Henry
15 Raymond Smith
16 Joseph Edgar and Genevieve Weaver
17 Gavin and Elianna Ann Smith
18 Thomas Alexander and
   Beatrice Mary Parisien
19 Emile Ernest Lepine
20 D.E. and Violet Smith
21 Joseph and Mary Cora Arcand

22 Patrick and Mathilde Conway
23 Joseph Amadee and Dorilda Conway
24 Remauld Frank Xavier Gosslin
   and Julia Hogg
   Patrick Henry
25 Joseph Adolphes and Marie Adele Vandal
26 Leo Paul and Helen Elizabeth Berard
27 William (Jr.) and Agnes Dunnick
28 John and Marie Josephine Paddison
29 Paul Napoleon and Bernice Parisien
   Arthur Parisen
   Ida Parisian
30 Michael and Ellen Slemko
31 Thomas and Christine Paquin
32 William and Lilly Smith
33 Albert Stephen and Lillian Ethel Wilson
34 Thomas and Grace Adele Jenkins
35 John and Alice Nolin
36 Gordon and Delia Margaret Parker
37 Henry Edward Lafrance and
   Amelia Grace Parker
38 Stanley and Julia Theresa Parker
39 Herbert Edwin and Clara Parker
40 Joseph Francois and Marie Adele Parisien

41 Leo and Margaret Vandal
42 William and Frances Malvina Smith
43 Arthur and Agnes Belvah Cardinal
44 William and Rachel Ogidile Anne Roussin
45 Amable and Alice Hogg
46 Ernest Joseph and Edmee Parisian
47 James Charles and Marie Louise Parisien
48 Charles Maxime and Elise Sais
49 Frederick and Alphonsine Parisian
50 Adolph Joseph and Marie Josephine Pilon
51 Joseph Amadee and Margaret Pilon
52 Paul Laramee
53 Alphonse and Frances Cora
   Theresa Laramee
54 Philias and Alice Laramee
55 Kenrick Peter Campbell
56 Joseph and Marie Rose Marcoux
57 Edward Scott and Mary Grace Smith
58 Joseph Louis and Marie Adele Laramee
59 Leonard Gabrielle and Rose Cardinal

*Note: Names in italics represent householders who no
longer reside within the perimeters of Rooster Town
but continue to be a part of Rooster Town community.*

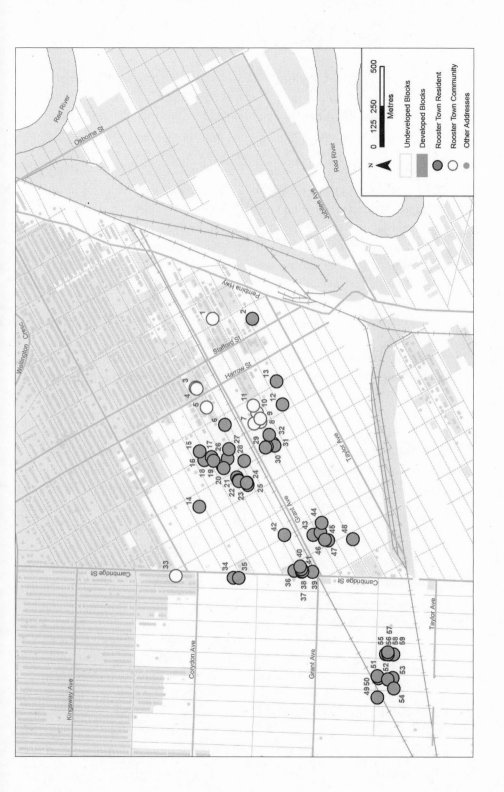

and appears to be paved. William and Frances Smith's house at 1249 Scotland Avenue is away from the developed area of Fort Rouge, and it is surrounded by extensive gardens. While the Smiths bought the property, the 1941 assessment rolls valued the house at only $250, so it was likely a small one.[83] The area where Henry Parker lived contains numerous buildings, some of them possibly occupied by his grown and married children. In 1948, the *Winnipeg Tribune* published a picture of Henry Parker standing in front of his house and reported, inaccurately, that he had been the first resident on the street in 1902 and that now two of his daughters and sons also lived on the street.[84] The railway still runs along what will later become Grant Avenue. In the 1948 aerial photo, there are extensive gardens around Paul and Bernice Parisien's house at 1065 Weatherdon Avenue. The dotting of small residences and lack of access to city services can be made out further west on what will become Grant Park Mall. It is this area, as well as the clusters of houses at Oak and Ash, that in 1948 the general public perceived as Rooster Town.

A description of what must have been a common housing configuration for many Rooster Town households accompanies newspaper coverage of two tragic deaths in 1946 and 1947. The two accidents orphaned eleven Tanquay children living at 1092 Hector Avenue. The small house was owned by Rooster Town resident Frank Gosselin, who moved in with Julia Hogg, and it was valued by the city at $100 in 1941.[85] Louise Tanquay was killed in June of 1946 when the family's stove exploded, leaving her seventeen-year-old daughter to care for the household. The family's father, Albert Tanquay, died in March 1947 when the ditch he was helping to dig as part of his employment with the city, collapsed on him. The *Winnipeg Free Press* reporter who visited the family described the house as a "crude one and a half storey frame shack, set off by itself in the woods at 1092 Hector avenue. . . . A sparsely furnished medium-sized room where three of the children sleep—a stove, table, one bed, two chairs and a rickety ladder leading up to a tiny attic. . . . The other eight [children] bundle together up there to keep warm when they sleep."[86]

The Tanquay case illustrates another aspect of Rooster Town housing at the time—some residents rented to other community members, further complicating Rooster Town tenure status. Frank Gosselin had originally moved and repaired the small shack on Hector in 1937, "all to the satisfaction of Health Dept.," and he lived there with his wife, who died the following year.[87] By 1945, Frank was living with Julia Hogg in her house at 1141 Lorette Avenue and, as a result, he was able to rent out his former dwelling. Louis Parisien, his brother

Joseph Francois Parisien, and their cousin James Charles (Jim) Parisien also rented houses to other Métis families. Their names are listed in association with 1065, 1069, and 1144 Weatherdon Avenue buildings, all of which were occupied by other Métis households at various times.[88] In an interview, Sandra Monro, one of the Birston daughters who lived in Rooster Town in the 1950s, identified James Charles (Jim) Parisien as "the landlord."[89]

Rooster Town continued to remain under the radar of Winnipeg's government and social services between 1931 and 1946. The number of households increased every year until, in 1946, the community reached its maximum size of fifty-nine households, with an estimated population of more than 250 people. Most of the increase was internal, with descendants marrying other Rooster Town residents. The growing population suggests that living in Rooster Town was a practical strategy for those facing the hardships of low incomes and discrimination. As Rooster Town residents struggled to make better lives for themselves and their families, they challenged the established attitudes that their living situation represented an inability to adapt to the urban economy. Poverty and unemployment associated with the depression and Winnipeg's chronic housing shortages meant that squatting, buying inexpensive unserviced land on urban fringes, and self-building remained attractive ways to access the city's labour market.

Patterns of settlement, shared housing, and choosing to reside near Rooster Town show that Métis culture and community was valued by these urban dwellers, and helped them to cope with an often hostile environment, rather than preventing them from adapting to urban life. The inadequate social safety net meant that Rooster Town residents relied on kin and community. During the Great Depression, in unprecedented levels they doubled up as families shared residences in order to reduce expenses. This period also witnessed relatives moving to the community, and more economically successful residents choosing to relocate to serviced lots that still were near Rooster Town. Clearly, community ties remained important, even next to socio-economic mobility. However, the following decade would see the destruction of the community through the intervention of social service organizations and municipal government.

CHAPTER FIVE

Stereotyping, Dissolution, and Dispersal: Rooster Town, 1951–1961

IN THE 1950S, ROOSTER TOWN RESIDENTS EXPERIENCED interventions into their lives and community by health, education, and municipal authorities to an extent that they had not previously experienced. In earlier decades, the media had occasionally posted some information about Rooster Town, most commonly reports on petty crime, bootlegging convictions, and homebrew-fuelled parties. The 1950s, however, ushered in prying and sensationalist reports by two of Winnipeg's major daily newspapers, the *Winnipeg Free Press* and the *Winnipeg Tribune*. Reporters moved in with their cameras, knocking on doors, entering houses, and taking photographs of the poorest dwelling units, the messiest surroundings, and, in some instances, the shabbiest home interiors. Their articles would describe Rooster Town people and their living conditions in ways that would titillate and distance the community from the largely middle-class readership. In the process, reporters simplified and homogenized residents and their housing, obliterated the complex processes and histories that created the community, and embarrassed Rooster Town residents. Newspaper reproductions of decades-old stereotypes of Indigenous people and their supposed unsuitability for city life demonstrated the dogged persistence of these tropes, despite extensive evidence to contradict them.

Rooster Town's last decade began with more tragedy for Julia Hogg. In June 1951, her sister Marie, estranged from William Smith and living in the North End, died.[1] In December of the same year her son, Mab, was struck by a train and killed. Less than one month later, Mab's wife Alice died.[2] In 1952, Julia's brother, Patrick, who now lived with Julia and Frank, died.[3] Julia continued to live at 1141 Lorette Avenue until 1955, when the house was torn down and burned.[4] By then suburban development had surrounded the small house and Julia was likely able to sell the property so that it could be developed. After that, she and Frank Gosselin moved to 1157 Weatherdon Avenue. Frank died in 1958 at seventy.[5] Julia continued to live at 1157 Weatherdon after Frank died and her sister Mathilda, now widowed, moved in with her.[6] In 1959, *Winnipeg Free Press* reporters again visited Rooster Town, this time to document its destruction, and one of the houses they visited was Julia and Mathilda's.[7] The grainy photo of the two widows, taken by the newspaper, represents one of the few remaining pictures of the community (Figure 5.1). The reporter, Joan Cohen, described the widows and their domestic situation in some detail: "Mrs. Julia Hogg and Miss [sic] Conway [Mathilda Henry, Julia's sister and Patrick Conway's widow], two old age pensioners, shared one of the smallest of these homes, along with nine cats, a large shaggy, part-collie mongrel, and a black-wood-stove that kept the room hot and musky. A table was squeezed into the centre of the room, littered with dishes from breakfast. They . . . live on their old-age pensions. They spend their money on food." Cohen also commented on the wedding picture hanging on the wall, noting that it showed "a young and pretty" Julia with her "dapper husband," Peter.

By 1953, Julia's brother Arthur and his family were listed by the city's voters lists and the Henderson's Directories as having left Rooster Town to live in Winnipeg's North End. The introduction of the old age security pension must have created a modicum of economic security for the widows, but the absence of husbands and male relatives made the lack of conveniences in Rooster Town challenging. The community made certain that Julia and Mathilda were taken care of: Frank Sais, who was born and grew up in the area, remarked that he used to bring them water and chop wood for them.[8] Julia and Mathilda were Frank's great aunts. He indicated that by the 1950s Julia was largely bedridden, likely a result of the hard life she had led.[9] Frank also insisted that he had "only ever seen two cats and a dog," but he suggested that the other cats may have been away "visiting," when he was at the widows' house.[10]

There is no information about how Julia found other housing or whether she received city assistance to move. As with other Rooster Town households, the Henderson's Directories indicate that by the end of 1959 she was

FIGURE 5.1. Rooster Town images from the *Winnipeg Free Press*, 1969. They appeared with Bill Leader's article "Winnipeg's Rooster Town . . . Remembrance of Things Past," 22 November 1969. Along with the photo of Julia Hogg and Mathilda Conway (bottom left), the newspaper page also shows Rose Halachaker ironing (bottom right) and her daughter Audrey (upper left). The Halchakers were a non-Metis family living in Rooster Town. The houses (upper right) could not be identified.

living in the North End, at 510 Elgin Avenue. She shared her home with another former Rooster Town family, Paul and Bernice Parisien, who were likely continuing the patterns of community support established in their old neighbourhood. By the time Julia moved, she had inhabited Rooster Town for almost six decades, and the relocation and the loss of community must have been devastating. The house at 1157 Weatherdon Avenue, where she had dwelled after 1955, was likely one of the buildings that were bulldozed and burned, along with other Rooster Town houses.[11] Warren Mills, who lived near Rooster Town, remembered the sight of burning homes and said that it "looked like Armageddon."[12] Julia died in November 1973, at eighty-eight, with only her brother Arthur (Archie) surviving her.[13]

Julia's last decade in Rooster Town was similar to that of other Rooster Town residents. It included continuing efforts to attain housing and economic security, dealing with media disruption and prying, and eventually the forced dissolution of the long-standing community, which would scatter throughout Winnipeg's North End. In the 1950s, the newspaper reports reproduced established narratives of Métis inability to cope with the modern urban economy and depicted them as out of place in urban space. In part, they helped to justify the destruction and dispersal of the community. We present alternative interpretations drawn from Rooster Town residents' perceptions of themselves and from their economic and housing strategies. The survival and prosperity of the neighbourhood's inhabitants for over sixty years challenge media depictions and show how powerful and dangerous racist stereotypes are when used in interpreting Indigenous peoples' experiences of urban life.

Newspaper reporting in the 1950s may appear an easy target, as journalists wrote sensationalist pieces in order to entertain, for the most part, the middle-class readership. The content of the articles, however, embarrassed Rooster Town inhabitants—with the result that, to this day, many former residents are reluctant to speak to non–Rooster Town dwellers about their experiences.[14] Such reporting also helped to construct Rooster Town as not worth saving, hid the effects of dissolution on community members, and helped the city to justify their forced relocation with very little compensation and support. The newspapers, then, were a powerful force in vindicating the eradication of Rooster Town and in denying the colonial history that led to its formation. In this context, it is appropriate to contradict the media's account of Rooster Town.

Winnipeg, 1951–1961

The Canadian economy expanded at an unprecedented rate after the Second World War. The increase in global commodity prices, as Europe and Japan began to rebuild from the devastation of war, was beneficial to Canada's primary sector, and the policies of full employment for Canadians and free education for veterans were successful in helping a large number of Canadians improve their socio-economic status. The Canadian gross national income increased from less than $12 billion in 1945 to approximately $30 billion in 1955.[15] Both job prospects and wages grew faster than the population, and the official unemployment rate between 1945 and 1956 averaged 2.5 percent.

Nevertheless, near full employment did not bring an end to poverty. A Statistics Canada study of non-farm families in 1961, which defined low-income families as those who paid more than 70 percent of income on food, shelter, and clothing, found that 27 percent of Canadian families were poor. If the definition was adjusted to count families who paid more than 60 percent of their income on these items, the proportion of low-income Canadian families who were poor increased to 41 percent.[16]

The welfare state that emerged after the war was relatively weak.[17] Large numbers of the short-term unemployed were covered by unemployment insurance throughout the 1950s, and an even larger cross-section of the short-term and seasonally unemployed were covered following the passage of the Unemployment Assistance Act in 1956, but individuals experiencing long-term unemployment did not benefit. The 1951 Old Age Security Act (which replaced the Old Age Pensions Act of 1927) provided a guaranteed base income of $40 to all people over seventy who met the requirements of twenty years residency in Canada.[18] The Disabled Persons Act (1954) and Blind Persons Act (1951), however, were limited in extent and few people estimated to be disabled in 1955, actually received aid from these governmental sources.[19] Still, universal hospital insurance was legislated at the federal level in the form of the Hospital Insurance and Diagnostic Services Act (1957).[20]

Housing conditions for low-income residents were poor throughout the 1950s, but particularly so in the early years of the decade. The 1944 Housing and Community Planning Subcommittee of the federal wartime Advisory Committee on Reconstruction reported that 10 percent of all dwelling units in Canada needed to be replaced, that another 25 percent needed major repairs and that one-fifth of households was overcrowded.[21] The subcommittee also found that one-third of households would not be able to pay enough rent to allow landlords to maintain dwellings and make a modest profit. While the subcommittee recommended a long-term program of building social housing for low-income renters, the federal government, supported by other levels of government, favoured programs to increase home ownership.

Winnipeg was no exception. The housing report of the 1952 Committee on Public Health and Welfare once again mentioned overcrowding, poor inner-city conditions, and overcrowding in emergency shelters.[22] For the first time, however, "poor housing in fringe areas within the City limits" was also addressed. Clearly Rooster Town was not the only fringe development in Winnipeg: the report mentioned "95 houses without plumbing in the City of Winnipeg, located on streets where there are no sewer mains."[23] The committee described the conditions of the dwelling units as being small, with six containing only one room, seven being overcrowded, and thirteen that were not clean. It also documented the extreme poverty of about half of these households: "The average monthly wage of 47 of the householders gainfully employed from whom we have received reports is $173.62."[24] There were even more houses reported without sewer main connections (107) in Winnipeg the following year, of which fourteen were on streets where sewer mains *did* exist.[25] The shortage of housing for low-income residents throughout the decade was demonstrated by a 1959 *Winnipeg Tribune* article that reported that the city council had been informed that there were eighty-one units in the North End that had collected 1,497 violations of the Health Act between 1955 and 1958, but could not be shut down because there was nowhere else to put the tenants.[26]

At the same time, this decade saw rapid suburbanization, and in the five years following the Second World War, metropolitan Winnipeg had a higher per capita rate of new house construction than any other large city in Canada.[27] The depression and the war had delayed family formation for many adults. Returning veterans, the beginning of the baby boom, relative prosperity, and state support for home ownership all meant that there was an enormous demand for new housing. Inexpensive land on the urban fringes, which the city had held onto for decades, was rapidly purchased by real estate companies assembling large tracts for housing development.[28] They hired architects and planners and they built or subcontracted extensive areas and vacant land in the southwest; Fort Rouge was rapidly transformed into row after row of neatly lined up similar-looking modest houses. Developers, planners, and politicians assumed that suburban residents desired nearby shopping centres, which took up additional land. Wildwood, Winnipeg's first fringe shopping centre, built in 1947, was soon replicated in other suburban communities.[29] It was suburbanization, not an effort to provide better housing for low-income residents, that brought Rooster Town into public view during the decade of the 1950s, and led to its eventual dissolution.

Newspaper Stereotyping

Media interest in Rooster Town was piqued with a report on 12 December 1951 by Mrs. Nan Murphy, school trustee member of the Child Health Services Board. She related to the Board of Education that there was a number of children living in Rooster Town with no plumbing and that other school children were told by parents not to play with them because they had skin infections.[30] Within a week, Rooster Town residents woke up to *Winnipeg Free Press* photos of tar paper shacks and outhouses, and a front-page article titled "Village of Patched-Up Shacks Scene of Appalling Squalor."[31] Not to be outdone, the *Winnipeg Tribune* also ran a front page-article on Rooster Town, claiming that it presented "one of the stickiest social problems in the Winnipeg Area."[32] The *Tribune* reporter knocked on one family's door and rewarded the courtesy of the residents, who asked him in out of the cold, with a description of their appearance as "bedraggled and—frankly—filthy" and the interior of their house as crowded and "not clean."[33] Like the *Winnipeg Free Press*, the *Tribune* printed pictures only of the poorest housing. Then, the neighbourhood faded from media attention until 1959, when the city began to dissolve the community and Rooster Town hit the front pages again.[34] In 1969, the *Winnipeg Free Press* would somewhat nostalgically describe the community that had once existed where the Grant Park Mall now stands.[35]

But the media reports in the 1950s echoed the ways that a variety of commentators had used to depict Indigenous people as out of place in early settler cities. The descriptions of "squalor," "filth," "dilapidated shacks," and "bedraggled children" peppered the reports. Rooster Towners were depicted as a threat to the growing city because of their disease. The *Winnipeg Free Press*'s 1951 article insisted that the lack of water and crowding resulted in "impetigo, scabies and other skin diseases, whooping cough, chicken-pox and so on."[36] Several strategies were used to emphasize that Rooster Town did not belong in the growing Fort Rouge suburb. The first was the contrast between the Métis community and other housing developments. The 1952 *Winnipeg Tribune* compared "the dilapidated shacks scattered through the brush" with the "bright paint of the newly built-up area, south of Corydon Avenue."[37] The *Winnipeg Free Press* repeated the contrast seven years later, describing the "tar-paper and wood shacks" next to the "bright bungalows of a new housing development" across the street, "shielded by a pile of dirt which was once a railway line."[38] The railway would have been the CNR's Harte subdivision line, which once ran down what is now part of Grant Avenue. The use of the term "shielded" brings us to another trope, which communicated that Rooster Town was so dilapidated that it needed to be removed from sight.

The fear of contagion underlies many of the newspaper reports. The suggestion that other school children avoided their Rooster Town classmates for fear of disease was repeated again and again. Using self-interested colonial reasoning, John Dafoe described Rooster Town as a threat because suburban development was encroaching on the community. He explained that "The town drew little attention while it was still an isolated spot on the prairie. But now city housing is threatening to engulf it so that it is becoming an acute social problem."[39] Earlier articles about housing conditions in the immigrant North End were also apprehensive about the spread of disease as a result of poor sanitary conditions. Now, for the first time in the media, there were similar concerns about Rooster Town. As long as Rooster Town was isolated, Winnipeg was not viewed as being threatened, but once Rooster Town was surrounded by modern housing developments, it was seen to pose a threat to the rest of the city.

By the late 1950s, Rooster Town was not seen as an everyday neighbourhood but had been almost completely exoticized as a colourful aspect of Winnipeg's history. John Dafoe of the *Winnipeg Free Press* reported that Rooster Town was "dying," but that it had had its "wild days": "There was plenty of social life though. They would party together and some of the parties got pretty rough. The police were always being called out after the parties."[40] Ten years later, Bill Leader remembered that "There'd been some pretty good time in old Rooster Town, some pretty wild parties and always an abundant supply of home-made liquor. . . . It may not have surpassed Wellington Crescent in elegance but in social life, by all accounts, it took some beating."[41] Leader explained Rooster Town's lack of belonging and forced removal rather euphemistically: "But the city encroached. There was no place in modern Winnipeg for such non-conformists as the Rooster Town residents and they were ousted."[42] In other words, the supposed "lifestyle" of Rooster Town had no place in gleaming modernity.

Rooster Town was also perceived as a problem because of its supposedly high cost to Winnipeg taxpayers. The assumption that all Rooster Town residents were squatters and living tax-free had surfaced in previous years, but now the complaints regarding the costs in terms of health nurse visits and public welfare were added. Ignoring the fact that most Rooster Town family heads were employed most of the year, media constructed a homogeneous picture of the community's inhabitants as uniformly welfare dependent, all unemployed, and all living on land they did not own, in so, avoiding taxes. Nan Murphy insisted that Rooster Town "cost the city unlimited funds in health and welfare."[43] Gerald O'Brien, assistant director of Winnipeg's Welfare Department, stated that "almost every family in the area during the depression was receiving municipal relief" and warned that even though Rooster Town families would move, "the problems of the Rooster Towners and the city that must care for them will remain the same."[44] His implication was that these predominantly Métis inhabitants would always be a liability and they would never fit in and prosper as Winnipeggers.

In the same vein, the media reproduced classic tropes associated with poverty and marginalization, and made Rooster Town seem "placeless"— ephemeral, unstable, and constantly moving, which suggested that dissolving the community had few consequences for the residents. Indeed, the *Winnipeg Free Press* put the word "community" in scare quotes, suggesting that it was too loosely organized to be a real community. According to reporters, even Rooster Town dwellers had difficulty describing where Rooster Town was: "Where is Rooster Town? That's a good question—one even a resident couldn't answer properly. 'We don't exactly have an address here' J.E. Cloutier told a *Winnipeg Free Press* reporter."[45] Journalists mentioned how difficult it was to find the Rooster Town residences in the bush, and stated that when buildings were identified for the purposes of tax collection, the shacks were often moved to another area. In 1959, Dafoe told the *Winnipeg Free Press* readership that "as the city moved the Rooster Towners loaded their scrapwood shacks and moved on, farther into the prairies."[46] By 1969, Leader's romanticized article "Winnipeg's Rooster Town . . . Remembrance of Things Past" stated that "it was impossible to find anyone who lived in the old town or even anybody who knew somebody who lived there. Rooster Town is a chapter in Winnipeg's history that has been largely unwritten. Where did all the people go?"[47] Rooster Town and its residents were ghost-like, and Leader suggested that the only source of information about Rooster Town might be in the wind, blowing through the Grant Park Mall parking lot: "But if you're interested why not take a stroll late one night, when the shoppers have all gone, across the deserted car park.... Maybe in the prairie wind you'll hear the far away call of a rooster and the echo of some wild party; maybe the secret is with the prairie wind?"[48] By ignoring Métis presence that has been and continues to be integral to the history of Canadian prairie cities, and by focusing on Indigenous absence, Leader demonstrated the strategy of erasure we discussed at the beginning of the book.

Finally, it bears emphasis that the media demonstrated no understanding of the history and processes of displacement and systemic racism leading to the formation of Rooster Town. Again and again, they incorrectly stated that Rooster Town was formed during the Great Depression. They also blamed Rooster Town residents for their situation. The 1951 interview with school trustee Nan Murphy, seemingly completely oblivious to the stigma of handouts and of sending children to school in second-hand clothes, reported that "the children are good at school . . . but the parents have no moral responsibility. They are shiftless and even when clothes and things are given to them they sell them."[49] Blaming their poverty and marginalization on their lack of ambition, the *Winnipeg Tribune* claimed that Rooster Town residents were satisfied with their situation: "The discouraging thing to welfare workers is that they're not sure the people of Rooster Town want anything better. Certainly the people to whom we spoke Wednesday were not bitter about their living conditions—they seemed to accept them as normal."[50] Failing to acknowledge a colonial history of dispossession as well as contemporary housing shortages, poverty, and discrimination, O'Brien, assistant director of Winnipeg's welfare department, suggested that that Rooster Town residents had chosen to move to the fringes of the developed city so they could live "Indian style."[51] Therefore, as a result of their parents' carelessness, the reporter Bill McPherson maintained, Rooster Town children "really didn't have a chance from the moment they were born."[52]

Alternative Perspectives of Rooster Town

Winnipeg's newspapers provided very little real insight into the beliefs, experiences, and perspectives of Rooster Town residents themselves. Reporters were not interested in exploring the history of Rooster Town or developing

FIGURE 5.2. Frank Sais, his wife Elaine, and his parents on Frank and Elaine's wedding day, 23 November 1963.

FIGURE 5.3. Laramees on Ash Street.

a deeper understanding of its origins. While there are no known surviving texts that would provide an alternative to the narrative woven by the media and social services, obituaries, a few photos, newspaper interviews with two Métis women who reached very old ages, and an examination of housing strategies provide a much more nuanced and less homogeneous portrait of the community.

A small number of available pictures from a variety of sources provide a different side of Rooster Town than the image of dirty, ragged people and an isolated, backward community fashioned by the media. Frank Sais pointed out that while the newspapers talked about Rooster Town residents as nothing but scum, dirt, and diseased, the Métis inhabitants used the same schools, churches, medical facilities, and stores that their neighbours did.[53] For example, Frank's wedding, held just a few years after the family moved out of Rooster Town and into the North End, took place at St. Ignatius Church, which the family had attended while they lived in Rooster Town.[54] The wedding photo of Frank, his beautiful wife Elaine, and Frank's parents Charles and Elice shows elegantly dressed participants who would have fitted in at any local place of worship (Figure 5.2).

A picture of Joseph Noel and Marguerite (Mary) Laramee's family in front of their house on Ash Street, estimated to be taken in the early 1940s, shows the family in Sunday best, nicely dressed, with Joseph again in a suit (Figure 5.3). Joseph Noel and wife Mary are in the back, Mary, Joseph Jr., and Adrianne are in the middle, and Yvonne and Hubert are in the front. The house, which can barely be made out in the background, is small, but it is not the tarpaper shack favoured by the media, and there are no heaps of garbage, old cars, or piles of lumber found in the early 1950s newspaper pictures.

A 1950 *Winnipeg Free Press* photo of "Four Generations of Laramees" showed handsome men in suits and ties, looking completely at ease in the clothing.[55] The photograph featured patriarch Paul, seventy-six, his son Joseph, fifty-six, Joseph's son Basil, twenty-four, and Basil's son Ronald, seven months old (Figure 5.4). In the earlier mentioned 1927 photo of four generations of Omands, the men also wore suits. Occasional pictures and accompanying obituaries or golden wedding celebrations similarly showed individuals who would be difficult to distinguish from middle-class Winnipeggers.

Two pictures featuring members of Paul Parisien's family send a similar message. The first is of Paul and his wife Bernice shortly after they moved from Rooster Town to 510 Elgin Street. Paul is probably dressed in his working

FIGURE 5.4. Four Generations of Laramees.

ROOM 25

Grade 6   Miss I. Clement

THE PARLIAMENT

One day in February we went down to the Parliament Buildings as a class. As we entered the Buildings we saw the grand staircase of 39 steps. Above we saw the Pool of the Black Star, also the rooms and chairs on which the King and Queen sat when they met the Lieutenant-Governor. We walked around happily enjoying the interesting things we were shown. We took pictures of the Golden Boy and of our class. The guide was very kind. He answered every question. We thanked him and home we came quietly and our teacher went home happily.

Yvonne Parisien
Room 25

ROOM 25

Thirteen come to our room
Wayne Mason and Sammy Broome.

Judy Wach comes bouncing in
But she can't beat Yvonne Parisien.

Did you ever see our Stella Lavallee
Make knitted squares like 1, 2, 3?

Dolores Karn is a whizz with yarn,
She crochets around every afghan square.

Dianne Harrison and Donald Howard
Always come in before the hour.

George Cardinal and Mervin Cahpiel
Hit the ball far out in the field.

Bobby Cherniak is our army cadet
At tumbling and swimming he's our best bet.

Edna Williams fell on the floor,
The desk that she broke can't be used any
more.

Bill Parker from Fort Garry travels by bus
He comes to our school without any fuss.

No room is so busy as Room 25
We work and we play like bees in a hive.

45

FIGURE 5.5. Yvonne Parisien's yearbook page.

clothes, but neither he nor his wife wear ragged or dirty clothing (Figure 5.6). The Grade Six St. Ignatius school, yearbook picture of Yvonne Parisien (she is to the teacher's left) shows her in a white blouse and dark jumper like all of her schoolmates. At the bottom, she is shown sewing, and she was chosen to write the entry describing their visit to the parliament building, featured on the class page (Figure 5.5). A photo of Adolph Joseph Pilon and Marie Josephine Laramee, likely on their 1921 wedding date, also shows both of them dressed up (Figure 5.7).[56]

FIGURE 5.6. Paul and Bernice Parisien at 510 Elgin Avenue, probably in the early 1960s.

Of course, there were celebrations and over the years the newspapers documented police raids on "homebrew-fueled" parties. To focus only on this facet of social life, however, provided an extremely biased representation of the community's life. As Frank Sais stated, "Yes, there were parties, and yes, sometimes they lasted all weekend, but nobody died and the police never came. And on Monday morning everybody got up and went to work."[57] In an earlier interview, Frank also mentioned that the Sais family would clear out the main room of their house and there they would hold parties with fiddling and jigging. He noted that William Roussin and Archie Cardinal were very good fiddlers.[58] Donald Laramee still has his grandfather's, Joseph Noel Laramee's, fiddle, and he said that his grandfather used to fiddle the Red River

FIGURE 5.7. Adolph Joseph Pilon and Marie Josephine Laramee, likely on their wedding date, 16 July 1921.

jig.[59] Frank Sais mentioned numerous examples of his family visiting other families, and it seems likely that "visiting" was a common social practice in the community.[60] The newspapers broadcast the negative aspects of Rooster Town gatherings, but these cultural and community-based activities were not of interest to reporters.

The material in a sampling of obituaries and other references—where Rooster Town residents it represent themselves—emphasizes individuals' historic and contemporary contributions to Manitoba's and Winnipeg's economy and challenges media interpretations of inhabitants' uniform dependency and cost to social welfare budgets. The photo of four generations of Omands was introduced by the statement: "For more than four generations has Manitoba boasted the name of Omand." The paragraph underneath the photo indicated that the patriarch James entered the services of the HBC at Fort Garry when he was fourteen years old and that he was "in government employ" for thirty years.[61] The 1912 obituary of James's wife, Jane, noted that she was the "wife

FIGURE 5.8. Frank Sais's water cart, 1951.
Winnipeg Tribune photograph appearing with MacPherson's article "Have You Heard of Rooster Town? It's Our 'Lost Suburb'" 20 December 1951, 1, 8.

of the government mail carrier who has been a well-known figure around Winnipeg for years."[62] William Peppin's obituary called him a "Pioneer Railroader," mentioning his many years of employment with the CNR.[63] Louis Parisien's 1941 obituary identified him as "a well-known farmer" in St. Norbert.[64] In a more recent example, Joseph Noel Laramee's 1988 obituary emphasized that: "He was employed with the Engineering Department of the City of Winnipeg for 32 years."[65] These examples significantly depart from the media's and social services' depictions of dependency and a drain on public coffers.

Other evidence of Métis participation in the urban labour force similarly contradicts the newspapers' emphasis on unemployment and reliance on social assistance. According to Doreen Pound, daughter of Frank Pound, who owned the nursery and greenhouses on Mulvey Avenue for many decades and employed Métis labourers there and in his snow-clearing and soil-packing businesses, the Métis were hard workers.[66] Warren Mills, who grew up at 1392 Dudley Avenue, near Rooster Town, emphasized that "the Kane [Cambridge

FIGURE 5.9. Ernest and Elizabeth Stock, 1959.
Photograph included with the article "Shack-towners to Lose Homes," in *Winnipeg Free Press*, 4 March 1959.

Riding Club], Pound [florist] and Van Walleghem [Royal Dairy] empires ran on Metis labour."[67] Moreover, even in 1951 when school trustee Nan Murphy complained of the "unlimited funds in health and welfare" spent on Rooster Town residents, W. Palmer, superintendent of the city department of public welfare, identified only six families on relief. A later article noted as well that, like many other unskilled labourers, numerous Rooster Town men on welfare worked seasonally, only applying for relief in wintertime.[68] Even small contributions helped low-income households. Frank Sais delivered water to the houses around Oak and Ash Streets. He said he was paid $0.25 per barrel, and that his father had delivered water before him. A picture of Sais's water cart appeared in the 1951 *Winnipeg Tribune* piece on Rooster Town (Figure 5.8).

The construction of Rooster Town as a uniformly tax-free squatter's community was both an exaggeration and a failure to acknowledge the economic and housing contexts that faced Rooster Town residents. As earlier chapters have shown, Rooster Town inhabitants attempted, again and again, to purchase land and create stability for their families. Poverty levels and the lack of economic security made this a risky strategy. With home ownership came city taxes and the possibility that with any financial setback, families could lose their home and the equity they had put into it. The newspapers failed to acknowledge that many Rooster Town households did arrange to pay property taxes in an attempt to create housing security. In fact, there is evidence that the city saw Rooster Town as a partial solution to the challenges of providing housing assistance and encouraged some poverty-stricken households to move to Rooster Town to meet their housing needs. Ernest Stock, a non-Métis resident, explained to a reporter in 1959 that a "city man" had suggested his family move to the area in the early 1950s when they had to leave their house on Ellice Street because of unsanitary conditions (Figure 5.9).[69]

It is important to acknowledge that the newspapers did document a part of the Rooster Town reality. There was desperate poverty and very poor housing. At times, some household heads did receive social assistance. There were parties that the police raided. Squatting was a strategy some families pursued. What the newspapers completely ignored, though, was the evidence that parents endeavoured and were often successful in making a better life for their children, that households tried to gain housing security through buying land and building houses or paying taxes, that Rooster Town heads of families were employed for the most part and contributing to the city's economic fabric, and that, in contrast to the police-raided parties, there were also community and cultural celebrations. The sensationalizing of the community may have sold newspapers, but it hid and distorted much of what was happening in Rooster Town.

The overall stability of Rooster Town, and many of its families, conflicts with newspaper constructions of ephemerality. Framed as a ghostly presence in the later newspapers, the community and its reality were significantly more complex. On the one hand, many Rooster Town descendants found their way out of Rooster Town, moving to other areas of Winnipeg, or to other towns or rural areas, contradicting reporters' predictions that Rooster Town children had "no chance." We know this from tracking some of the families, for whom information is available, but also by extrapolating this from the fact that many Rooster Town families were large, and if all descendants had continued to live in the community, its population would have been much larger. On the other hand, many families stayed in the community for decades. Records document three generations of many families and two generations of others. Out of the forty-three heads of household living in Rooster Town in 1901, over half, twenty-two, lived there until their deaths.[70]

The available records connect Rooster Town's stability to its inhabitants' very strong sense of rootedness and relationship to the history of the Red River valley. Obituaries of early Rooster Town residents spoke of origins before settlers flooded into Manitoba and before Winnipeg became a city. In her 1937 interview with the *Winnipeg Tribune*, Elice Minnie remembered when

TABLE 5.1. Changes between 1946 and 1951.

GONE FROM ROOSTER TOWN	
Deaths	1 individual
Not listed or moved	2 individuals, 5 families
Integrated	12 families
ADDED TO ROOSTER TOWN	
Without obvious kin links to Rooster Town	0
With kin links to Rooster Town	1 family
Married widow or formed with previous families or descendants	4 families

Sources: 1946 to 1951 City of Winnipeg Henderson's Directories; City of Winnipeg, City Clerk's Department, Election Rolls, 1946–1951, City of Winnipeg Archives and Record Centre (CWARC). Details about these changes are found in Appendix B.

FIGURE 5.10. Map of Rooster Town, 1951.

1   *Marcien Peter and Marguerite Cardinal*
2   *Patrick and Elsie Morrisette*
    Adelaide Morrisette
3   *Alphonse Peter and Caroline Courchene*
4   *Orlando and Marie Adele Weaver*
5   *Rene Alexander and Marie Parisian*
6   *Edward Scott and Mary Grace Smith*
7   *Walter and Denise Weaver*
8   *Joseph Noel and Marie Marguerite Laramee*
9   *Arthur Edmond and Marguerite Laramee*
    Paul Laramee
10 *Joseph Alphonse and Mary Louise Hamel*
11 *Edward and Marion V. Parisian*
12 *Basil and Marie Ellen Laramee*
13 *Florida Smith*
14 *John and Marie Josephine Paddison*
15 *Arthur and Esther Catherine Henry*
16 *Joseph Edgar and Genevieve Weaver*
17 *Thomas Alex and Beatrice Mary Parisien*
    Philias Laramee
18 *Patrick and Mathilde Conway*

19 *Joseph Amadee and Dorilda Conway*
20 Remauld Frank Xavier
    Gosselin and Julia Hogg
    Patrick Henry
21 Joseph Adolphes and Marie Adele Vandal
22 Paul Napoleon and Bernice Parisien
    Jackans Alphonse Parisian
23 James Charles and Marie Louise Parisien
24 Michael and Ellen Slemko
25 Joseph and Marie Rose Marcoux
26 Albert Stephen and Lillian Ethel Wilson
27 *Thomas Grace and Adele Jenkins*
28 *John and Alice Nolin*
29 William and Frances Malvina Smith
30 Arthur and Agnes Belvah Cardinal
31 Amable (Matt) and Alice Hogg
    Emile Ernest and Julia Lepine
32 William and Rachel Ogidile Roussin
33 Charles and Lucy Villebrun
34 Gordon and Delia Margaret Parker
35 Henry Edward Lafrance Parker

36 Joseph Francois and Marie Adele Parisien
37 Herbert Edwin and Clara Parker
38 William Smith
39 Joseph Edward and Marie Jane Cloutier
40 Thomas and Agnes Dunnick Birston
41 Joseph and Mary Cora Arcand
42 Charles Maxime and Elsie Sais
43 Frederick Parisian
44 Adolph Joseph and Marie Josephine Pilon
45 Joseph Amadee and Margaret Pilon
46 Josephat Gabriel and Marie
    Ernestine Mondor
47 James Charles and Rose Land
48 Julia Theresa and Stanley Parker
49 Kenrick Peter Campbell
50 Josephine St. Germaine
51 Joseph Louis and Marie Adele Laramee
    Peter Laramee

Note: Names in italics represent householders who no longer reside within the perimeters of Rooster Town but continue to be a part of Rooster Town community.

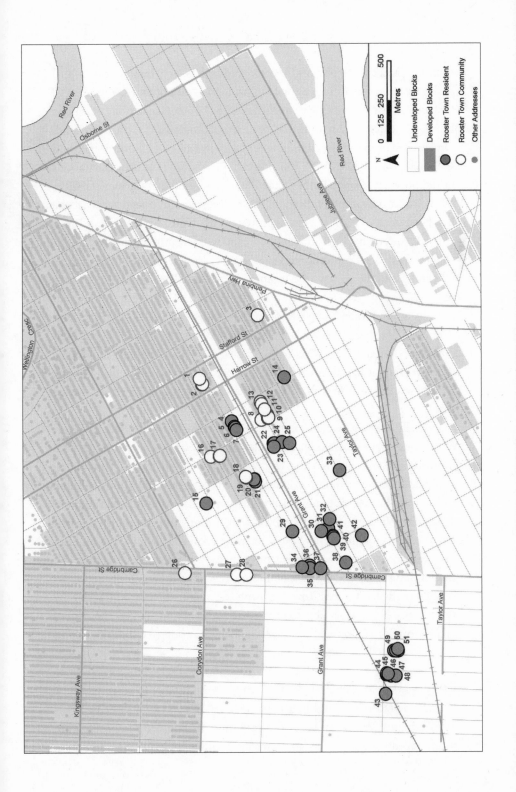

Winnipeg had only three stores and she sold "kinikinac" (traditional tobacco) at the HBC fort for $0.25 a pound.[71] The 1927 photo of four generations of Omands in the *Winnipeg Free Press* was titled "Four Generations Manitoba Born."[72] The description under the *Free Press* photo noted that patriarch James Omand had been born in the Red River valley in 1840, and the three men and the three-year-old boy in the photo were representatives of their generations in the province. Nancy Poitras (née Plante), who died at the age of 106 in 1939, was regularly interviewed on her birthday and told reporters that she had been born in 1833 at Fort Augustus on the North Saskatchewan River, and that she and her husband Joseph moved to the southern banks of the Assiniboine River in Fort Rouge in 1853. She recalled the buffalo hunts, the Riel rebellions, and the growth of Winnipeg.[73] Katherine Parisien's 1932 obituary in the *Winnipeg Free Press* listed her as a "Pioneer of the West," noting that she was an "old-timer" who was born in St. Norbert in 1857 and lived near Winnipeg all of her life.[74] Similarly, William Peppin's 1932 *Winnipeg Free Press* obituary referred to him as "one of Winnipeg's pioneer citizens."[75] The choice of terms is not insignificant. The Métis of Rooster Town knew their history, and these obituaries must have been one way of signalling to newer settlers that "We were here first."

Finally, the newspapers completely ignored the history of Rooster Town or the causes for its formation. Blaming Rooster Town residents for their own misfortune, they obscured the colonial history of land dispossession and fraudulent practices around scrip that created Métis poverty. They also failed to acknowledge the continuing discrimination Metis people in urban communities, like Winnipeg, experienced and how it must have impacted their employment possibilities. While some reporters acknowledged that the community was close-knit, their emphasis on pathology and instability clouded any recognition that dissolving the community would be economically and emotionally costly for Rooster Town residents. Such reporting paved the way for the city and its social services to rationalize and even congratulate themselves on destroying a community that many residents considered to be their home.

Rooster Town, 1951–1961

The trend of Rooster Town houses being overtaken and families being largely indistinguishable from those of surrounding developments was even more pronounced by 1951. A dozen families were now a part of the developing

Fort Rouge suburb and connected to city services. Only one family moved into Rooster Town, and four new households were formed with existing Rooster Town residents (Table 5.1). Figure 5.10 shows the Rooster Town community including inhabitants who had moved into the developed area nearby. The cluster of houses on Scotland Avenue, including Julia Hogg's house and the Vandals' dwelling, had been there since the late 1920s, but by now, they were probably connected to water, sewers, and electricity. The 1950 aerial photo map, though, shows that the buildings are less uniform and smaller than those of the surrounding housing developments.[76] The Parker family housing cluster was likely similar to nearby housing, but it was still on the fringes of the developed area. The city had identified one house on Ebby Avenue as part of Rooster Town;[77] it presumably belonged to Josephine Henry and John Paddison.

Figures 5.11 and 5.12 show the 1950 aerial photo with the 1951 Rooster Town households superimposed, and display the encroachment of the developed area of Fort Rouge, as well as households that had been overtaken by development. The railroad track is still in existence on what will eventually become Grant Avenue. Parts of Weatherdon Avenue appear not to be paved, and the graded road that extends Weatherdon a block past Wilton Avenue ends abruptly. Paths connect the houses. The households near Cambridge Street are still relatively isolated, as is the cluster of houses on Oak and Ash Streets between the tracks west of Cambridge. What appear to be a few dotted farms lie outside Rooster Town.

Likely in response to the newspaper reports on Rooster Town conditions, city council conducted its own investigation. In 1952, the committee on finance wrote to the city solicitor that "there are two groups of undesirable dwellings in the extreme southern portion of Winnipeg. None of these dwellings is on a street provided with sewer or water mains. Both groups have been the cause of considerable difficulty to our Health Department from a standpoint of health and sanitation."[78] The finance committee identified the first group as the Elm, Oak, and Ash Street cluster, all of which were on private property, paying taxes, and not on relief. With respect to these residents, wrote the committee on finance, the city could only enforce health regulations, and only one property appeared to be in bad shape. The other cluster between Carter, Weatherdon, Beaumont, and Jaffrey, with a single dwelling on Ebby Avenue (likely 819 Ebby), constituted ten shacks, with nine adults and sixteen children on relief. Despite evidence that many of the household

FIGURE 5.11. Aerial photo with 1951 eastern Rooster Town households identified.

1 *Marcien Peter and Marguerite Cardinal*
2 *Patrick and Elsie Morrisette*
  Adelaide Morrissette
3 *Alphonse Peter and Caroline Courchene*
4 Orlando and Marie Adele Weaver
5 Rene Alexander and Marie Parisian
6 Edward Scott and Mary Grace Smith
7 Walter and Denise Weaver
8 *Joseph Noel and Marie Marguerite Laramee*
9 *Arthur Edmond and Marguerite Laramee*
  Paul Laramee
10 *Joseph Alphonse and Mary Louise Hamel*
11 *Edward and Marion V. Parisian*
12 *Basil and Marie Ellen Laramee*

13 *Florida Smith*
14 John and Marie Josephine Paddison
15 Arthur and Ester Catherine Henry
16 *Joseph Edgar and Genevieve Weaver*
17 *Thomas Alex and Beatrice Mary Parisien*
  Philias Laramee
18 *Patrick and Mathilde Conway*
19 *Joseph Amadee and Dorilda Conway*
20 Remauld Frank Xavier
  Gosselin and Julia Hogg
21 Joseph Adolphes and Marie Adele Vandal
22 Paul Napoleon and Bernice Parisien
  Jackans Alphonse Parisian
23 James Charles and Marie Louise Parisien
24 Michael and Ellen Slemko

25 Joseph and Marie Rose Marcoux
26 William and Frances Malvina Smith
27 Arthur and Agnes Belvah Cardinal
28 Amable (Matt) and Alice Hogg
  Emile Ernest and Julia Lepine
29 William and Rachel Ogidile Roussin
30 Joseph Edward and Marie Jane Cloutier
31 Thomas and Agnes Dunnick Birston
32 Joseph and Mary Cora Arcand
33 Charles and Lucy Villebrun

Note: *Italicized names identify households that have been connected to city services.*

FIGURE 5.12. Aerial photo with 1951 western Rooster Town households identified.

1   Arthur and Esther Catherine Henry
2   *Patrick and Mathilde Conway*
3   *Joseph Amadee and Dorilda Conway*
4   Remauld Frank Xavier Gosselin
    and Julia Hogg
    Patrick Henry
5   Joseph Adolphes and Marie Adele Vandal
6   *Albert Stephen and Lillian Ethel Wilson*
7   *Thomas Grace and Adele Jenkins*
8   *John and Alice Nolin*
9   William and Frances Malvina Smith
10 Arthur and Agnes Belvah Cardinal

11 Amable (Matt) and Alice Hogg
    Emile Ernest and Julia Lepine
12 William and Rachel Ogidile Roussin
13 Charles and Lucy Villebrun
14 Gordon and Delia Margaret Parker
15 Henry Edward Lafrance Parker
16 Joseph Francois and Marie Adele Parisien
17 Herbert Edwin and Clara Parker
18 William (Jr.) Smith
19 Joseph Edward and Marie Jane Cloutier
20 Thomas and Agnes Dunnick Birston
21 Joseph and Mary Cora Arcand
22 Charles Maxime and Elsie Sais

23 Frederick Parisian
24 Adolph Joseph and Marie Josephine Pilon
25 Joseph Amadee and Margaret Pilon
26 Josephat Gabriel and Marie
    Ernestine Mondor
27 James Charles and Rose Land
28 Julia Theresa and Stanley Parker
29 Kenrick Peter Campbell
30 Josephine St. Germaine
31 Joseph Louis and Marie Adele Laramee
    Peter Laramee

Note: Italicized names identify households that have been connected to city services.

heads in this cluster were wage labourers and that some had purchased their lots, paid taxes, and improved their housing, the city characterized all the households in this second cluster as squatters, on relief, with shacks worth $50 each. The opinion of the Finance Department was that the inhabitants had no title to their residences and could be evicted "by appropriate legal proceedings." There was a cautionary note to the letter, however, that evictions could "increase the City's relief burden." In other words, the city realized that on some level, with their independence and ability to live in rudimentary living conditions, Rooster Town residents saved Winnipeg money. Whatever the debates among the members of the finance committee, they wrote a letter to the city solicitor's office instructing him to "take the necessary action to evict the squatters on City Land."[79]

In addition to the pressure on city council from health and welfare departments, Rooster Town residents were also threatened by the desires of the growing Fort Rouge population. The inhabitants of the developed area wanted greater access to a shopping centre, and the possibility that the city could reduce its inventory of decades-old land held for defaulted property taxes. In the spring of 1953, the city council found out that the 1954 CNR budget included money to remove the little used tracks of its branch line running on part of what is now Grant Avenue.[80] By the fall, the city had granted options on fifty-eight acres of city-owned land to Arle Realty Ltd. The company was to construct a $10,000 business and shopping centre in the area, "bounded by Frederic Avenue, Wilton and Nathaniel streets" and the CNR branch line, an area that contained the eastern cluster of Rooster Town houses. Later, the city gave the same firm the option of first refusal in extending the tract to Cambridge Street.[81] However, the track removal process was slow, and as a result, the development of a shopping centre was delayed.[82] Probably because of the delay, Arle Realty lost its bid for development, and in 1957 the real estate firm of Aronovitch and Leipsic started advertising building lots for sale on the site and asking for a shopping centre builder.[83]

In the meantime, the city began to remove some Rooster Town residents from the neighbourhood at the fringes of Fort Rouge development where they had lived for decades. Mindful of the severe housing shortage for low-income residents, the city was anxious not to create additional hardships, such as eviction, fines, or jail time, that would increase families' dependence on city relief.[84] Moreover, according to Burley, "One thing that city government disliked more than Rooster Town was the prospect of finding housing for low-income families that it dislocated."[85] In a 1952 description of Rooster Town, the *Winnipeg Tribune* reported that "some of the Rooster Town families are on relief, and over those the city has some control," suggesting that the government might threaten to withhold relief unless families moved.[86]

The changes between 1951 and 1956 foreshadowed the eventual demise of Rooster Town, as the number of households in the community decreased to only thirty-seven in total. There were a surprising number of deaths—ten people, on average just fifty-five years old. More people left Rooster Town than in the previous period—eighteen compared to thirteen residents who left between 1946 and 1951 (Table 5.2). Very few households joined Rooster Town. The destitute non-Métis Halchaker parents and their five children moved into the two-room shanty left empty by Archie and Belvah Cardinal. The Cardinals had relocated their large family into the small house built by William Roussin, whose wife was Archie's sister. Archie had suffered an injury working as a city labourer and was therefore on social assistance.[87] The family's move into a house with their relatives raises questions about whether the municipal government was threatening to cut off relief if they didn't leave. It certainly attests to the difficulty the Cardinals had finding affordable

TABLE 5.2. Changes between 1951 and 1956.

GONE FROM ROOSTER TOWN	
Deaths	6 individuals, 2 families
Not listed or moved	3 individuals, 7 families
Integrated	1 family
ADDED TO ROOSTER TOWN	
Without obvious kin links to Rooster Town	1 family
With kin links to Rooster Town	1 individual
Married widow or formed with previous families or descendants	3 families

Sources: 1951 to 1956 City of Winnipeg Henderson's Directories; City of Winnipeg, City Clerk's Department, Election Rolls, 1951–1956, City of Winnipeg Archives and Record Centre (CWARC). Details about these changes are found in Appendix B.

housing while being on relief. By 1961 the Cardinal family was living in Winnipeg's North End, where other Rooster Towners would eventually end up. Meanwhile, as noted above, Mathilda Conway moved in with her sister Julia Hogg into 1141 Lorette Avenue, upon the death of her husband. Three families of descendants were added to the community, two living in the Ash and Oak Street cluster, and one living in the developed area, just a few blocks away from the shanties at the site of the future Grant Park Shopping Centre. Figure 5.12 shows the shrinking community and the increasing incorporation of Rooster Town households into the developing Fort Rouge suburb.

The city government contradicted itself as it attempted simultaneously to minimize assistance for low-income residents and to maximize development.[88] In 1927, William Roussin purchased a lot, at what later became 1261 Carter, for $127 and built a 12 x 18–foot shanty valued at $150.[89] He paid no taxes, and in 1954, the city repossessed the property and attempted to charge rent, which Roussin also did not pay.[90] In 1956, the *Winnipeg Free Press* reported that a writ had been issued to evict "the landscape labourer, his wife and three children from the shed they live in on vacant land in the southwest corner of the city," but the city admitted it had little to gain by forcing the family out.[91] The Henderson's Directories show that the Roussins were still there in 1959.

The city's contradictory strategies led to another, obviously short-sighted move. This became clear from a 1959 municipal dispute with the Winnipeg School District, related to the building of the Grant Park High School. In a March 1959 letter to the city clerk, the solicitor for the School District of Winnipeg No. 1 wrote that "the surveyor brought to my attention the fact that the land was occupied by some fourteen squatters, some of whom stated that the City had moved them there a number of years ago," possibly to clear the site of the proposed Grant Park Shopping Centre.[92] The school district demanded that the city hand over a vacant plot of land. While city solicitors equivocated, suggesting that who had the responsibility for moving the squatters was "not well settled," the city solicitor recommended paying the Rooster Town families to move and asked that the school district pay half the costs.[93]

Many Rooster Town residents were reluctant to move. Part of their opposition stemmed from the lack of alternative, affordable housing in other parts of the city. Frank Sais reported that when his father knew he had to move his family, he asked, "Where will we move? We have no place to go."[94] Some Rooster Town residents had improved their houses, even if they did not own the land, and moving meant a loss of their investment. Ernest Stock, a non-Métis resident, explained to a reporter in 1959 that he had put money into the house he and his wife lived in, and wanted the city to tell him where he could move it.[95] James Charles (Jim) Parisien, who owned several houses and rented them out, stood to lose a fair share of his livelihood. He told a journalist that he hoped the city would move these houses to another area. Part of the reluctance to relocate must also have stemmed from a feeling of community among the Rooster Town families.[96] Gerald O'Brien, of the welfare department, told a reporter that the community was very close-knit.[97] Like the "shacktowners" of Vancouver's shoreline documented by Jill Wade, residents had "friendships, family connections and ethnic ties."[98]

The city, however, wanted to erase the six-decades-old community. In 1959, city council approved a grant of $75 per household to assist with the costs of a move, and the city welfare committee offered the householders a list of Winnipeg neighbourhoods they could move to.[99] The grant stipulated

FIGURE 5.13. Rooster Town photo accompanying Joan Cohen's article, "No Fuss, No Excitement, Squatters 'Just Moving,'" *Winnipeg Free Press*, 8 April 1959, 3.

FIGURE 5.14. Map of Rooster Town, 1956.

1   Leonard and Barbara Cardinal
2   Elsie Morrisette
    Adelaide Morrisette
3   Peter and Caroline Courchene
4   Joseph Edgar and Genevieve Weaver
5   Thomas Alexander and Beatrice Mary
    Parisien
    Philias Laramee
6   Orlando and Marie Adele Weaver
7   Walter and Denise Weaver
8   Joseph Noel and Marie
    Marguerite Laramee
9   Florida Smith
10 Basil and Mary Ellen Laramee
11 Edward and Marion V. Parisian
12 Joseph Amadee and Margaret Pilon
    Arthur Edmond and Marguerite Laramee
    Paul Laramee
13 Rene Alexander and Marie Parisian

14 Joseph Adolphes and Marie Adele Vandal
15 James Charles and Marie Louise Parisien
    Marie Adele Parisien
16 Paul Napoleon and Bernice Parisien
17 Joseph and Marie Rose Marcoux
18 Albert Stephen and Lillian Ethel Wilson
19 Thomas and Grace Adele Jenkins
20 Henry Edward Lafrance Parker
    Lucy Villebrun
21 James and Rose Halchaker
22 Emile Ernest and Julia Lepine
23 William and Rachel Ogidile Anne
    Roussin
24 Arthur and Agnes Belvah Cardinal
    Ernest H and Elizabeth Stock
25 Remauld Frank Xavier Gosselin and
    Julia Hogg
    Mathilde Conway
    Patrick Henry

26 Joseph and Mary Cora Arcand
27 Charles Maxime and Elsie Sais
28 Gordon and Delia Margaret Parker
29 Frederick Parisian
30 Olivier and Anne Parisian
31 Adolph Joseph and Marie
    Josephine Pilon
32 Josephat Gabriel and Marie
    Ernestine Mondor
33 James Charles and Rose Land
34 Stanley and Julia Theresa Parker
35 Kenrick Peter Campbell
36 Thomas and Agnes Dunnick Birston
37 Joseph Louis and Marie Adele Laramee

Note: Names in italics represent householders who no
longer reside within the perimeters of Rooster Town
but contiue to be a part of Rooster Town community.

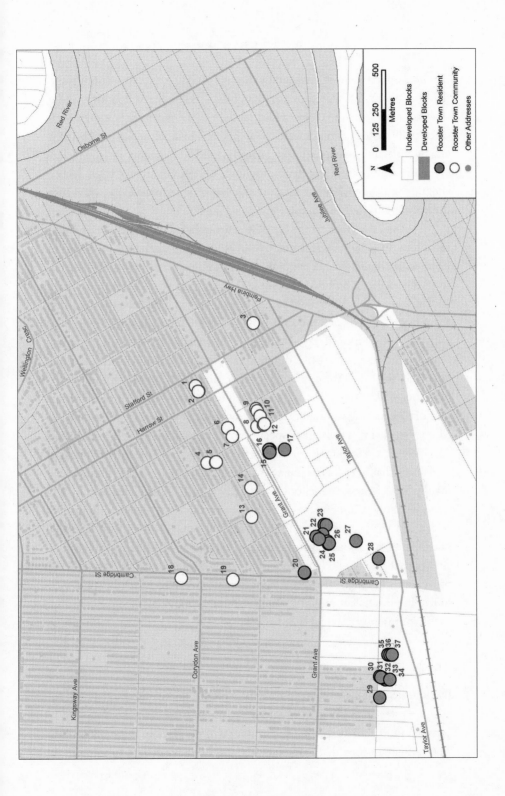

that homes had to be abandoned by the end of May to receive the full grant, that the inhabitants would receive $50 if they left by the end of June, and if they did not move, the city would evict them. The *Winnipeg Free Press* indicated that fourteen families were still living in Rooster Town in March 1959, and by June, there were only seven families left.[100] The grants and the threatening eviction notices targeted households on the Grant Park High School site; the Ash and Oak Street lots must have been sold to developers, because the households in this location were also gone by 1959.

By 1961, the Henderson's City Directories listed only one household as remaining in what had previously been Rooster Town, and it belonged to Charles Maxime Sais. He had purchased the house and land at 1501 Hector Street in 1943, and had kept up with municipal taxes.[101] Frank Sais told us that when his mother went to pay taxes, likely in 1959, she was told that the school board owned the land. Frank's father and uncle went to city hall with the paperwork and stayed in Rooster Town while the issue was resolved. Frank noted that at least five different lawyers contacted his father and encouraged him to sue the city, but his father refused. When the last one came, his father walked out of the house with an unloaded shotgun and frightened him off. According to Frank, the Sais household eventually received about $1,200 for the lot, which Frank speculated was probably worth about $150 to $200. Nevertheless, Frank felt that the land had been stolen from the family, explaining that "when someone sells something that isn't theirs [the city selling the Sais's land to the school board], that's theft."[102] The Henderson's Directories show that, like other Rooster Town residents, the Sais family then relocated to Winnipeg's North End. While they may have profited from the sale of the lot, they also lost the opportunity for homeownership, the possibility that they could have bettered their economic position through improvements on the house or through rising property values, and their ability to live in a Métis community. The Sais family's move marked the end of a Métis community that had lasted six decades.

By 1959 Rooster Town was almost sixty years old, and it represented remarkable persistence in the face of settler racism and the colonizers' stubborn contention that Métis people and culture had no place in the modern city. The settlement provided a unique and innovative Métis response to settler colonialism and dispossession. Disregarding almost six decades of evidence of the inhabitants' socio-economic mobility and determination to gain economic and housing security for themselves and their families, newspapers repeated stereotypes of Rooster Towners' inability or unwillingness to adapt to urban conditions. Reporters from both of Winnipeg's daily papers visited the community, took pictures of the poorest conditions, and published sensationalist articles that humiliated the residents. The journalists ignored the heterogeneity of situations within the settlement and the dispossession and discrimination faced by the Métis. In failing to acknowledge the stability of the community, as well as the ties of kinship and ethnicity that bound Rooster Town residents together and made them extremely reluctant to leave, the newspapers were complicit with administrators in the destruction of the neighbourhood and in the dissolution of Rooster Town inhabitants.

By 1956, the city had begun the process of moving families out of Rooster Town and by 1961, only one family was listed as still living there. Clearly some of the housing in Rooster Town was very poor, but moving to Winnipeg's North End was probably not an attractive alternative. David Burley noted that the households that can be traced moved to tenements or rooming houses in the slum areas of the core, and less than a year after their move several families lost their new homes due to a fire.[103] Besides having to occupy poor housing after their relocation, many Rooster Town families also suffered other losses. These included the ability to live in a largely Métis community, the social support networks of neighbours, the independence and the ability to exert some control over their residence and land, and the low cost of housing. Some also lost the opportunity of homeownership and part of their livelihood in the form of rent. Individuals employed at nearby businesses in Fort Rouge would have found it extremely difficult to continue to work and commute to a suburban location, far from their new homes in Winnipeg's North End. We do not romanticize the extreme poverty experienced by many Rooster Town residents. In contrast to newspaper depictions, however, we emphasize what the Rooster Town community lost when it was dissolved.

Conclusion

THE PRESENCE OF MÉTIS FRINGE COMMUNITIES on the prairies and in British Columbia has been almost completely ignored in Canadian urban geography and history disciplines, even though a substantial number of people lived there and some communities lasted for more than half a century. Lagassé's 1959 government-supported research on Métis in Manitoba reported that more than a quarter (26 percent) of this population lived on the fringes of urban settlements.[1] However, this urban fringe Métis history has not been researched in larger literature on Métis history and communities. Rooster Town was a settlement composed largely of Métis who had been dispossessed of their lands in Manitoba. Often, the households which comprised the settlement moved from the intense poverty in the rural parishes to experience access, if limited, to the urban labour market. Given evidence of extreme prejudice against the Métis, throughout the decades Rooster Town was in existence, it is also likely that choosing to live in a largely Métis community protected residents from these attitudes to some extent. Living near each other also allowed them to maintain their language, as well as their ways of socializing and of community support. While one parish, St. Norbert, was the main source of the original families that moved to the area, later arrivals came from a variety of locations. Because they made their income mostly in labouring occupations, most Rooster Town residents originally squatted on city-owned land at the fringe of the developed area of southwest Winnipeg. They built their own residences or moved structures onto the land and repaired them. Over time, some families were able to purchase lots and to improve their housing, but this was a precarious strategy when incomes were low and not dependable, and families risked losing their investments through foreclosure on unpaid taxes. Rooster Town reached its maximum population in 1941, with fifty households and an estimated population of around 250 people. It was one of the largest Métis fringe communities in Manitoba. Lagassé's 1959 list of twenty-five other fringe communities in the province identified only two with populations larger than Rooster Town: Pine Falls with 300 residents and St. Eustache with 434 residents.[2] Rooster Town dissolved in the 1950s as some residents were able to purchase land and build modest housing on nearby suburban blocks. A few families appear to have been relocated through city social service departments, and the remaining households were forced by the city to move to make way for suburban development in the late 1950s and early 1960s.

The characteristics of Rooster Town may differ from those of other fringe communities, but this study raises many questions that could fruitfully be explored in order to begin to understand the urban roots of Métis experiences. The formation of Rooster Town was rooted in the failure of settler governments to implement the provisions of the Manitoba Act, in setting aside a land base for the province's Métis population. While poverty and dispossession likely form the basis for the formation of fringe communities in many areas, the processes may be different because of varying colonial histories and practices. Other aspects to explore include the reasons for the formation of these communities, their composition, the nature of land tenure, the relationships between the fringe and nearby urban areas, the length of time these neighbourhoods existed, and the mechanisms of their dissolution. Further research of these communities would contribute to a fuller understanding of Métis and urban history and geography in Canada.

Métis People and Settler Colonialism

Many Métis fringe communities were formed as a direct result of the processes of settler colonialism, but the mechanisms differed from those directed toward First Nations people. The dispossession of Métis from their lands occurred through the implementation of land title regimes (including land scrip) rather than through treaties, which led to Department of Indian Affairs' policing and administrative practices strictly directed towards First Nations people, registered under the Indian Act. In Manitoba, delays and irregularities associated with the implementation of the 1870 Manitoba Act provisions meant that many Métis did not receive title to the river lots they or their ancestors had initially been promised by the HBC. In what is now Alberta and Saskatchewan, the federal government delayed recognition of land title to the Métis who had moved there, as well as to the Métis born in those areas, and, as a result, settlers once more displaced Métis people. In more northern areas, the signing of treaties differentiated Métis from First Nations and the Métis were denied access to reserve lands. The administration of trapline and fishing licencing and the development of commercial fisheries interrupted the ability of both Métis and First Nations people in northern areas to make a living from these activities.[3]

Researchers exploring the links between settler colonialism and Indigenous experiences of urbanization have identified containment, expulsion, and erasure as the main mechanisms through which colonizers attempted to remove Indigenous presence from cities. These processes, however, were directed primarily toward First Nations people registered under the Indian Act. Métis people were not subject to legislation or administrative practices that confined them to particular areas. Hence, Rooster Town residents came from many parishes in Manitoba and were free to choose where they settled; of course, their choices were limited to what they could afford and their willingness to tolerate the discriminatory settler attitudes toward them.

The Métis were not expelled from urban areas like the First Nations people who were registered under the Indian Act. While prejudice and discrimination almost certainly made urban life difficult for many Métis people, Winnipeg's census documents between 1901 and 1921 identified Métis individuals and families who continued to live within city boundaries, primarily working as labourers or as domestics in non-Métis households.[4] Although some residents worked in commercial operations near Rooster Town, others worked for the city of Winnipeg, the railways, for themselves and others as teamsters, and in other occupations that would have taken them into the city. They attended nearby churches, shopped in nearby retail establishments, used city services, and sent their children to school with other suburban residents. In other words, the Métis inhabitants were not cut off from urban areas the way most First Nations people were at the time.

Finally, while colonizers attempted to erase Métis as well as First Nations histories and cultures from urban life, the mechanisms through which they did this vary. Like those of First Nations, Métis cultures were seen as incompatible with urban life, and they were expected to disappear in the face of settlement. Similarly, the influences of both Indigenous groups in urban areas have largely been obscured. However, for the Métis this process was more indirect as they just ceased to be identified in the census after 1901, making it difficult to pinpoint their contribution to city life. Secondly, many urban Métis residents ceased to identify themselves as such, in an attempt to avoid discrimination. Identifying the cultural origins of Rooster Town residents required extensive genealogical research and the consultation of scrip records. An exploration of the differences between Métis and First Nations urban experiences represents an important contribution to a more nuanced understanding of settler colonialism and Indigenous peoples.

Challenges to Settler Attitudes and Expectations

The existing emphasis in scholarship—on the role of settler institutions, attitudes, and actions in shaping the experiences of urban Indigenous people—obscures the ways Indigenous citizens have resisted and challenged colonial power. An examination of the ways Indigenous individuals have undermined colonial strategies is not meant to minimize the power differences between the settlers and the Indigenous nations they encountered. However, it is important not to deny their agency by neglecting the ways that Indigenous people attempted to limit the effect of colonialism on their lives, either through explicit resistance or by pursuing ways to better their circumstances.

Rooster Town residents did not move to Rooster Town primarily to challenge settler perceptions about the incompatibility of Métis and urban cultures or to undercut colonial expectations that Métis people and their customs would disappear. However, in accessing urban employment opportunities and in finding ways to make housing near the city affordable, Rooster Town households did call into question the stereotypes that Métis people were unable to adapt to the demands of urban life. In fact, some of the early Rooster Town households were Métis families who, upon leaving their long lots, would live and work in Winnipeg for many years. Over the years, many Rooster Town residents were successful in moving away from the fringe community and into the developed area of Winnipeg. Moreover, in creating a largely Métis community and preserving elements of Métis culture such as fiddling, jigging, socializing, and supporting one another, Rooster Town residents denied expectations about the inevitable dissolution of their culture and assumptions that it did not fit into urban areas. By establishing a largely Métis settlement, they created a space of some cultural safety in the city. In their attempt to create a better life for themselves and their families, Rooster Town residents undermined colonial attitudes and expectations.

Research on Métis fringe communities in Canada makes important contributions to our understanding of geography as well as urban and Métis history, and to a more nuanced picture of the nature of settler colonialism. There are other reasons, though, why this research is important. It is clear that in some areas the dissolution of these fringe communities has created an ongoing legacy of distrust and anger. In Smithers, British Columbia, for example, the unresolved history of what happened to the "Indian Town," which existed on the fringe of the city, has created tension in the relationship between the local Indigenous people and the municipality.[5] In others, such as Rooster Town in Winnipeg, patronizing and derogatory newspaper articles and remarks by city officials created depictions of the community and its residents that humiliated them and failed to provide an accurate depiction of their lives and motivations. These depictions hid the losses the community experienced when it was dissolved. The lack of information about these communities denies them their rightful places in urban histories, economies, and cultures. Exploring the nature of fringe communities and the role settler colonial institutions and attitudes had in creating and destroying them represents an important step in the process of reconciliation.

Fort Rouge as
Métis Space:
Losing the Land

AS NOTED IN CHAPTER 1, THE 1870 CENSUS of the new province of
Manitoba shows that 99 percent of the population (over 300 people) living in what would become Fort Rouge was Métis.[1] Figure 1.2 depicts land
use and river lot layouts for the area southwest of Winnipeg. River lots 14
to 64 in the parish of St. Boniface comprise land annexed by the city of
Winnipeg in 1882 and named Fort Rouge. Most of the land was woodlot,
and only small plots were cultivated near the Red River in the area's southern portion. The HBC land register book recorded only 148.6 acres of the
total area of 4500.58 acres in cultivation in 1873, although 231.33 acres
had previously been cultivated (Table A.1). Crops failed regularly in the
early 1870s because of grasshopper infestations. Gerhard Ens indicates
that even though crops were better by 1876, many Métis who had taken
grain mortgages in the previous years could only pay them by selling their
river lot farms.[2] He also suggests that troops sent to the Red River Settlement in 1870 were a deterrent and contributed to the dispersal of Métis
in the region and that this may have been particularly felt by households
near Winnipeg.[3] Nevertheless, in 1873 almost half (48 percent) of the lots
still had houses on them, almost one-third (32 percent) had stables or other
buildings, and many were still actively being used as homesteads. With the
exception of lot 62, for which information is missing, all of the lots had
been occupied for decades.

TABLE A.1. Characteristics of River Lots in Fort Rouge, 1872.

LOT #	ADDRESS OF OCCUPANT	SIZE IN ACRES	HOUSE	STABLES OR OTHER	CULTIVATED ACRES	YEARS OCCUPIED
14	St. Boniface	61.4	1	5	33	50
15	St. Boniface	35.78	1		10	50
16	St. Boniface	43.3	1	2	10.8	50
17	St. Boniface	156.3	1	2	12.6	50
18	Not recorded	105				50
19	St. Boniface	52.4				50
20	Not recorded	52.5				50
21	Not recorded	52.5				50
22	St. Boniface	99.88	1	2	6.8	50
23	St. Boniface	98.54	1	2	9.9	50
24	St. Boniface	232.6	1	2	10.6	50
25	St. Boniface	145.6	1	1		50
26	St. Boniface	145.6				50
27	Winnipeg	51.9			7	50
28	St. James	66.2				50
29	St. Boniface	64.91	1	1	9	50
30	Winnipeg	107.8	2	3		50
31	St. Boniface	149.2	1	1	6	50
32	St. Boniface	58.66	1	1		50
33	Winnipeg	88.72	2	2		60
34	St. Boniface	191.8				60
35	Winnipeg	129.5	1			60
36	Winnipeg	48	1	1		50
37	Winnipeg	49.8	1			50
38	Winnipeg	3.53				50
39	Winnipeg	3.6				139
40	St. Boniface	2.29	1	1	2	139
41	St. Boniface	55.89	1	1	10	21
42	St. James	41.8	3	5		40
43	Winnipeg	106.4	1	1		30
44	St. Boniface	14.25	1	1	2.9	30
45	Winnipeg	87.45				30
46	St. James	193.2				30
47	Winnipeg	101.14	1	1	11	30
48	Winnipeg	87.29	1	1	5	5
49	St. James	87.29				16
50	St. James	161.52				25
51	St. James	106.2				18
52	St. James	105				19
53	St. Boniface	103.5				19
54	St. James	102.6				19
55	St. Boniface	98.09				17
56	St. James	102				17
57	St. James	103.2				17
58	St. Boniface	102.3	1	1	2	23
59	St. Boniface	100.8	"on buffalo"	"on buffalo"	"on buffalo"	25
60	St. James	99				13
61	St. Boniface	97.8				18
62	St. Boniface	48.75				
63	St. Boniface	97.8				24

Source: Land Register Book B, describing lots granted by Lord Selkirk and the HBC to various individuals, including the name of the grantee, the measurement of the lot in acres, rods and poles, the date of grant and the price per acres, 1830–1871, Location H1-30-4 (E.6/2) Microfilm 4M105 (Winnipeg: Provincial Archives of Manitoba).

According to the terms of the Manitoba Act of 1870, existing land holdings were guaranteed upon proof of ownership and river lots were to be resurveyed according to existing boundaries. The process of establishing ownership began in 1873. In 1875, after owner testimonies were given to the Dominion Lands agent in Winnipeg, the Canadian government began issuing patents to river lot holders. Despite the fact that the Hudson's Bay's land records were, according to Ens, "a hodgepodge system of land tenure,"[4] it is possible to piece together a rough history of land disposition of the Métis in Fort Rouge (Table A.2).

Table A.2 describes lot occupants and owners in 1870: the year occupants or their heirs were granted patent to their lands and what were their occupations; main purchasers and their occupations; and finally, the estimated sale price of the land received by Métis families, who owned or occupied the land in 1870. Leaving out institutions, speculators (such as Irishman James Mulligan and the Honourable James H. McKay), and occupants who sold their land before the process of assigning patents could be worked out, most of the 1870 occupants received patents to their properties fairly quickly. However, there were delays in some cases, as disputes over ownership worked their way through the courts. The Métis of Fort Rouge, then, did not face the problem of delayed title to land to the same extent Métis households in other parts of the Red River Settlement appear to have experienced them.[5] While many Métis occupants sold their entire lot to one individual, a few sold theirs gradually and to many buyers—the main or only buyers are listed on the table. The occupations of the majority of purchasers were ascertained from the Henderson's Directories and the *Manitoba Free Press* newspaper archives, but a few persons were identified as speculators by the fact that they rapidly turned over the lots they had purchased, especially during the 1881–1882 real estate boom. It should also be noted that many of the individuals not identified as speculators in Table A.2 were, nevertheless, speculating in Métis lands.

The estimate of the amounts of money Métis households received for their river lots deserves some additional attention. We followed the methodology developed by Flanagan and Ens for establishing benefits from sales in the Land Titles Office Property Abstracts.[6] This includes accepting the transaction that led to later recognition of title when there were indications of this in the property abstracts and accepting the later and higher prices when the land was sold more than once—on the assumption that there was

TABLE A.2. Sales of Fort Rouge Lands.

LOT #	1870 OWNERS	YEAR OF PATENT	OCCUPATION OF 1870 OCCUPANT	MAIN PURCHASER	OCCUPATION OF MAIN PURCHASER	YEAR OF LAST SALE	TOTAL VALUE OF SALES
14	Emanuel Champagne	1877	Farmer	Edward Morrow	Real estate	1881	$2,300
15	Moise Carriere	1877	Farmer	Edward Morrow	Real estate	1881	$1,600
16	Baptiste Laroque	1877	Farmer	Unclear	Unclear	Unclear	Unclear
17	Philiberte Laderoute	1875	Farmer	James Fisher	Barrister	1882	$12,700
18	Roger Goulet	1878	Civil servant	Hon. J. Cauchon	Lt Governor	1880	$2,300
19	Baptiste Laderoute	1877	Farmer	Auguste Lalonde	Unknown	1878	$300
20	Nicholas Mouard	1875	Farmer	Dosithe Bonneau	Quebec farmer	1890	$93
21	John Baptiste Laderoute	1875	Farmer	Various buyers	Speculator	1888	$4,680
22	R.C. Mission	1878	Religious				
23	Honore Parisien	No patent	Farmer	Hon. L. Betourney	Judge	1873	$900
24	Hoseph Genthon	1875	Farmer	L. Murray	Wife	1881	$255
25	Charles Genthon	No pat.	Farmer	Hon. J.E. Cauchon	Lt. Governor	1882	$2,000
26	Louis Galerneau	No patent	Farmer	Archbishop Taché	Archbishop	1878	$1,000
27	Joseph Galerneau	No patent	Farmer	H.J. Clarke	Judge	1880	$200
28	James Mulligan	1875	Speculator				
29	Jean Baptiste Morin	1875	Farmer	F. Buller	Unknown	1881	$3,195
30	James Mulligan	No Patent	Speculator				
31	Baptiste Berard	1875	Farmer	Various buyers	Speculators	1883	$17,900
32	Sisters of Charity	1880	Religious				
33	Baptiste Bruce	No patent	Farmer	Daniel Carey	Barrister	1873	$840
	John H. McTavish	No patent	HBC Com.	Daniel Carey	Barrister	1873	$240
34	R.C. Mission	1878	Religious				
35	James Mulligan	1875	Speculator				
36	Joseph Lemay	No patent	Farmer	Hon. H.J. Clarke	Judge	1883	$1
37	James Mulligan	1875	Speculator				
38	James Mulligan	1887	Speculator				
39	HBC	1875					
40	HBC	1894					
41	Andre Harkness	1882	Farmer	Various	Speculator	1883	$2,345
42	Hon. James McKay	1877	MP				
43	Paul Boucher	1878	Farmer	Various	Speculator	1883	$2,275
	James Mulligan	1878	Speculator				
44	Joseph Stanley	No patent	Farmer	Lewis H. Hunter	Barrister	1888	$175
45	James Mulligan	1877	Speculator				
46	James Mulligan	Np patent	Speculator				
47	James Stewart	1875	Farmer	Joseph Monkman	Unknown	1879	$1,550
				A.W. Murdoch	Business man		
48	Robert Collier	No patent	Farmer	George Taylor	Speculator	Unclear	$300
49	James Mulligan	No patent	Speculator				
50	Hon. James McKay	No patent	MP				
51	James Mulligan	No patent	Speculator				
52	Hon. James McKay	No patent	MP				
53	Andre Harkness	No patent	Farmer	Archibald & Howell	Barristers	1880	$460
54	John Moyses*	1878	Livery owner	Kennedy & Mullholland	Barristers	1881	$1,100
55	Robert Collier	No patent	Farmer	George Taylor	Speculator	1872	$300
56	James Hallett	1876	Farmer	Various		1882	$18,559
57	John Omand	1881		Various		1900	$3,625
58	Pierre Allary	No patent	Farmer	William C. Eaton	Unknown	1875	$750
59	Pierre Allary	1878	Farmer	William C. Eaton	Unknown	1875	$1,000
60	James Mulligan	No patent	Speculator				
61	Joseph Caplet	No patent	Farmer	Archibald Wright	Speculator	1882	$1,819
62	Joseph Caplet	Unclear	Farmer	Archibald Wright	Speculator	1882	$1,800
63	Vital Turcotte	1875	Farmer	Archibald Wright	Speculator	1877	$3,750

Sources: Land Register Book B, describing lots granted by Lord Selkirk and the HBC to various individuals, including the name of the grantee, the measurement of the lot in acres, rods and poles, the date of grant and the price per acres, 1830–1871, Location H1-30-4 (E.6/2) Microfilm 4M105 (Winnipeg: Provincial Archives of Manitoba); St. Boniface West Lot 14–63, Property Abstracts, Land Titles Registry Office, Winnipeg, Manitoba; Donald N. Sprague and R.P. Frye, The *Genealogy of the First Metis Nation* (Winnipeg: Pemmican Press, 1983).

a problem with the first transaction. However, Flanagan and Ens did not address the problem that, particularly during the boom years of 1881–1882, property changed hands very quickly, and it is clear from an examination of both the property abstracts and the city's assessment rolls that many buyers subsequently failed to discharge their mortgages. Frenzied land sales and the lack of a legal requirement to record transactions until 1885 meant that many of these recorded sales did not actually translate into substantial monetary benefits for the Métis, as Flanagan and Ens suggest.

Two prominent Red River investors owned lots in the Fort Rouge area. James Mulligan owned almost one-half (45.5 percent) of the dozen lots in St. Boniface West. Arriving in the Red River Settlement in 1848 as part of a contingent of British troops, he received land on the north side of the Assiniboine River.[7] He was serving as a police officer in 1869 and was part of the group of "Canadians" who opposed Riel. Mulligan purchased land in what is now River Heights and Fort Rouge. The 1879 Alexander Begg and Walter Nursey account of Winnipeg's early history referred to Mulligan as "one of our largest property holders at the present time in the city."[8] Likely subscribing to the view that incoming settlers would sweep away Métis people and culture, Mulligan was prepared to profit from that process. Another major land owner of the Fort Rouge lots, as well as others, was the Honourable James H. McKay, the son of Scotsman James McKay and First Nations or Métis mother Marguerite Gladu. He was an HBC employee and an interpreter for many of the numbered Treaties.[9] He left Red River during the time of Riel's provisional government but returned to be appointed to the Manitoba Legislative Assembly from 1871 to 1876. He was elected to the legislature in 1877.[10]

Sixteen of the twenty lots fronting the Red River, lots 14 to 33, were farmed by Métis families or by non-Métis men married to Métis women in 1870. Only five lots were owned by speculators, religious institutions, or the HBC, which owned part of lot 33. Although most of the acreage of these river lots was brush or grass, they represented the most extensively cultivated of the Fort Rouge river lots (Figure 1.2). There were only four farmers on the block of lots 34 to 44, and their land was quickly purchased by members of Winnipeg's elite for low prices. The eighteen lots (45–63) fronting the Assiniboine River were much less cultivated. Only three were listed as having buildings and some acres under cultivation. Mulligan owned four of these lots, and James McKay owned one. Archibald Wright was a major purchaser of land in this area, buying a few entire lots and some parts of lots other individuals had initially purchased. Like Mulligan, Wright was one of the "Canadians" who opposed Riel and was imprisoned by him in 1869.[11] Wright was a prominent Winnipeg citizen who served on the first school board and the first city council. By the time of his death in 1912, he had assembled 2,300 acres of land on the south bank of the Assiniboine River, including the property now occupied by Assiniboine Park.

Ens has argued that the Winnipeg boom in 1881–1882 made nearby river lots prime real estate and that the Métis used the money from their lot sales to acquire land more appropriate for larger farming operations.[12] Flanagan and Ens reiterated that between 1880 and 1882, because of railway construction, land prices near Winnipeg soared and that Métis advantageously "sold their river lots to re-establish themselves in the North-West Territories or in other parts of Manitoba."[13] However, the land titles abstracts for these properties tell a much more complicated story of the ways the Fort Rouge Métis were dispossessed of their lands and allow us to evaluate these statements at least for Fort Rouge residents.

Ten of the twenty-five lots, not owned by speculators or absentee owners, were sold before the Winnipeg boom of 1881–1882 for an average of $11.22 per acre. If civil servant Roger Goulet, who received a healthy $2,300 for his land, and Vital Turcotte, who reportedly sold his land for $3,750, are removed from the total, the average price is $9.91 per acre. This is higher than the average price of $7.30 per acre for lands sold in all parts of the Red River Settlement before 1881, but choice lots near to Winnipeg and with river frontage should have commanded higher prices.[14] Moreover, these prices fall far short of the prices buyers received during the boom. Flanagan and Ens reported that lots within St. Boniface, one kilometre from Winnipeg, sold for an average of $34.44 per acre between 1871 and 1899.[15] About one-third (32 percent) of the Fort Rouge families, then, did not benefit from high land prices created during the Winnipeg boom. It is possible that these were farmers who were caught by the poor farming conditions in the early 1870s and were forced to cover their expenses by selling their lands. Most of these lots were sold to Winnipeg's elite—including prominent lawyers, judges, and ministers—who were, like many others, speculating in Métis lands.

The remaining fifteen lots had all been sold by 1890, with eight lots sold during the real estate boom of 1881–1882. The average price per acre was

$41.54, considerably higher than the pre-1881 Métis land sales in the Fort Rouge area. These prices compare favourably with the average of $36.06 for lots sold between 1881 and 1890, in all parts of the Red River Settlement, as well as the average price of $34.44 for lots sold in St. Boniface near the city of Winnipeg between 1871 and 1899, as documented by Flanagan and Ens.[16] As discussed earlier, in 1901 ordinary labourers in the Winnipeg building trade were reported to earn $1.75 per day,[17] and so a Canadian unskilled seasonal labourer at the time,[18] working six-day weeks for eight months, would earn $336. Using these figures, Vital Turcotte's sale, for example, represented at least ten years of a labourer's wages. Baptiste Berard's sale represented an astonishing fifty-three years of wages. However, the subsequent locations of residence and socio-economic characteristics of these families raise questions about the dependability of the property abstract information and the conclusions that Métis farmers in Fort Rouge profited handsomely from the sale of their properties (Table A.3).

TABLE A.3. Subsequent Location of Fort Rouge Families Who Presumably Obtained Good Prices for their River Lots after 1880.

LOT #	1870 OCCUPANT	YEAR OF SALE	ESTIMATED VALUE OF SALE	SOURCE	LOCATION	OCCUPATION	# OF ROOMS
14	Emanuel Champagne	1881	$2,300	1891 census	Rural MB	Farmer	6
15	Moise Carriere	1881	$1,600	1891 census	Rural MB	Farmer	2
17	Philiberte Laderoute	1881	$12,700	1891 census	Rural MB	Farmer	4
25	Charles Genthon	1882	$2,000	1891 census	Rural MB	Farmer	4
29	Jean Baptiste Morin	1881	$3,195	1891 census	Rural MB	Farmer	4
63	Heir of Vital Turcotte	1877	$3,750	1891 census	Rural NWT	Farmer	3
21	Heir of Jean Baptiste Laderoute	1888	$4,680	1891 census	St. Boniface	Farmer	2
43	Paul Boucher	1883	$2,450	1891 census	St. Laurent, NWT	Hunter	2
41	Heir of Andre Harkness	1881	$2,345	1891	Winnipeg	Real Estate	4
61,62	Joseph Caplet	1882	$3,600	1891 census	Moose Jaw, NWT	Farmer	1
31	Baptiste Berard	1883	$17,900	1891 census	St. Boniface	Farmer	2

Sources: St. Boniface West Lot 14–63, Property Abstracts, Land Titles Registry Office, Winnipeg, Manitoba; MS Census 1891, Manitoba.

By 1891, six of the nine families that seemed to receive good prices for their river lots (defined as at least $1,500, or slightly less than five years of a labourer's wages) appear to have purchased land for farming elsewhere in the Red River parishes or established themselves in the urban economy.[19] Most lived modestly, even though raising and feeding their large families could be costly, and only David Champagne, who had received title to river lot 14, had a two-story, six-room house. Jean Baptiste Laderoute, who had supposedly received almost $5,000 for his river lot, could not be found subsequently. The only descendant who could be located was his oldest son Chrystosteme, who was still farming the lot in St. Boniface in 1891 and lived in a two-room house, and who appeared as a labourer in St. Vital in the 1901 census. These records further suggest that it is highly unlikely that the Laderoute family profited as greatly as the existing records suggest. Similarly, in 1891, Paul Boucher occupied a two-room house in St. Laurent, Saskatchewan, and was engaged in subsistence hunting and fishing. His oldest son lived nearby, carrying on a subsistence lifestyle. Andre Harkness's only surviving son joined the urban workforce. He and his family lived in a four-room house in Ward 1 in Winnipeg, and he worked as a real estate agent. The sum his father's estate generated for the family likely assisted them, but hardly represented a windfall. Joseph Caplet's children split up the estate after his death in 1875, each receiving small allotments. Son Paul, who sold in 1882, reportedly received $2,700 of the estate sale, but by 1891 he had moved to Saskatchewan and was farming, living in a one-room wooden house. Finally, the 1891 census still lists Baptiste Berard as a farmer in St. Boniface, but the ten-member Berard family lived in a small two-room house, emphasizing the likelihood that they did not receive the full amount recorded in the property abstracts.[20]

The available records, then, suggest that the majority of the Fort Rouge Métis did not gain economic security from the sales of their river lots. Many sold early and for very modest amounts. Only six 1870 occupants, or their families, seemed to profit enough from the Winnipeg real estate boom to be able to purchase land elsewhere, and all of these families appeared to live very modestly when the inevitable bust occurred. Others joined the urban economy and two of the families moved to Saskatchewan. The extensive involvement of Winnipeg's legal circle in purchasing Fort Rouge land may have discouraged Métis farmers from pursuing land sale debts. In their 1879 history of Winnipeg, Alexander Begg and Walter R. Nursey lamented that "as every lawyer in the city, to say nothing of most of our merchants, who were all, more or less, large land owners . . . the margin of profit where such competition existed was painfully reduced."[21] While the Fort Rouge river lots represent only a small proportion of Métis lots sold in the Red River Settlement, these results suggest caution in reaching a conclusion that many Métis were able to capitalize on and profit from the real estate market in Manitoba after 1870.

Rooster Town Population Change Details

TABLE B.1. Population Changes between 1901 and 1906.

GONE FROM ROOSTER TOWN	
Deaths	Poitras, Joseph (b. 1835)* Smith, William (Sr.) (1853–1902) Omand, Francis James (1877–1904) and Sarah (née Mowat) (1876–1905)
Not listed or moved	Henault, Roger (b. 1843) and Silvia/Celine (née Berard) (b. 1846) Roy, Joseph (b. 1869) and Rosalie Angelique (née Zastre) (b. 1867)

ADDED TO ROOSTER TOWN	
Without obvious kin links to Rooster Town	Parker, Henry (1877–1960) (not Métis) and Amelia Grace (née Armitt) (not Métis) (1882–1950)
With kin links to Rooster Town (Extended Berard family)	Berard, Alfred (1866–1909) and Georgeline (née Ritchot) (b. 1870) Berard, Florent (1866–1944) and Mary Louise (née Morin) (b. 1881) Berard, Francois (1837–1912) and Marguerite (née Roussin) (1843–1918) Berard, Frederick Joseph (1879–1918) Berard, Peter (1877–1934) and Sarah (née Morin) (b. 1887) Berard, Pierre (1852–1909) and Harriet (née Cook) (1856–1911)
With kin links to Rooster Town (Extended Morrisette family)	Atkinson, Thomas (1825–1907) and Josephte/Suzette (née Morrisette) (1847–1918) Fountaine, Jean Baptiste (non-Métis) (b. 1868) and Mary Rose (née Morrisette) (b. 1881) Morrisette, Abraham (b. 1871) and Mary Christine (née Marcellais) (b. 1885) Morrisette, Elie (b. 1874) and Euphrosinna (née Grouette) (b. 1875) Morrisette, William (b. 1845) Mulvaney, John James (1873–1916) and Florence (née Atkinson) (1876–1922) Paquin/Pocha, Henry George (1870–1940) and Mary/Madeline (née Lund) (b. 1875
Married widow or formed with previous families or descendants	Chassie, Frederick (b. 1877) and Eleanor Gertrude (née Omand) (1882–1969) Fisher, Isadore (b. 1874) and Marie/Mary Louise (née Desmarais) (b. 1884) Griffiths, Henry (not Métis) (b. 1869) and Charlotte (née Omand) (1867–1955) Parisien, Henry (1865–1934) and Catherine (née Parisien) (1857–1932) Smith, Alexander (1880–1937) and Agnes (née McMillan) (1880–1935)

* Even though we do not know the exact date of Joseph Poitras's death we know he died during this time period because his wife is listed as a widow in 1906.

TABLE B.2. Population Changes between 1906 and 1911.

GONE FROM ROOSTER TOWN	
Deaths	Berard, Pierre (1852–1909) and Harriet (née Cook) (1856–1911) Marie Logan (née Dupuis) (b. 1828)* Morrisette, Abraham (b. 1871)
Not listed or moved	Griffiths, Henry (not Métis) (b. 1869) and Charlotte Chipperfield (née Omand) (1867–1955) Logan, John (b. 1831) Marcellais, Elice (née Vandal) (b. 1847) Morrissette, Mary Christine (née Marcellais) (b. 1885) Morrisette, Elie (b. 1874) and Euphrosinna (née Grouette) (b. 1875) Wendt, William (b. 1875) (not Métis) and Marie Adele (née Hogg) (b. 1873)
ADDED TO ROOSTER TOWN	
Without obvious kin links to Rooster Town	Cyr, Alfred (b. 1876) and Nathalie (née Delorme) (b. 1882) Ritchot, Bruno (1877–1959) and Ernestine (née Grouette) (1884–1984) St. Arnaud, Jean Baptiste (b. 1847) and Marguerite (née Laderoute) (b. 1843) Villebrun, Edward (b. 1881) and Jessie (née Morin) (1886–1933)
With kin links to Rooster Town	Boyer, Joseph Arthur (b. 1893) and Edith (née Land) (b. 1894) Morrissette, Alexander (b. 1881–1947) and Adelaide (née Miller) (not Métis) (1888–1962) Parisien, Alexander (1859–1923) and Cecile (née Lund) (b. 1886) Smith, James Albert (b. 1871) (not Métis) and Florence (née Paquin) (1875–1934)
Married widow or formed with previous families or descendants	Dunnick, William Exavier (1884–1939) (not Métis) and Mary Jane (née Smith) (1885–1946) Land, George (1887–1936) and Hilda Grace (née Omand) (1882–1927) Omand, John William (1872–1956) and Catherine (née Mowat) (b. 1880) Parisien, James Charles (1889–1972) and Marie Louise (née Minnie) (1888–1970) Smith, William (1889–1953) and Marie (née Henry) (1887–1951) Souchereau, Nola (1877–1927) (not Métis) and Susan Jane (née Atkinson) (1887–1963)

* John Logan is listed as widowed in the 1911 census.

TABLE B.3. Population Changes between 1911 and 1916.

GONE FROM ROOSTER TOWN	
Deaths	Arcand, Isadore (b. 1852) Atkinson, Thomas (1825–1907) Berard, Francois (1837–1912) Comptois, Pierre (b. 1842–1912) Fisher, Isadore (b. 1849) Henry, John (1851–1914) Omand, Jane (née Birston (1842–1912)
Not listed or moved	Berard, Margeurite (née Roussin) (1843–1918) (no record) Boyer, Joseph Arthur (b. 1893) and Edith (née Land) (b. 1894) (move to Woodlands, MB), labourer Chassie, Frederick (b. 1877) and Eleanor Gertrude (née Omand) (1882–1969) (move to Selkirk, bought farm) Cyr, Alfred (b. 1876) and Nathalie Cyr (née Delorme) (b. 1882) (St. Vital, bought farm) Fountaine, Jean Baptiste (non-Métis) (b. 1868) and Mary Rose (née Morrissette) (b. 1881) (move to north end) Land, George (1887–1936) and Hilda Grace Germain Land (née Omand) (1882–1927) (moved to 160 Clarke St.) Omand, Alexander Septisen (1875–1947) and Rachel Anne (née Ballendine) (350 Power, bought farm)
ADDED TO ROOSTER TOWN	
Without obvious kin links to Rooster Town	Richard, Alfred (b. 1880) and Marie Francoise (née Cardinal) (b. 1895) Cardinal, Modeste (1874–1940) and Sarah (née Richard) (b. 1874)
With kin links to Rooster Town	Orvis, Alexander (1859–1943) and Elizabeth (née Morrissette) (b. 1892) Parisian, Louis Raphael (1891–1941) and Ida (née Parisien) (1899–1966) Parisien, Pascal (1859–1933) and Veronique (née Parisien) (b. 1870) Savage, Frederick W J (1866–1943) and Isabella (née Morrisette) (1862–1929) (back)
Married widow or formed with previous families or descendants	Phidme Gagnon (not Métis) (b. 1864) Henderson, Albin (not Métis) (1884) and Marie Grace (née Curran) (1896) Griffiths, Henry (not Métis) and Charlotte (née Omand) (1867–1955) (back on Jessie with father, mother died) McDougall, Duncan Archibald (1884) and Mary Alice (née Todd) (1894)

TABLE B.4. Population Changes between 1916 and 1921.

Deaths	Josephte/Suzette Atkinson (née Morrissette) (1847–1918) Berard, Frederick Joseph (1879–1918) Curran, William (1872–1917) Henderson, Albin (1886–1918) Minnie, Mary (née McCorrster) (1879–1919) Mulvaney, John James (1873–1916)
Not listed or moved	Marie Arcand (née Chartrand) (b. 1860) Berard, Peter (1877–1934) and Sarah (née Morin) (b. 1887) Berard, Daniel (1895) Cardinal, Modeste (1874–1940) and Sarah (née Richard) (b. 1874) Fisher, Adeline (née Arcand) Fisher, Isadore (b. 1874) and Marie/Mary Louise (née Desmarais) (b. 1884) Griffiths, Henry (not Métis) and Charlotte (née Omand) (1867–1955) Land, George (1887–1936) and Hilda Grace Germain Land (née Omand) (1882–1927) Minnie, Mary (née McConister?) (1879–1919) McDougall, Aime/Amade (b. 1859) and Josephte (née Berard) (b. 1864) Omand, James Septisen (1841–1927) Orvis, Alexander (1859–1943) and Elizabeth (née Morrissette) (b. 1892) Parisien, Alexander (1859–1923) and Cecile Parisien (née Lund) (b. 1886) Richard, Alfred (b. 1880) and Marie Francoise (née Cardinal) (b. 1895) Savage, Frederick W J (1866–1943) and Isabella (née Morrisette) (1862–1929) Souchereau, Nola (not Métis) (1877–1927) and Susan Jane (née Atkinson) (1887–1963)

Without obvious kin links to Rooster Town	Laramee, Philius (1875–1961)
With kin links to Rooster Town	Parisien, Joseph Eduard (1861–1939) and Marie Julienne (née Courchene) (1870) Parisien, Ovide Phillip (b. 1890) and Marie Louise (1888) Sais, Francois (b. 1853–1921) and Marie Sais (née Parisien) (1860–1938) Vandal, Joseph Adolphes (1894–1978) and Marie Adele Vandal (née Parisien) (1892–1980)
Married widow or formed with previous families or descendants	Butchart, David (1882)

TABLE B.5. Population Changes between 1921 and 1926.

GONE FROM ROOSTER TOWN	
Deaths	Peppin, Virginia (née Muloin) (1871–1926)
Not listed or moved	Berard, Frank (1886–1946) seems to move to Fisher Branch with the Chassies, then enlists Berard, Florent (1866–1944) and Mary Louise Berard (née Morin) (b. 1881) can't trace Butchart, David (b. 1882) (not Métis) and Victoria Curran Butchart (née Migneault) (not Métis) (1875–1937) no record Smith, James Albert (b. 1871) and Florence (née Paquin) (b. 1934) no record Smith, George Albert (b. 1896) and Blanche Rose (née Curran) (b. 1898) no record

ADDED TO ROOSTER TOWN	
Without obvious kin links to Rooster Town	Campbell, Kenrick Peter (1884–1965) Berard, Joseph Andre (1893–1973) and Alexandrina Evangeline (née Nault) (1903–1971)
With kin links to Rooster Town	Cardinal, Marcien Peter (1896–1976) and Marguerite (née Peppin) (1903–1973) Cardinal, Maxime Michael (1893–1960) and Marie Josephine (née Larocque) (1899–1987) Land, George (1887–1936) and Hilda Grace Germain (née Omand) (1882–1927) (back) Laramee, Joseph Louis (1899–1983) and Marie Adele (née Parisian) (1903–1977) Laramee, Paul (non-Métis) (1872–1956) and Marie Julie (née Courchene) (1868–1943) Lepine, Emile Ernest (1889–1958) and Marie Julia/Julie Ann (née Cardinal) (1900–1942) Parisian, Frederick (1880–1964) and Alphonsine (née Morand) (1881–1947) Pilon Joseph Alexandre (1868–1949) and Aurelia (1885–1971) Pilon, Adolph Joseph (1891–1976) and Marie Josephine (née Laramee) (1897–1976) Roussin, William (1901–1993) and Rachel Adile/Ogidile Anne (née Cardinal) (1904–1981)
Married widow or formed with previous families or descendants	Henry, Arthur (1896–1979) and Patrick Henry (b. 1885) Peppin, John (b. 1895) and Agnes Peppin (née Muir) (1894–1971) Minnie, Adele (née Parisien) (b. 1904)

TABLE B.6. Population Changes between 1926 and 1931.

GONE FROM ROOSTER TOWN	
Deaths	Hilda Grace Germain Land (née Omand) (1882–1927)
Not listed or moved	Smith, Marie (née Henry) (1887–1951)

ADDED TO ROOSTER TOWN	
Without obvious kin links to Rooster Town	Butchart, David (b. 1882) (not Métis) and Victoria Curran (née Migneault) (1875–1937)
With kin links to Rooster Town	Arcand, Joseph (1887–1959) and Mary Cora (née Henry) (1883–1956) Berard, Florent (1866–1944) and Mary Louise (née Morin) (b. 1881)
Married widow or formed with previous families or descendants	Conway, Joseph Amadee (1905–1970) and Dorilda (née Parisian) (1910–1997) Henry, Arthur (1896–1979) and Esther Catherine (née St. Germaine) (b. 1907) Jenkins, Thomas (1907–1968) and Grace Adele (née Parker) (b. 1901) Laramee, Philias (b. 1902) and Alice (née Rieux) (b. 1915) Parker, David (b. 1903) and Violet May (née Evans) Peppin, Maurice (b. 1904) and Winona Louise (née Steuart) (1894–1972) Smith, Edward Scott (1914–1976) and Mary Grace (née Germain) (1909–1959)

TABLE B.7. Population Changes between 1931 and 1936.

GONE FROM ROOSTER TOWN	
Deaths	Henry, Melanie (née Vandal) (1857–1932)
	Land, George (1887–1936)
	Parisien, Henry (1865–1934) and Catherine Smith (née Parisien) (1857–1932)
	Peppin, William (1871–1932)
	Smith, Agnes (née McMillan) (1880–1935)
	Villebrun, Jessie (née Morin) (1886–1933)
Not listed or moved	Berard, Joseph Andre (1893–1973) and Alexandrina Evangeline (née Nault) (1903–1971)
	Berard, Florent (1866–1944) and Mary Louise Berard (née Morin) (b. 1881)
	Cardinal, Maxime Michael (1893–1960) and Marie Josephine (née Larocque) (1899–1987)
	Gagnon, Phidme (not Métis) (b. 1864)
	Lepine, Emile Ernest (1889–1958) and Marie Julia/Julie Ann (née Cardinal) (1900–1942)
	Parker, David Edward (b. 1903) and Violet May Parker (née Evans)
ADDED TO ROOSTER TOWN	
Without obvious kin links to Rooster Town	None
With kin links to Rooster Town	Cardinal, Charles H. (1863–1938) and Marie Josephine (née Parisien) (1871–1943)
	Cardinal, Modeste (1874–1940) and Sarah (née Richard) (b. 1874)
	Larocque, Francois (b. 1853) and Marie Sais (née Parisien) (1860–1938)
	Weaver, Joseph Edgar (1886–1986) (not Métis) and Genevieve (née Sais) (1896–1985)
	Weaver, Orland (1889–1981) (not Métis) and Marie Adele (née Sais) (1890–1961)
Married widow or formed with previous families or descendants	Cardinal, Arthur (1906–1991) and Agnes Belvah (née Dunnick) (1916–1980)
	Cardinal, Leonard (1932–1983) and Barbara (née Young?)
	Courchene, Alphonse Peter (1906–1993) and Caroline (née Dunnick) (1912–1970)
	Courchene, Joseph Leon (b. 1902) and Florence (née Smith) (b. 1912)
	Henry, Patrick (b. 1885)
	Gosselin, Remauld Frank Xavier (1888–1958) and Adeline Fisher (née Arcand) (1877–1938)
	Hogg, Amable/Matt (1900–1951) and Alice (née Parisien) (1902–1952)
	Paddison, John (non-Métis) (1889–1954) and Marie Josephine Parisien (née Henry) (1901–1954)
	Parisian, Joseph Arthur (b. 1909) and Marion (no information)
	Parisien, Joseph Francois (1888–1954) and Marie Adele (née Roy) (1886–1964)
	Smith, Adrich (1913–1945) and Florida Smith (née Laramee) (1903–1999)
	Nolin, John (1899–1986) and Alice Nolin (née Dunnick) (1913–1954)
	Smith, Blanche Rose (née Curran) (b. 1898)

TABLE B.8. Population Changes between 1936 and 1941.

GONE FROM ROOSTER TOWN	
Deaths	Butchart, Victoria Curran (née Migneault) (1875–1937)
	Cardinal, Charles H (1863–1938)
	Dunnick, William Exavier (1884–1939)
	Gosselin, Adeline Fisher (née Arcand) (1877–1938)
	Larocque, Marie Sais (née Parisien) (1860–1938)
	Parisian, Louis Raphael (1891–1941)
	Smith, Alexander (1880–1937)
Not listed or moved	Cardinal, Modeste, and Sarah (née Richard) (b. 1874)
	Henry, Patrick (b. 1885)
	Hogg, Peter (1877–1939)
	Larocque, Francois (b. 1853)
	Minnie, Adele (née Parisien) (b. 1904)
	Minnie, Elice (née Comptois) (b. 1851)
	Nolin, John (1899–1986)
	Peppin, John (1895–1963) and Agnes Peppin (née Muir) (1894–1971)
	Peppin, Maurice (b. 1904) and Winona Louise Peppin (1894–1972) (née Steuart)
	Parisian, Ida (née Parisien) (1899–1966)
ADDED TO ROOSTER TOWN	
Without obvious kin links to Rooster Town	Marcoux, Joseph (1899–1972) (not Métis) and Marie Rose (née L'Heaureaux) (not Métis)
With kin links to Rooster Town	Cardinal, Joseph and Mary
	Lepine, Emile Ernest (1889–1958) and Marie Julie Ann Lepine (née Cardinal) (1900–1942)
	Parisien, Thomas Alexander (1898–1972) and Beatrice Mary (née Fielder)
	Sais, Charles Maxime (1893–1970) and Elise Sais (née Arcand) (1919–1991)
	St. Germaine, Joseph George (1865–1941) and Josephine St. Germaine (née Blondin) (b. 1864)
	St. Germain, Laurel (b. 1904) and Anne Jean (née Courchene) 1213 Weatherdon
	Weaver, Orland (1889–1981) (not Métis) and Marie Adele (née Sais) (1890–1961)
Married widow or formed with previous families or descendants	Dunnick, William (Jr) (b. 1915) and Agnes Dunnick Birston (née Lepine) (1925–1991)
	Laramee, Alphonse (1913–1985) and Frances Cora Theresa (née Dunnick) (1919–2008)
	Laramee, Horamidos (1916–1997) and Angeline (née Ricard) (1924–2004)
	Morrisette, Patrick (1912–1953) and Elsie Morrissette (née Anderson) (1909–1983)
	Parisian, Edward (1916–1993) and Marion V. (1922–2007)
	Parker, Gordon (not Métis) (1916–1999) and Delia Margaret Parker (née Parisian) (1919–1999)
	Parker, Herbert Edwin (1912–1952), (not Métis) and Clara (née Moors) (not Métis)
	Smith, Gavin (1905–1968) and Elianna Ann (née Richard) (1905–1983)
	Smith, Raymond (b. 1918)

TABLE B.9. Population Changes between 1941 and 1946.

GONE FROM ROOSTER TOWN	
Deaths	Butchart, David (1882–1945) (not Métis)
	Cardinal, Marie Josephine (née Parisien) (1871–1943)
	Laramee, Marie Julie (née Courchene) (1868–1943)
	Lepine, Marie Julia/Julie Ann (née Cardinal) (1900–1942)
	St. Germaine, Joseph George (1865–1941)
	Smith, Adrich (1913–1945)
	Minnie, Alex (1876–1941)
Not listed or moved	Cardinal, Joseph and Mary
	Courchene, Joseph Leon (b. 1902) and Florence (née Smith)
	Laramee, Horamidos (1916–1997) and Angeline (née Ricard) (1924–2004)
	Larson, Herman and Lydia
	Parisien, Marion (no information)
	St. Germain, Laurel (b. 1904) and Anne Jean (née Courchene)
	Smith, Blanche (née Curran)
Intergrated	Laramee, Arthur Edmond (1895–1969) and Marguerite (no information)
	Laramee, Joseph Noel (1893–1988) and Marie Marguerite (née Parisian) (1909–2002)
	Laramee, Philius (1875–1961) and Mary Jane (née Smith) (1885–1946)
	Morrisette, Alexander (1881–1947) and Adelaide (née Miller) (1888–1962)
	Morrisette, Patrick (b. 1912–1953) and Elsie Morrisette (née Anderson) (1909–1983)
	Parisian, Edward (1916–1993) and Marion V (1922–2007)
	Smith, Florida (née Laramee) (1903–1999)
ADDED TO ROOSTER TOWN	
Without obvious kin links to Rooster Town	Berard, Leo Paul (1915) and Helen Elizabeth (née Morrow) (not Métis) (1917)
	Paquin/Pocha, Thomas (no information) and Christine (no information)
With kin links to Rooster Town	Parisien, Paul Napoleon (1908–1972) and Bernice Parisien (née Parisian) (1917–1992)
	Smith, D.E. (unknown) and Violet (unknown)
	Smith, William (1919) and Lily (unknown)
	Parisian, Ida (née Parisien) (1899–1966)
	Weaver, Orland Alem (1889–1981) (not Métis) and Marie Adele (née Sais) (1890–1961)
Married widow or formed with previous families or descendants	Laramee, Arthur Edmond (1895–1969) and Marguerite (no information)
	Nolin, John (1899–1986) and Alice (née Dunnick) (1913–1954)
	Parisian, Ernest Joseph (1922–1962) and Edmee (née Parisien) (1925–2012)
	Parker, Stanley (1920–1965) (not Métis) and Julia Theresa (née Parisian) (d. 2005)
	Pilon, Joseph Amadee (1917–1994) and Margaret (née Cardinal) (no dates)
	Vandal, Leo and Margaret (née Berg)

TABLE B.10. Population Changes between 1946 and 1951.

GONE FROM ROOSTER TOWN	
Deaths	Parisien, Alphonsine (née Morand) (1881–1947)
Not listed or moved	Berard, Leo Paul (1915) and Helen Elizabeth (née Morrow) (not Métis) (1917) 1064 Dudley Cardinal, Leonard Gabrielle (1910–1996) and Rose (née Smith) (1916–1968) Dunnick, William (b. 1915) Laramee, Philias (b. 1902) and Alice (née Rieux) (b. 1915) Parisian, Ernest Joseph (1922–1962) and Edmee (née Parisien) (1925–2012) Smith, Gavin (1905–1968) and Elianna Ann (née Richard) (1905–1983) (not Métis) Vandal, Leo and Margaret (née Berg)
Intergrated	Cardinal, Marcien Peter (1896–1976) and Marguerite (née Peppin) (1903–1973) Conway, Joseph Amadee (1905–1970) and Dorilda (née Parisian) (1910–1997) Conway, Patrick (1880–1956) and Mathilde (née Henry) (1876–1965) Jenkins, Thomas (1907–1968) and Grace Adele (née Parker) (b. 1901) Nolin, John (1899–1986) and Alice (née Dunnick) (1913–1954) Paquin, Thomas (no information) and Christine (no information) Parisien, Thomas Alexander (1898–1972) and Beatrice Mary (née Fielder) (no dates) Parker, Gordon (not Métis) (1916–1999) and Delia Margaret (née Parisian) (1919–1999) Smith, Edward Scott (1914–1976) and Mary Grace (née Germain) (1909–1959) Weaver, Joseph Edgar (1886–1986) (not Métis) and Genevieve (née Sais) (1896–1985) Weaver, Orliff/Orland Alem (1889–1981) (not Métis) and Marie Adele (née Sais) (1890–1961) Wilson, Albert Stephen (1899–1966) and Lillian Ethel (née Parker) (1910–2005)
ADDED TO ROOSTER TOWN	
Without obvious kin links to Rooster Town	None
With kin links to Rooster Town	Cloutier, Joseph Edward (1904–1978) and Marie Jane (née Parisien) (1912–1972)
Married widow or formed with previous families or descendants	Birston, Thomas (1914–1970) and Agnes (née Lepine) (1925–1991) Land, James Charles (1914–1965) and Rose (née Laramee) (1925–1965) Lepine, Emile Ernest (1889–1958) and Julia (née Arcand) (1923–1991) Mondor Josephat Gabriel (1919–2006) and Marie Ernestine (née Parisian) (1920–2005)

TABLE B.11. Population Changes between 1951 and 1946.

GONE FROM ROOSTER TOWN	
Deaths	Conway, Patrick (1880–1956) Hogg, Amable/Matt (1900–1951) and Alice (née Parisien) (1902–1952) Morrisette, Patrick (1912–1953) Nolin, Alice (née Dunnick) (1913–1954) Paddison, John (1889–1954) (not Métis) and Marie Josephine (née Henry) (1901–1954) Parisien, Joseph Francois (1888–1954) Smith, William (1889–1953) Villebrun, Charles (1905–1953)
Not listed or moved	Cloutier, Joseph Edward (1904–1978) and Marie Jane (née Parisien) (1912–1972) Conway, Joseph Amadee (1905–1970) and Dorilda (née Parisian) (1910–1997) Henry, Arthur (1896–1979) and Esther Catherine Henry (née St. Germaine) (b. 1907) Nolin John (1899–1986) Parker, Herbert Edwin (1912–1952) and Clara Parker (née Moors) St. Germaine, Josephine (née Blondin) (b. 1864) Slemko, Michael and Ellen Smith, Edward Scott (1914–1976) and Mary Grace (née Germain) (1909–1959) Smith, Frances Malvina (née Cardinal) (b. 1888) Laramee, Peter and Mary Parisian, Jackans Alphonse (1932–1999)
Intergrated	Cardinal, Leonard (1932–1983) and Barbara Cardinal (née Young?)

ADDED TO ROOSTER TOWN	
Without obvious kin links to Rooster Town	Halchaker, James and Rose Halchaker
With kin links to Rooster Town	Conway, Mathilde (née Henry) (1876–1965)
Married widow or formed with previous families or descendants	Parisian, Olivier (no dates) and Anna Parisian (née Simmons) (b. 1933) Parisian, Rene Alexander (1921–1979) and Marie (née Petrie) (1925–1996) Weaver, Walter/William and Denise Weaver (née Roussin)

NOTES

PREFACE

1   The database on which this book is based is available on the University of Manitoba Archives website, http://digitalcollections.lib.umanitoba.ca/islandorg/object/uofm%3Aroostertown.

2   Richard Harris, *Unplanned Suburbs: Toronto's American Tragedy, 1900 to 1950* (Baltimore: The Johns Hopkins University Press, 1996).

3   Ibid., 262.

4   Richard B. Andrews, "Elements in the Urban-Fringe Pattern," *The Journal of Land and Public Utility Economics* 18, no. 2 (1942): 171.

5   Ibid., 174.

6   Jill Wade, "Home or Homelessness? Marginal Housing in Vancouver, 1886–1950," *Urban History Review/Revue d'histoire urbaine* 25, no. 2 (1997): 19–29.

7   Jon Tatrie, "Africville," *The Canadian Encyclopedia*, 2014, http://www.thecanadianencyclopedia.ca/en/article/africville/.

8   Wade, "Home or Homelessness?" 27.

9   Arthur K. Davis, *Edging into Mainstream: Urban Indians in Saskatchewan* (Bellingham: Western Washington State College, 1965).

10 Ibid., 457–58.

11 Jean H. Lagassé, *A Study of the Population of Indian Ancestry Living in Manitoba* (Winnipeg, MB: Manitoba. Department of Agriculture and Immigration. Social and Economic Research Office, 1959).

12 Ibid., 66.

13 Ibid., 68.

14 Ibid., 69–70.

15 Ibid., 70.

16 Mike Evans and Lisa Krebs, *A Brief History of the Short Life of the Island Cache* (Edmonton: University of Alberta Press, 2004).

17 Ibid., 13.

18 Ibid., 56–57.

19 Ibid., 5–55.

20 Ibid., 101–114.

21 Ibid., 115–31.

22 Ibid., 78–99.

23 Ibid., 112–139.

24 Gail Morin, *Métis Families: A Genealogical Compendium* (Pawtucket, RI: Quintin Publications, 2001); Douglas N. Sprague and R.Frye, *The Genealogy of the First Metis Nation* (Winnipeg: Pemmican Press, 1983).

25 The Rooster Town digital collection can be found at http://roostertown.lib.umanitoba.ca/.

26 "Running a Raffle," *Manitoba Free Press*, 30 September 1909, 5.

27 City of Winnipeg meeting with Rooster Town families to discuss nature of Rooster Town commemorative makers, Grant Park High School, Winnipeg, MB, 25 November, 2017.

28 Ibid.

CHAPTER ONE: SETTLER COLONIALISM AND THE DISPOSSESSION OF THE MANITOBA MÉTIS

1   Nicholas Blomley, *Unsettling the City: Urban Land and the Politics of Property* (New York: Routledge, 2004), 108.

2   I use the term "Indigenous peoples" to refer to First peoples internationally. In Canada, these peoples include the First Nations, Métis, and Inuit people. I also use "First Nations" and "Métis" to refer to specific groups. At the same time, I recognize that many Indigenous people prefer to identify with a specific Indigenous community, for example Mi'kmaq, Cree, or Red River Métis. .

3   First Nations individuals who were not registered under Canada's Indian Act likely experienced settler colonialism in similar ways to the Métis.

4   Evelyn Peters, "'Urban' and 'Aboriginal': An Impossible Contradiction," in *City Lives and City Forms: Critical Research and Canadian Urbanism*, ed. John Caulfield and Linda Peake (Toronto: University of Toronto Press, 1996), 47–62; Evelyn J. Peters and Chris Andersen, "Introduction," *Indigenous in the City: Contemporary Identities and Cultural Innovation* (Vancouver: UBC Press, 2013), 1–25; Ryan Walker and Sarem Nejad, "Urban Planning, Indigenous Peoples, and Settler States," in *Urbanization in a Global Context,* ed. Allison Baine and Linda Peake (Toronto: Oxford University Press, 2017), 136–54.

5   Kay Anderson, "Science and the Savage: The Linnean Society of New South Wales, 1874–1900," *Ecumene* 5 (1998): 125–43; Robert Berkhoffer, *The White Man's Indian: Images of the American Indian from Columbus to the Present* (New York: Vintage, 1979); Terry Goldie, *Fear and Temptation: The Image of the Indigene in Canadian, Australian, and New Zealand Literatures* (Montreal: McGill-Queen's University Press, 1989); Jane M. Jacobs, *Edge of Empire: Post-colonialism and the City* (New York: Routledge, 1996), 103–131.

6   Anne McClintock, *Imperial Leather: Race, Gender, and Sexuality in the Colonial Contest* (New York: Routledge, 1995), 40.

7   Blomley, *Unsettling the City*, 11–135; David Hamer, *New Towns in the New World: Images and Perceptions of the Nineteenth-Century Urban Frontier* (New York: Routledge, 1990); Jacobs, *Edge of Empire*, 103–31; Jordan Stanger-Ross, "Municipal Colonialism in Vancouver: City Planning and the Conflict Over Indian Reserves, 1928–1950s," *The Canadian Historical Review* 89, no.4 (2008): 541–80.

8   Penelope Edmonds, *Urbanizing Frontiers: Indigenous Peoples and Settlers in 19th-Century Pacific Rim Cities* (Vancouver: UBC Press, 2010), 198.

9   Cole Harris, *Making Native Space: Colonialism, Resistance, and Reserves in British Columbia* (Vancouver: UBC Press, 2002), 265, 268.

10 Jean Barman, "Erasing Indigenous Indigeneity in Vancouver," *BC Studies* 155 (Autumn 2007): 3–30; Edmonds, *Urbanizing Frontiers*, 10; Patricia K. Wood, "Pressured from All Sides: The February 1913 Surrender of the Northeast Corner of the Tsuu T'ina Nation," *Journal of Historical Geography* 30 (2004): 112–129.

11 Stanger-Ross, "Municipal Colonialism in Vancouver," 542.

12 Ibid., 555.

13 Edmonds, *Urbanizing Frontiers*, 10.

14 Stewart Raby, "Indian Land Surrenders in Southern Saskatchewan," *Canadian Geographer* 17 (1973): 36–52; Stanger-Ross, "Municipal Colonialism in Vancouver," 541–80.

15 Canada, Department of Indian Affairs (hereafter DIA), *Annual Report* (Ottawa: King's Printers, 1911), xxi.

16   Edmonds, *Urbanizing Frontiers*, 137.

17   Ibid., 207, 209, and 217.

18   Jaimy Miller, "The Papaschase Band: Building Awareness and Community in the City of Edmonton," in *Aboriginal Peoples in Canadian Cities: Transformations and Continuities*, eds. Heather Howard and Craig Proulx (Waterloo: Wilfrid Laurier Press, 2011), 53–68.

19   Coll Thrush, "The Crossing-Over Place: Urban and Indian Histories in Seattle" (PhD diss., University of Washington, 2002), 174.

20   F. Laurie Barron, "The Indian Pass System in the Canadian West, 1882–1935," *Prairie Forum* 13, no.1 (Spring 1988): 30.

21   Blomley, *Unsettling the City*, 109–14.

22   Evelyn J. Peters, "Conceptually Unclad? Feminist Geography and Aboriginal Peoples," *Canadian Geographer* 48, no. 3 (2004): 255.

23   See, for example: John E. Foster, "The Plains Metis," in *Native Peoples: The Canadian Experience*, ed. R. Bruce Morrison and C. Roderick Wilson (Don Mills, ON: Oxford University Press, 2004), 297–319; Jacqueline Peterson and Jennifer S.H. Brown, *The New Peoples: Being and Becoming Métis in North America* (Winnipeg: The University of Manitoba Press, 1985); Alexander Ross, *The Red River Settlement: Its Rise, Progress, and Present State* (Edmonton: Hurtig Publishers); Fred J. Shore, "The Emergence of the Metis Nation in Manitoba," in *Metis Legacy: A Metis Historiography and Annotated Bibliography*, ed. Lawrence J. Barkwell, Leah Dorion, and Darren R. Préfontaine (Winnipeg: Pemmican Publications); and George F.G. Stanley, *The Birth of Western Canada: A History of the Riel Rebellions* (Toronto: University of Toronto Press, 1961).

24   Renisa Mawani examines the 1923 and 1925 trials regarding the hardships of mixed-blood people living in Stanley Park, Vancouver, but focuses primarily on the way they were positioned as neither Indian nor white, and how the fact that they were not considered First Nations prevented them from asserting legal claims to the land. Renisa Mawani, "Genealogies of the Land: Aboriginality, Law, and Territory in Vancouver's Stanley Park," *Social and Legal Studies* 14, no. 3 (2005): 315–39. Cheryl Troupe's 2009 MA thesis does explore the emergence of a largely Métis neighbourhood enclave in Saskatoon around the 1930s. Cheryl L. Troupe, "Métis Women: Social Structure, Urbanization and Political Activism, 1850–1980" (MA thesis, University of Saskatchewan, 2009).

25   Renisa Mawani, "'Half-breeds,' Racial Opacity, and Geographies of Crime: Law's Search for the 'Original' Indian," *Cultural Geographies* 17, no.4 (October 2010): 499–500.

26   Ibid., 499.

27   Bradford Groves and Robert K. Groves, "Canada's Forgotten Peoples: The Aboriginal Rights of Métis and Non-Status Indians," *Law and Anthropology* 2 (1987): 139–167. While recent court cases have challenged provincial and national responsibilities with regards to Métis people somewhat, they were not relevant at the time of this study.

28   Cole Harris, "How did Colonialism Dispossess? Comments from an Edge of Empire," *Annals of the Association of American Geographers* 94, no.1 (2004): 166–67.

29   Nihal Perera, "Indigenising the Colonial City: Late 19th-century Columbo and its Landscape," *Urban Studies* 39, no. 9 (2002): 1704, 1706.

30   Edmonds, *Urbanizing Frontiers*, 195, 207, 206–229. See also Barman, "Erasing Indigenous Indigeneity."

31   Mawani, "Genealogies of the Land."

32   Kathi Wilson and Evelyn J. Peters, "'You Can Make a Place for It.' Remapping

Urban First Nation Spaces of Identity," *Society and Space* 23 (2005): 395–413.

33 David Newhouse, "From the Tribal to the Modern: The Development of Modern Aboriginal Societies," in *Expression in Canadian Native Studies*, ed. Ron F. Laliberte, et al. (Saskatoon: University of Saskatchewan Extension Press, 2000), 406.

34 David Newhouse, "The Invisible Infrastructure: Urban Aboriginal Institutions and Organizations," in *Not Strangers in These Parts: Urban Aboriginal Peoples*, ed. David Newhouse and Evelyn Peters (Ottawa: Policy Research Initiative, 2003), 251.

35 Evelyn J. Peters and Carol Lafond, "'I Basically Mostly Stick with My Own Kind': First Nations Appropriation of Urban Space in Saskatoon, Saskatchewan, Canada," in *Indigenous in the City: Contemporary Identities and Cultural Innovation*, ed. E.J. Peters and C. Andersen (Vancouver: UBC Press, 2013), 123–53.

36 Jay Johnson, "Dancing into Place: The Role of the Powwow within Urban Indigenous Communities," in *Indigenous in the City: Contemporary Identities and Cultural Innovation*, ed. E.J. Peters and C. Andersen (Vancouver: UBC Press, 2013), 216–30.

37 Walker and Nejad, "Urban Planning," 139–151.

38 Gerhard J. Ens, *Homeland to Hinterland: The Changing Worlds of the Red River Metis* (Toronto: University of Toronto Press, 1996), 127.

39 Marcel Giraud, *The Métis in the Canadian West*, vols. I and II, trans. George Woodcock (Edmonton: University of Alberta Press, 1986), 381. Also, Ens, *Homeland to Hinterland*, 127.

40 Lagassé, *A Study of the Population of Indian Ancestry*, 142.

41 Walter E. Boek and Jean K. Boek, *The People of Indian Ancestry in Greater Winnipeg* (Winnipeg: Manitoba Department of Agriculture and Immigration. Social and Economic Research Office, 1959).

42 Foster, "The Plains Metis," 297.

43 Margaret McWilliams, *Manitoba Milestones* (Toronto: J.M. Dent and Sons, 1928), 39.

44 Stanley, *The Birth of Western Canada*, 13.

45 Michel Hogue, *Metis and the Medicine Line: Creating a Border and Dividing a People* (Regina: University of Regina Press, 2015), 25.

46 Foster, "The Plains Metis," 305.

47 Alexander Begg and Walter H. Nursey, *Ten Years in Winnipeg: A Narration of the Principal Events in the History of the City of Winnipeg from the Year A.D. 1870 to the Year A.D. 1879 Inclusive* (Winnipeg, MB: Times Printing and Publishing House 1879), 49.

48 Foster, "The Plains Metis," 303.

49 Ibid., 305.

50 Ross, *The Red River Settlement*, 246–62.

51 Stanley, *The Birth of Western Canada*, 14.

52 Ens, *Homeland to Hinterland*, 127.

53 McWilliams, *Manitoba Milestones*, 97.

54 Shore, "The Emergence of the Metis Nation in Manitoba," 76.

55 McWilliams, *Manitoba Milestones*, 108.

56 The Royal Commission on Aboriginal Peoples (RCAP), *Volume 4: Perspectives and Realities* (Ottawa: Canada Communication Group — Publishing Ottawa, 1996), 223–4, 334–42.

57 For a summary of this debate, see Brad Milne, "The Historiography of Métis Land Dispersal, 1870–1890," *Manitoba History* 30, Autumn (1995): 30–41.

58 RCAP, *Volume 4: Perspectives and Realities*, 342.

59 Manitoba Metis Federation Inc. v. Canada (Attorney General) 2013 SCC 14.

60 Giraud, *The Métis in the Canadian West*, vol. II, 470–75.

61 Ens, *Homeland to Hinterland*, 139–73.

62 Todd Paquin, Patrick Young, and Darren Prefontaine, *Métis Farmers* (Saskatoon: Gabriel Dumont Institute's The Virtual Museum of Métis History and Culture, 2003), http://www.metismuseum.ca.

63 Nicole St. Onge, "Race, Class, and Marginality in a Manitoba Interlake Settlement 1850–1950," *Socialist Studies/ Etudes Socialistes* Annual No. 51989 (1989): 124.

64 Frank Tough, "Race, Personality and History: A Review of Marcel Giraud's *The Métis in the Canadian West*," *Native Studies Review* 5, no. 2 (1989): 55–93.

65 Giraud, *The Métis in the Canadian West*, vol. II, 476.

66 Ibid.

67 Ibid.

68 Ens, *Homeland to Hinterland*, 139.

69 Begg and Nursey, *Ten Years in Winnipeg*, 13.

70 William L. Morton, *Manitoba: A History* (Toronto: University of Toronto Press, 1967), 166.

71 The location and boundaries of early Winnipeg can be seen on Figure 1.2.

72 Alan F. J. Artibise, *Winnipeg: A Social History of Urban Growth, 1874–1914* (Montreal: McGill-Queen's University Press, 1975), 130.

73 Ruben Bellan, *Winnipeg First Century: An Economic History* (Winnipeg: Queenston House Publishing, 1978), 25–31.

74 Artibise, *Winnipeg*, 133–35.

75 Sinclair, Duncan and George McPhillips. Plan of River Lots in the Parishes of St. John, St. James and St. Boniface Province of Manitoba [map]. Scale not given. Ottawa: Dominion Lands Branch, 1874. Source: Library and Archives Canada. https://www.flickr.com/photos/ manitobamaps/2079199096/in/album-72157603347076165/.

76 Randolph R. Rostecki, *Crescentwood: A History* (Winnipeg: Crescentwood Home Owners Association, 1993).

77 Joyce Solonecki, *Fort Rouge Through the Years: Souvenir Booklet* (Winnipeg: Fort Rouge Centennial Brochure Committee, 1974), 1.

78 The population counts that follow may slightly underestimate the population of the area that became Fort Rouge. The census does not identify the river lots that families were settled on. Census returns for St. Boniface were matched to HBC lists of individuals who received patents to their land and this comparison established that census takers travelled north in conducting the census. David Champagne received title for lot 14, which represents the southern boundary to Fort Rouge, so the Champagne household and all of the population to the north were counted as resident in Fort Rouge.

79 Ens, *Homeland to Hinterland*, 166, 168.

80 Thomas Flanagan and Gerhard Ens, "Métis Land Grants in Manitoba: A Statistical Study," *Histoire Sociale/Social History* 27, no. 53 (May 1994): 77.

81 Like many of the people who eventually lived in Rooster Town, the Berards were French Métis and the French spelling of their names would have included an accent to make it "Bérard." Most of the records used in this study, however, contained anglicized Métis names and we have used those forms for consistency.

82 Sprague and Frye, *The Genealogy of the First Metis Nation*.

83 Ibid.

84 Ibid.

85 *Property Abstract for Lot 31, St. Boniface West* (Winnipeg: Property Registry Office, various dates).

86   Canada, Department of Labour, "Wages and Hours in the Building Trades, Canada. Table 8 Builders, Labourers," *Labour Gazette* (Ottawa: Queen's Printer, 1905–6), 8405.

87   MS Census 1891, Manitoba, District 8 (Provencher), Subdistrict 1 (St. Boniface), 44 #78.

88   1911 City of Winnipeg Assessment Rolls, Ward 1, no. 1291, City of Winnipeg Archives and Record Centre (CWARC).

89   We do not give page numbers for the Manitoba and Henderson's Directories since this would make the number of endnotes unmanageable. These Directories are available for Winnipeg for every year of this study and organized alphabetically by street and name of the household heads.

90   1883 City of Winnipeg Assessment Rolls, Ward 1, no. 1291, CWARC.

91   James Struthers, *No Fault of Their Own: Unemployment and the Canadian Welfare State 1914–1941* (Toronto: University of Toronto Press, 1983), 3–4.

92   "In the courts," *Manitoba Free Press*, 3 July 1885, 4.

93   Artibise, *Winnipeg*, 130.

94   MS Census 1891, Manitoba, District 8 (Provencher), Subdistrict 1 (St. Boniface), 44 #78.

95   Solonecki, *Fort Rouge Through the Years*, 1; W.Thompson, *Fort Rouge Neighbourhood Walking Tour* (Winnipeg, 1994), http://www.winnipeg.ca/ppd/historic/pdf/Fort_Rouge_Walking_Tour_1994.pdf.

96   Randolph R. Rostecki, *Crescentwood: A History* (Winnipeg: Crescentwood Home Owners Association, 1993).

97   Artibise, *Winnipeg*, 166–67.

98   Rostecki, *Crescentwood*, 23–28.

99   See 1946 map of lands seized for non-payment of taxes "Greater Winnipeg Tax Forfeited Lands (1946)" in Metropolitan Planning Committee and Winnipeg Town Planning Commission, *Background for Planning Greater Winnipeg* (Winnipeg 1946) plate 9, http:/www.flickr.com/photos/manitobamaps/3130341037/in/set-72157611557215976.

CHAPTER TWO: THE ESTABLISHMENT AND CONSOLIDATION OF ROOSTER TOWN, 1901–1911

1   Manitoba Vital Statistics, Marriage Registration no. 1901, 001824, Pierre Hogue and Marie Julienne Henry.

2   MS Census 1901, Manitoba, District 10 (Provencher), Subdistrict m-5 (St. Boniface Municipality), 1 #3.

3   A 1969 *Winnipeg Free Press* article about Rooster Town displaying a 1959 photo of widowed Julia Hogg in her Rooster Town shanty described a photo of Julia and her husband Peter on their wedding day displayed on the wall. Bill Leader, "Winnipeg's Rooster Town . . . Remembrance of Things Past," *Winnipeg Free Press*, 22 November 1969, 3.

4   MS Census 1901, Manitoba, District 10 (Provencher), Subdistrict m-5 (St. Boniface Municipality), 1 #3.

5   MS Census 1891, Manitoba, District 8 (Provencher), Subdistrict h-1 (St. Norbert Parish), 12 # 54 for Julia; Attestation Papers of Peter Hogg, 22 July 1915, box 442-24, accession 92-93, Ministry of the Overseas Military Forces of Canada, RG150, LAC.

6   Sprague and Frye, *The Genealogy of the First Metis Nation*.

7   MS Census 1901, Manitoba, District 12 (Winnipeg), Subdistrict a-3 (Ward 1), 11 #113 for the Wendts; 14, #147 for the Logans; 14 #148 for the Henrys.

8   They are listed in the Rooster Town area in the 1902 City of Winnipeg Assessment Rolls.

9   MS Census 1906, Manitoba, Winnipeg District, Subdistrict 1-b, 68 #531.

10 1911 City of Winnipeg Assessment Rolls, Ward 1, no. 8033, CWARC.

11 Bellan, *Winnipeg First Century*, 114.

12 Ibid., 115; and Artibise, *Winnipeg*, 130–31.

13 Artibise, *Winnipeg*, 187–89.

14 Ibid., 189.

15 Eric Strikwerda, *The Wages of Relief: Cities and the Unemployed in Prairie Canada 1929–1939* (Edmonton: Athabasca University Press, 2013), 37.

16 Bellan, *Winnipeg First Century*, 78–99.

17 "Foreigners and Overcrowding," *Manitoba Free Press*, 1 May 1909, 11.

18 Lawrence Barkwell, *The Reign of Terror Against the Métis of Red River*, Virtual Museum of Métis History and Culture, 12 February 2008, http://www. metismuseum.ca/media/document. php/07260.THE%20REIGN%20 OF%20TERROR.pdf; Barron, "The Indian Pass System in the Canadian West, 1882–1935"; Davis, *Edging into Mainstream*; and Lagassé, *A Study of the Population of Indian Ancestry*.

19 Murray Dobbin, "The Métis in Western Canada Since 1945," in *The Making of the Modern West: Western Canada Since 1945*, ed. A.W. Rasporich (Calgary: University of Calgary Press, 1984), 186.

20 Métis were identified mainly through the column recording colour, and the column recording racial or tribal origin. Some individuals were not identified as "halfbreeds," the terminology of the census, but we knew their identities because they subsequently became part of the Rooster Town population and had been identified by Sprague and Frye (1983) or through various Métis genealogies. (Manitoba Census, 1870,

Public Archives of Manitoba, MG 2 B3; MS Census 1901, Manitoba, District 12 [Winnipeg]; Gail Morin, *Métis Families*.

21 MS Census 1901, Manitoba, District 12 (Winnipeg).

22 Sprague and Frye, *Genealogy*; MS Census 1891, Manitoba, District 10 (Winnipeg), Subdistrict 1 (Ward 1), 16 #68.

23 MS Census 1901, Manitoba, District 12 (Winnipeg), Subdistrict a-3 (Ward 1), 11 #111, 11 #110, 16 #157, 11 #112.

24 MS Census 1901, Manitoba, District 12 (Winnipeg), Subdistrict a-3 (Ward 1), 11 #111, 11 #110, 16 #157, 11 #112.

25 1900 City of Winnipeg Assessment Rolls, Ward 1, no. 810, CWARC.

26 1900 City of Winnipeg Assessment Rolls, Ward 1, no. 1712, CWARC.

27 James Starr was First Nations, married to a Métis woman. Interview with Larry Morrissette, Winnipeg, 10 March 2014.

28 St. Norbert had been established on the shores of the La Salle and Red Rivers in the early 1850s when a population of about 700 justified the permanent presence of a priest (Giraud, *The Métis in the Canadian West*, 178). It was a French-speaking parish whose economy had emphasized hunting, including the summer buffalo hunt, more than agriculture (Giraud, *The Métis in the Canadian West*, 165).

29 Flanagan and Ens, "Métis Land Grants in Manitoba," 18.

30 MS Census 1901, Manitoba, District 12 (Winnipeg), Subdistrict e (Wards 5 and 6).

31 MS Census 1891, Manitoba, District 8 (Provencher), Subdistrict m (St. Boniface Town) 55 #114.

32 MS Census 1901, Manitoba, District 12 (Winnipeg), Subdistrict a-3 (Ward 1) 14 #144.

33 MS Census 1901, Manitoba, District 12 (Winnipeg), Subdistrict a-3 (Ward 1) 14 #143.

34 1903 City of Winnipeg Assessment Rolls, Ward 1, no. 788, CWARC.

35 1902 City of Winnipeg Building Permits, Ward 1, no. 484530, CWARC.

36 1902 City of Winnipeg Assessment Rolls, Ward 1, no. 444, CWARC.

37 1905 City of Winnipeg Building Permits, Ward 1, no. 2792, CWARC.

38 1905 City of Winnipeg Building Permits, Ward 1, no. 2705, CWARC.

39 Richard Harris, "Self-building in the Urban Housing Market," *Economic Geography* 67 no.1 (January 1991): 12.

40 Ibid.

41 Ibid., 9–10.

42 "Houses for Sale," *Manitoba Free Press*, 3 July 1901, 1; "Houses for Sale," 21 March 1901, 12; "Houses for Sale," 13 October 1901, 11.

43 Artibise, *Winnipeg*, 166.

44 Manitoba Vital Statistics, Marriage Registration no. 1906,002717, Henri [Henry] Parisien and Catherine Smith. MS Census 1906, Manitoba, Winnipeg District, Subdistrict 1-b, 45 #336.

45 Street directories were compiled for every year, and these were searched extensively for Rooster Town addresses and occupations. Providing a reference for every individual piece of data would multiply the number of references exponentially. Where there is a reference to an address with no specific reference provided, the source is the street directory for that year. Interested readers can also consult the Rooster Town project database on the University of Manitoba website for confirmation of the source.

46 "Smith and his 'Water Wagon,'" *Manitoba Free Press*, 6 March 1906, 1.

47 "City to Install Sewer Connection," *Manitoba Free Press*, 5 February 1907, 7.

48 "Criminal Cases Today," *Winnipeg Tribune*, 12 June 1912, 5.

49 Sprague and Frye, *Genealogy*.

50 Nicole St. Onge, "Memories of Metis Women in Saint-Eustache, Manitoba—1910–1980," *Native Studies Review* 17, no. 2 (2008): 48.

51 Sprague and Frye, *Genealogy*.

52 "Running a Raffle," *Manitoba Free Press*, 30 September 1909, 5.

53 Ibid.

54 "Mrs. Ed. Villburn Makes Statement," *Manitoba Free Press*, 18 December 1911, 24.

55 Details about individuals and families are contained in Appendix B.

56 Details about individuals and families are contained in Appendix B.

57 F.H. Leacy and M.C. Urquhard, eds., *Historical Statistics of Canada* (Ottawa: Statistics Canada and Social Science Federation of Canada, 1983). Hourly wage rates for labourers in Winnipeg did increase from $0.20 in 1901 to $0.28 in 1911, a 40 percent increase (Series # 248–267).

58 Canada, Department of Labour, "Cost/Week of a Family Budget of Staple Foods, Fuel and Lighting, and Rent in Terms of the Average Prices in Sixty Cities in Canada," *Labour Gazette* (Ottawa: Queen's Printer, 1926), 69.

59 James S. Woodsworth, *My Neighbour: A Study of City Conditions, A Plea for Social Services* (Toronto: The Missionary Society of the Methodist Church, 1911), 103.

60 Artibise, *Winnipeg*, 240.

61 1911 City of Winnipeg Assessment Rolls, Ward 1, no. 2004, CWARC.

62 1911 City of Winnipeg Building Permits, Ward 1, no. 2752, CWARC.

63 1911 City of Winnipeg Building Permits, Ward 1, no. 2264, CWARC.

64 1911 City of Winnipeg Building Permits, Ward 1, no. 902, CWARC.

65 "City to Install Sewer Connection," *Manitoba Free Press*, 5 February 1907, 7.

66 19071 City of Winnipeg Building Permit, Ward 1, no. 960, CWARC.

67 Richard Harris, *Unplanned Suburbs*.

68 "Action Against City," *Winnipeg Tribune*, 4 October 1906, 10.

69 "Comptroller's Annual Report," *Winnipeg Tribune*, 23 November 1907, 7; 1907 City of Winnipeg Assessment Rolls, Ward 1, no. 1059, CWARC.

70 St-Onge, "Memories of Metis Women of Saint-Eustache," 66.

CHAPTER THREE: DEVISING NEW ECONOMIC AND HOUSING STRATEGIES: ROOSTER TOWN DURING THE FIRST WORLD WAR AND AFTER, 1916–1926

1 These relationships can be pieced together from the Manitoba Vital Statistics, obituaries, and census information. Manitoba Vital Statistics, Marriage Registration no. 1915,174244, Joseph Arcand and Clara Henry; MS Census 1916, Manitoba, District 15 (Winnipeg South), Subdistrict 14, 37 #392; 39 #401; 38 #395; 36 # 382; "Obituaries, Patrick Conway," *Manitoba Free Press*, 19 December 1956, 30; "Obituaries, Marie Smith," *Manitoba Free Press*, 12 June 1951, 7; "Deaths and Funerals, William Smith," *Manitoba Free Press*, 8 April 1953, 17.

2 MS Census 1916, Manitoba, District 15 (Winnipeg South), Subdistrict 14, 37 #392; 39 #401; 38 #395; 36 # 382; Manitoba Vital Statistics, Death registration no. 1914,074278.

3 Attestation papers of Peter Hogg, 22 July 1915, box 442-24, accession 92-93, Ministry of the Overseas Military Forces of Canada, RG150, LAC. Attestation

papers are personal forms that volunteers for service in the First World War needed to fill out before they were accepted by the Canadian Expeditionary Force (CEF).

4 Desmond Morton, *Fight or Pay: Soldiers' Families in the Great War* (Vancouver: UBC Press), 44.

5 Interview with vocational counsellor, 26 February 1917, box 442-24, accession 92-93, Ministry of the Overseas Military Forces of Canada, RG150, LAC.

6 Ibid.

7 The fact that when he returned Peter Hogg was often listed as living with his wife also lends support to the possibility that they quarrelled but did not separate (Morton, *Fight or Pay*, 31).

8 MS Census 1921, Manitoba, Winnipeg South District, Subdistrict 42, 10 #202.

9 "Wounded," *Winnipeg Tribune*, 17 May 1916, 12.

10 Medical History of Individual, 15 May 1917, box 442-24, accession 92-93, Ministry of the Overseas Military Forces of Canada, RG150, LAC.

11 Proceedings on Discharge, 30 September 1917, box 442-24, accession 92-93, Ministry of the Overseas Military Forces of Canada, RG150, LAC.

12 Interview with vocational counsellor, 26 February 1917, box 442-24, accession 92-93, Ministry of the Overseas Military Forces of Canada, RG150, LAC.

13 MS Census 1921, Manitoba, Winnipeg South District, Subdistrict 42, 10 #202.

14 Medical History of an Invalid, 16 May 1917, box 442-24, accession 92-93, Ministry of the Overseas Military Forces of Canada, RG150, LAC.

15 Bellan, *Winnipeg First Century*, 132.

16 Artibise, *Winnipeg*, 281.

17 J.E. Rea, *The Winnipeg General Strike* (Toronto: Holt, Rinehart and Winston of Canada, 1973).

18   Hugh Amos Robson, *Royal Commission to Enquire into and Report Upon the Causes and Effects of the General Strike Which Recently Existed in the City of Winnipeg: For a Period of Six Weeks, Including the Methods of Calling and Carrying on Such Strike* (Winnipeg: Government of Manitoba, 1919), 6.

19   Bellan, *Winnipeg First Century*, 159.

20   "Night Visit to Foreign District," *Manitoba Free Press*, 13 May 1913, 16.

21   Artibise, *Winnipeg*, 239–45.

22   City of Greater Winnipeg, Committee on Public Health and Welfare (1919), Annual Report for the year ending December 31, 1918, CWARC, Box A 713, Vol. 9, 6.

23   City of Greater Winnipeg, Committee on Public Health and Welfare (1914), Annual Report for the year ending December 31, 1913, CWARC, Box A 711, Vol. 3, 100.

24   City of Greater Winnipeg. Committee on Public Health and Welfare. (1918), Annual Report for the year ending December 31, 1917, CWARC, Box A 713, Vol. 8, 70.

25   City of Greater Winnipeg, Committee on Public Health and Welfare (1925), Annual Report for the year ending December 31, 1924, CWARC, Box A 715, Vol. 11. City of Greater Winnipeg, Committee on Public Health and Welfare (1926), Annual Report for the year ending December 31, 1925, CWARC, Box A 715, Vol. 11.

26   Stefan Epp, "Class, Capitalism, and Construction: Winnipeg's Housing Crisis and the Debate over Public Housing, 1934–1939," *Histoire Sociale/Social History* 43, no. 86 (2010): 400.

27   Harris, *Unplanned Suburbs*, 2.

28   Cost of living surveys from *Labour Gazette*, 1914, quoted in Morton, *Fight or Pay*, 245.

29   Quoted in Artibise, *Winnipeg*, 187.

30   Artibise, *Winnipeg*, 285.

31   Ibid., 187.

32   Quoted in Artibise, *Winnipeg*, 188.

33   Artibise, *Winnipeg*, 190.

34   Ibid., 190–94.

35   Bellan, *Winnipeg First Century*, 180.

36   Ibid., 185.

37   The population number is an estimate because not all of the households were listed in the census. The estimate is based on household sizes reported in the census and the age of children from other census records.

38   St-Onge, "Race, Class and Marginality," 119.

39   Attestation papers of Modeste Cardinal, 29 February 1916, box 4930-35, accession 92-93, Ministry of the Overseas Military Forces of Canada, RG150, LAC.

40   MS Census 1916, Manitoba, District 15 (Winnipeg South), Subdistrict 14, 9 #76.

41   Natural Resources Canada Photo FA809_034 from National Air Photo Library. Aerial Photograph taken 10-17-1927. Scale 1:10,000.

42   1916 City of Winnipeg Assessment Rolls, Ward 1, 832, CWARC.

43   A. Bryan Cyr, *Métis Veterans of Manitoba: From Buffalo to Battlefields* (Winnipeg: Manitoba Métis Federation, 2010), 10.

44   Christopher Sharpe, "Recruitment and Conscription (Canada)," *1914–1918-online. International Encyclopedia of the First World War*, edited by Ute Daniel, Peter Gatrell, Oliver Janz, Heather Jones, Jennifer Keene, Alan Kramer, and Bill Nasson, issued by Freie Universität Berlin, Berlin 2015-06-2, http://dx.doi.org/10.15463/ie1418.10670.

45   Larry Morrissette (Rooster Town descendant), interview with Evelyn Peters, 10 March 2014, Winnipeg.

46   Morton, *Fight or Pay*, 23.

47 Medical Records of Peter Berard, 17 August, 1917, box 669-21, accession 92-93, Ministry of the Overseas Military Forces of Canada, RG150, LAC.

48 "Deaths and Funerals, Peter Berard," *Winnipeg Tribune*, 23 February 1934, 17.

49 Medical History Sheet of Frank Berard, 20 November 1917, box 683 - 6, accession 92-93, Ministry of the Overseas Military Forces of Canada, RG150, LAC.

50 Medical History of an Invalid, John Baptiste Fountaine, 4 November, 1918; Proceedings on Discharge, John Baptiste Fountaine, 11 November 1918, box 3241-13, accession 92-93/166, Ministry of the Overseas Military Forces of Canada, RG150, LAC.

51 MS Census 1911, Manitoba, Winnipeg, District 5, 37 #363, MS Census 1921, Manitoba, Winnipeg South District, Subdistrict 42, 2 #17.

52 Medical History Sheet of John Baptiste Peppin, n.d., box 7726 - 84, accession 92-93, Ministry of the Overseas Military Forces of Canada, RG150, LAC.

53 Medical History Sheet of Frederick Savage, n.d., box 8668 - 6, accession 92-93, Ministry of the Overseas Military Forces of Canada, RG150, LAC.

54 Casualty Form, Active Service for William Curran, 7 October, 1917, box 2227-24, accession 92-93, Ministry of the Overseas Military Forces of Canada, RG150, LAC.

55 Untitled document, 7 October, 1917, box 4246-47, accession 92-93, Ministry of the Overseas Military Forces of Canada, RG150, LAC.

56 "Deaths and Funerals, Albin Henderson," *Manitoba Free Press*, 2 August 1918, 3.

57 Untitled form, 4 October, 1916, box 6477-42, accession 92-93, Ministry of the Overseas Military Forces of Canada, RG150, LAC.

58 Morton, *Fight or Pay*, 245.

59 Ibid., 20.

60 Alvin Finkel, *Social Policy and Practice in Canada: A History* (Waterloo: Wilfrid Laurier University Press, 2006); Morton, *Fight or Pay*, 95.

61 War Service Gratuity to Dependents of Deceased Soldiers, 4 October, 1916, box 6477-42, accession 92-93, Ministry of the Overseas Military Forces of Canada, RG150, LAC.

62 Manitoba Vital Statistics, marriage registration 1888,001871, Joseph McDougall and Florence Atkinson.

63 Separation Allowance papers for John James Mulvaney, n.d., box 6477-42, accession 92-93, Ministry of the Overseas Military Forces of Canada, RG150, LAC.

64 Morton, *Fight or Pay*, 96.

65 MS Census 1916, Manitoba, District 15 (Winnipeg South), Subdistrict 23 10, #209.

66 MS Census 1916, Manitoba, District 15 (Winnipeg South), Subdistrict 23 31, #335.

67 Separation Allowance Record, John Baptiste Fountaine, no date, box 3241-13, accession 92-93/166, Ministry of the Overseas Military Forces of Canada, RG150, LAC.

68 War Service Gratuity for John Baptiste Fountaine, 11 April 1919, box 1482-31, accession 92-93/166, Ministry of the Overseas Military Forces of Canada, RG150, LAC.

69 MS Census 1916, Manitoba, District 15 (Winnipeg South), Subdistrict 14, 15 #170.

70 MS Census 1916, Manitoba, District 15 (Winnipeg South), Subdistrict 14, 16 #171.

71 For details about the families and individuals involved, see Appendix B.

72 "Prescription for Nags Used as Intoxicant," *Winnipeg Tribune*, 24 December 1919, 1.

73 "Drives Car While Drunk," *Winnipeg Tribune*, 17 July 1922, 2.

74 "Deaths and Funerals, William Dunnick," *Manitoba Free Press*, 13 February 1939.

75 See, for example, "In Memoriam," *Manitoba Free Press*, 30 August 1962, 33.

76 Sprague and Frye, *The Genealogy of the First Metis Nation*.

77 Sprague and Frye, *Genealogy*; Marcel Giraud, *The Métis in the Canadian West*, vol. I, 165.

78 Sprague and Frye, *Genealogy*.

79 See, for example: Louis Parisian, MS Census 1911, Manitoba, District 8, Subdistrict 49 (St. Norbert Parish), 6 #77; Henry Parisien, MS Census 1901, Manitoba, District 10 (Provencher), Sub-district h-2 (St. Norbert), 8 #6; Pascal Parisian, MS Census 1901, Manitoba, District 10 (Provencher), Subdistrict h-2 (St. Norbert), 8 # 71; Joseph Eduard Parisien, MS Census 1916, Manitoba, District 12 (Springfield), Subdistrict 3 (St. Norbert), 33 #254, James Charles Parisien, MS Census 1891, Manitoba, District 8 (Provencher), Subdistrict h-1 (St. Norbert Parish), 16 #76.

80 MS Census 1916, Manitoba, District 12 (Springfield), Subdistrict 3 (St. Norbert), 32 #248; Manitoba, Vital Statistics Agency, Death Registration no. 1921, 017769.

81 Manitoba, Vital Statistics Agency, Marriage Registration no. 1920, 019069.

82 MS Census 1921, Manitoba, Winnipeg South District, Subdistrict 42, 24.

83 Solonecki, *Fort Rouge Through the Years*, 23.

84 Doreen Pound (daughter of Frank Pound, greenhouse owner and florist), interview by Evelyn Peters, 30 November 2016, Winnipeg.

85 Leacy and Urquhard, eds., *Historical Statistics of Canada*.

86 "Cost/Week of a Family Budget of Staple Foods, Fuel and Lighting, and Rent in Terms of the Average Prices in Sixty Cities in Canada," *Labour Gazette* (Ottawa: Department of Labour, 1926), 69.

87 1921 City of Winnipeg Assessment Rolls, Ward 1, no. 5748, CWARC.

88 MS Census 1921, Manitoba, Winnipeg South District, Subdistrict 42, 19, #188.

89 1920 City of Winnipeg Assessment Rolls, Ward 1, no. 15456, CWARC; 1921 City of Winnipeg Assessment Rolls, Ward 1, no. 12521, CWARC.

90 1921 City of Winnipeg Assessment Rolls, Ward 1, no. 12521, CWARC.

91 "Retail Prices of Staple Foods, Groceries, Fuel and Lighting, and Rentals in Canada at the Beginning of December 1925," *Labour Gazette* (Ottawa: Department of Labour, 1926), 75.

92 Pulling together information about tenure, ownership, and building is extremely difficult. While it may seem obvious that property descriptions could be matched across different records, in practice this is not possible. Building permit property descriptors and addresses are often inaccurate or incomplete, the purpose of assessment rolls is to provide a contact for tax collection and they do not consistently identify owners and occupants. As plans change, so do property descriptors, and it is beyond the scope of this project to research these changes and apply them to the many pieces of scattered information collected in this project.

93 1922 City of Winnipeg Building Permits, Ward 1, no. 1554/5, CWARC.

94 1926 City of Winnipeg Assessment Rolls, Ward 1, no. 526, CWARC.

95 1918 City of Winnipeg Building Permits, Ward 1, no. 497, CWARC; MS Census 1916, Manitoba, District 15 (Winnipeg South), Subdistrict 14, 16 #70.

96   MS Census 1921, Manitoba, Winnipeg South census, Subdistrict 23, 24 #278.

97   Manitoba, Vital Statistics Agency, Dearth Registration no. 1927,009082.

98   1920 City of Winnipeg Building Permits, Ward 1, no. 1120, CWARC.

99   MS Census 1921, Manitoba, Winnipeg South District, Subdistrict 42; Subdistrict 23, 21, #205.

100 1926 City of Winnipeg Collector's Rolls, Ward 1, no. 4896, CWARC.

101 1921 City of Winnipeg Collector's Rolls, Ward 1, no. 4394, CWARC.

102 1921 City of Winnipeg Assessment Rolls, Ward 1, no. 4157, CWARC.

103 "He Escapes Taxes for Seven Years," 3.

104 1927 City of Winnipeg Building Permits, Ward 1, no. 3373, CWARC.

105 1923 City of Winnipeg Building Permits, Ward 1, no. 154, CWARC.

106 Harris, *Unplanned Suburbs*, 267.

107 1922 City of Winnipeg Building Permits, Ward 1, 3725, CWARC.

108 1921 City of Winnipeg Collector's Rolls, Ward 1, no. 5229, CWARC.

109 1921 City of Winnipeg Building Permits, Ward 1, no. 408, CWARC.

110 1926 City of Winnipeg Assessment Rolls, Ward 1, no. 5421, CWARC.

111 1929 City of Winnipeg Collector's Rolls, Ward 1, no. 3813, CWARC.

112 1932 City of Winnipeg Assessment Rolls, Ward 1, no. 3813, CWARC.

113 1923 City of Winnipeg Building Permits, Ward 1, no. 217 and 254, CWARC.

114 1926 City of Winnipeg Assessment Rolls, Ward 1, no. 5420, CWARC.

115 1926 City of Winnipeg Collector's Rolls, Ward 1, no. 5420, CWARC.

116 1927 City of Winnipeg Building Permits, Ward 1, no. 3834, CWARC.

117 Ron Poulton, "Before the Magistrate," *Manitoba Free Press*, 29 May 1928, 4.

118 1929–30 City of Winnipeg Assessment Rolls, Ward 1, no. 4822, CWARC.

119 Harris, *Unplanned Suburbs*.

120 Attestation Papers of William Omand, December 24, 1915, box 4930-35, accession 92-93, Ministry of the Overseas Military Forces of Canada, RG150, LAC. The Omands lived next door to the Curran residence at 916 Garwood. The family was listed as living on the lot in 1915.

121 1921 City of Winnipeg Building Permits, Ward 1, no. 2281, CWARC.

122 1924 City of Winnipeg Building Permits, Ward 1, no. 50, CWARC.

123 1926 City of Winnipeg Assessment Rolls, Ward 1, no. 6469, CWARC.

124 1913 City of Winnipeg Building Permits, Ward 1, no. 3717, CWARC.

125 1921 City of Winnipeg Assessment Rolls, Ward 1, no. 15230, CWARC.

126 1926 City of Winnipeg Assessment Rolls, Ward 1, no. 6015, CWARC.

127 MS Census 1916, Manitoba, District 15 (Winnipeg South), Subdistrict 14, 21 #244.

128 1922 City of Winnipeg Building Permits, Ward 1, no. 530, CWARC.

129 1928 City of Winnipeg Building Permits, Ward 1, no. 34866, CWARC.

130 City of Winnipeg Property Assessment Details, 787 Carter, http://www.winnipegassessment.com/asmttax/english/propertydetails/.

131 1911 City of Winnipeg Assessment Rolls, Ward 1, no. 7930, 7931, CWARC.

132 1921 City of Winnipeg Assessment Rolls, Ward 1, no. 5739, CWARC.

133 1922 City of Winnipeg Building Permits, Ward 1, no. 801, CWARC.

134 James Struthers, *No Fault of Their Own: Unemployment and the Canadian Welfare*

State, 1914–1941 (Toronto: University of Toronto Press, 1983), 4.

135 Attestation Papers of Marcien Cardinal, 22 November 1916, box 1482-29, accession 92-93, Ministry of the Overseas Military Forces of Canada, RG150, LAC Canadian Expeditionary Force (CEF); Discharge Papers of Marcien Cardinal, 18 December 1918, box 1482-29, accession 92-93, Ministry of the Overseas Military Forces of Canada, RG150, LAC Canadian Expeditionary Force (CEF); Attestation Papers of Maxime Michael Cardinal, 20 March 1917, box 1482-30, accession 92-93, Ministry of the Overseas Military Forces of Canada, RG150, LAC Canadian Expeditionary Force (CEF); Discharge Papers of Maxime Michael Cardinal, 25 February 1919, box 1482-30, accession 92-93, Ministry of the Overseas Military Forces of Canada, RG150, LAC Canadian Expeditionary Force (CEF); Discharge Papers of Joseph Andre Berard, 25 May 1918, box 668-63, accession 92-93, Ministry of the Overseas Military Forces of Canada, RG150, LAC Canadian Expeditionary Force (CEF); Discharge Papers of Joseph Andre Berard, 5 December 1919, box 668-63, accession 92-93, Ministry of the Overseas Military Forces of Canada, RG150, LAC Canadian Expeditionary Force (CEF); Attestation Papers of Adolph Joseph Pilon, 31 November 1918, box 7837-45, accession 92-93, Ministry of the Overseas Military Forces of Canada, RG150, LAC Canadian Expeditionary Force (CEF); Discharge Papers of Adolph Joseph Pilon, 6 December 1918, box 7837-45, accession 92-93, Ministry of the Overseas Military Forces of Canada, RG150, LAC Canadian Expeditionary Force (CEF); Manitoba, Vital Statistics Agency, Marriage Registration no. 1921,006195, Marcien Cardinal and Marguerite Peppin; Manitoba, Vital Statistics Agency, Marriage Registration no. 1921,010257, Maxime Cardinal and Marie Josephine Larocque; Manitoba, Vital Statistics Agency, Marriage Regis-

tration no. 1921,038356, Joseph Andre Berard and Alexandrina Evangeline Nault; Manitoba, Vital Statistics Agency, Marriage Registration no 1921, 026461 Delphis Pilon and Josephine Laramee.

136 There are scattered references to an F. Berard as well as Mary Louise Berard in the area in the Henderson's Directories and newspapers, but there is not enough supplementary information to confirm who these individuals were.

137 1920 City of Winnipeg Assessment Rolls, Ward 1, no. 13615 and 13616, City of Winnipeg Archives and Record Centre (CWARC).

138 Sonya Wright and Dwili Burns (nieces of Rooster Town residents Kenny Campbell), interview with Evelyn Peters, 9 December 2013, Winnipeg.

139 Sonya Wright, personal communication to Evelyn Peters, 16 December 2013.

140 Natural Resources Canada Photo FA809_034 from National Air Photo Library. Aerial Photograph taken 10-17-1927. Scale 1:10,000.

141 1926 City of Winnipeg Assessment Rolls, Ward 1, no. #4078, CWARC.

142 1926 City of Winnipeg Assessment Rolls, Ward 1, no. 6607, CWARC.

143 MS Census 1921, Manitoba, Winnipeg South District, Subdistrict 42, 19 #188.

144 Candace Hogue, personal communication to Evelyn Peters, 23 November 2017.

CHAPTER FOUR: PERSISTENCE, GROWTH, AND COMMUNITY: ROOSTER TOWN DURING AND AFTER THE GREAT DEPRESSION, 1931–1946

1 1931 City of Winnipeg Assessment Rolls, Ward 1, no. 4149, CWARC.

2 1931 City of Winnipeg Assessment Rolls, Ward 1, no. 4149, CWARC; "Deaths

and funerals, Joseph Edward Parisien," *Winnipeg Tribune*, 1 August 1939, 18.

3   Manitoba Vital Statistics, Death Registration no. 1932,044140, Melanie Gagnon; The Henry siblings are mentioned in Cora Arcand's obituary: "Deaths and funerals, Cora Arcand," *Winnipeg Free Press*, 5 September 1956, 20.

4   Reference in the previous chapter.

5   In 1929, Joseph Conway, son of Patrick Conway, purchased 1075 Dudley, and he and his wife Dorilda (née Parisian), and Patrick and Mathilda lived there. There were two buildings on the lot, worth about $200 each. They stay here until 1952. (1931 City of Winnipeg Assessment Rolls, Ward 1, no. 4157, CWARC.

6   We can piece together this information from Marie Smith's obituary, where she lists her siblings, her husband and her sons. Her sons are the same as those listed in William Smith's obituary, which refers to his wife as Frances. Archie Henry's wife Esther is identified in his obituary: "Deaths and Funerals, Marie Smith," *Winnipeg Free Press*, 12 June, 1951, 7; "Deaths and Funerals, William Smith," *Winnipeg Free Press*, 8 April 1953, 17; "Deaths and Funerals, Arthur Henry," *Winnipeg Free Press*, 26 June 1979, 56.

7   This information is pieced together by triangulating a number of sources including the Henderson's Directories and the City of Winnipeg voters lists. Manitoba Vital Statistics, Marriage Registration no. 1923,050104, Archie Pervian and Josephine Henry; "Deaths and Funerals, Joseph Arthur Eugene Parisien," *Winnipeg Free Press*, 10 January 1956, 26; "Deaths and Funerals, Marie Josephine Parisien," *Winnipeg Free Press*, 1 July 1954.

8   "Five Convicted of Liquor Act Breach," *Free Press*, 17 October 1936, 11; "Deaths and Funerals, Marie Josephine Parisien," *Winnipeg Free Press*, 1 July 1954, 31.

9   "Houses for Sale," *Winnipeg Free Press*, 19 June 1958, 36.

10 Leacy and Urquhard, eds., *Historical Statistics of Canada*, Series S298-322.

11 Poulton, "Before the Magistrate," 13.

12 "Man Badly Hurt by Locomotive," *Winnipeg Free Press*, 1 April 1939, 8; "65-Year Old Man Killed by Train," *Winnipeg Tribune*, 4 April 1939, 1.

13 1922 City of Winnipeg Building Permits, Ward 1, no. 3388, CWARC; "Deaths and Funerals, Adeline Gosselin," *Winnipeg Tribune*, 3 December 1938, 5.

14 "Deaths and Funerals, Frank Gosselin," *Winnipeg Free Press*, 14 June 1958, 47; 1941 City of Winnipeg Assessment Rolls, Ward 1, no. 3451-1, CWARC.

15 Udo Sautter, "Measuring Unemployment in Canada: Federal Efforts before World War II," *Histoire Sociale/Social History* 15, no. 30 (1982): 485.

16 James Struthers, *No Fault of Their Own*, 4.

17 Ibid., 5.

18 Michiel Horn, ed., *The Depression in Canada: Responses to Economic Crisis* (Toronto: Copp Clark Pitman, 1988): 278.

19 Struthers, *No Fault of Their Own*, 47.

20 City of Greater Winnipeg, City Council Minutes, 1933 Minute Book, note 866.

21 Struthers, *No Fault of Their Own*, 71.

22 Ibid., 48.

23 City of Greater Winnipeg, City Council Minutes, 1931 Minute Book, note 452 "Updated Relief Policy in Winnipeg."

24 Struthers, *No Fault of Their Own*, 71–74.

25 Bellan, *Winnipeg First Century*, 205.

26 Cost of living surveys from *Labour Gazette*, 1914 (quoted in Morton, *Fight or Pay*, 245).

27 City of Greater Winnipeg, Committee on Public Health and Welfare (1909), Annual Report for the Year Ending

December 31, 1908, City of Winnipeg Archives, Box A 711, Vol. 1, 62.

28 Bellan, *Winnipeg First Century*, 209–14.

29 Harold F. Greenway, *Housing in Canada: A Study Based on the Census of 1931 and Supplementary Data* (Ottawa: Edmond Cloutier, 1941), 541–42.

30 City of Greater Winnipeg, Committee on Public Health and Welfare (1939), Annual Report for the Year Ending December 31, 1938, City of Winnipeg Archives, Box A 717, Vol 14(a), 4.

31 Bellan, *Winnipeg First Century*, 221–30.

32 Ibid., 223.

33 John C. Bacher, *Keeping to the Marketplace: The Evolution of Canadian Housing Policy* (Montreal: McGill-Queen's University Press, 1993); John C. Bacher and J. David Hulchanski, "Keeping Warm and Dry: The Policy Response to the Struggle for Shelter Among Canada's Homeless, 1900–1960," *Urban History Review* 16, no. 2 (October 1987): 147.

34 City of Greater Winnipeg, Committee on Public Health and Welfare (1941), Report of the Twenty-Third Annual Survey of Vacant Houses and Vacant Suites in the City ALSO Total Housing Accommodation and Remarks on Housing in General – January 1941, CWARC, Box A 718, 6.

35 City of Greater Winnipeg, Committee on Public Health and Welfare (1946), Report of the Twenty-Seventh Annual Survey of Vacant Houses and Vacant Suites in the City ALSO Total Housing Accommodation and Remarks on Housing in General – January 1946. Retrieved from CWARC, Box A 723, 5.

36 Jody Perrun, *The Patriotic Consensus: Winnipeg, 1939–1945* (Ottawa: Library and Archives Canada/Bibliothèque et Archives Canada, 2010).

37 *Housing in Winnipeg: Report of Committee on Housing*, Winnipeg Council of Social Agencies (Winnipeg: The Committee on Housing, 1943), 21.

38 *Census of Canada 1941: Winnipeg Housing Atlas* (Ottawa: Dominion Bureau of Statistics, 1944); *Population and Housing Characteristics by Census Tracts: Winnipeg* (Ottawa: E. Cloutier, Queen's Printer, 1953).

39 Bacher and Hulchanski, "Keeping Warm and Dry," 159.

40 "Woman Attacked," *Winnipeg Tribune*, 3 August 1937, 3; "Before the Magistrate," *Winnipeg Tribune*, 4 December 1937, 3.

41 "Health Officer Would Banish Relics of Pioneering Days," *Winnipeg Tribune*, 3 February 1944.

42 David G. Burley, "Rooster Town: Winnipeg's Lost Métis Suburb, 1900–1960," *Urban History Review* 42, no. 1 (2013): 8.

43 See Appendix B.

44 1931 City of Winnipeg Building Permits, Ward 1, no. 1554/5, CWARC.

45 See, for example, John Omand's 1921 City of Winnipeg Building Permits, Ward 1, no. 2281, CWARC.

46 "Mayor to Present Gift," *Winnipeg Free Press*, 24 November 1931, 11.

47 "Social and Personal," *Winnipeg Free Press*, 24 November 1932, 8; "Society," *Winnipeg Free Press*, June 14, 1935, 9; "Deaths and Funerals, Agnes Morrissette," *Winnipeg Free Press*, 7 February 1940, 2.

48 Natural Resources Canada Photo A1221_009 from National Air Photo Library. Air Photo Taken 06-15-1929. Scale 1:10,000.

49 MS Census 1916, Manitoba, District 37 (Springfield), Subdistrict 13 (St. Vital), 9 #75; Attestation Papers for Modeste Cardinal, 29 February, 1916, box 4930-35, accession 92-93, Ministry of the Overseas Military Forces of Canada, RG150, LAC); Sprague and Frye, *The Genealogy of the First Metis Nation*.

50 Family relationships can be derived from Archie Cardinal's obituary, "Deaths and

Funerals, Arthur Cardinal," *Winnipeg Free Press*, 20 January 1991, 32.

51   Manitoba Vital Statistics, Birth registration no. 1906,004517, 1902,003924 (Courchenes) MS Census 1916, Manitoba, District 12 (Springfield), Subdistrict 3 (Ste. Anne), 19 #177.

52   Giraud, *The Métis*, 476.

53   Struthers, *No Fault of Their Own*, 4.

54   1931 City of Winnipeg Collector's Rolls, Ward 1, no. 3438, CWARC.

55   "Five Convicted of Liquor Act Breach," *Winnipeg Free Press*, 17 October 1936, 11.

56   "War Rumours Blamed When Three Charged With Theft of Scrap," *Winnipeg Tribune*, 22 April 1937, 21.

57   Steven Casey, *Thirty-Seven Years with the Jesuits* (Montreal: McGill-Queen's University Press, 2007), 32.

58   1935 Voters Lists, Federal Elections, 1935–1980. R1003-6-3-E (RG113-B). Library and Archives Canada, Ottawa, Ontario, Canada.

59   1933 City of Winnipeg Building Permits, Ward 1, no. 2679, CWARC; "Deaths and Funerals, Wasyl Uhryn," *Winnipeg Free Press*, 6 February 1950, 26.

60   Natural Resources Canada Photo A11320_205. Air Photo Taken by Energy, Mines and Resources 1948; City of Winnipeg Property Assessment Details, 1003 Weatherdon Avenue, http://www.winnipegassessment.com/asmttax/english/propertydetails/.

61   "Deaths and Funerals, Roger Parisien," *Winnipeg Free Press*, 22 April 1943; "Deaths and Funerals, Thomas Parisien," *Winnipeg Free Press*, 25 March 1972, 39.

62   1938 City of Winnipeg Building Permits, Ward 1, no. 459, CWARC.

63   John Dafoe, "Rooster Town Is Dying – but It Had Its Wild Days," *Winnipeg Free Press*, 11 April 1959, 1.

64   "Nail Tinting, '"No Good to Do,'" *Winnipeg Tribune*, 8 March 1937, 3.

65   Scrip affidavit for Elice Minnie, vol. 1323, sed. D-11-8-a, Interior Department, RG 15, LAC; MS Census 1901, Manitoba, District 12 (Winnipeg), Subdistrict a-3 (Ward 1).

66   "Region 3 Captain: Ron Nunn," BCMANR: British Columbia Assembly of Natural Resources, http//www.bcmanr.ca/captains/reg3.html.

67   Donald Laramee, personal communication, 17 February 2016.

68   Natural Resources Canada Photo A11320_205. Air Photo Taken by Energy, Mines and Resources 1948.

69   The photos related to the Pound greenhouses and delivery horses and truck were contributed by Susan Campbell, Doreen Pound's daughter, 13 December 2016.

70   Doreen Pound (daughter of Frank Pound, greenhouse owner and florist), interviewed by Evelyn Peters, 30 November 2016, Winnipeg.

71   Warren Mills (resident who grew up near Rooster Town), interviewed by Evelyn Peters, 2 December 2016, Winnipeg.

72   Frank Sais (Rooster Town resident), interviewed by Evelyn Peters, 28 September 2012; Warren Mills (resident who grew up near Rooster Town), interviewed by Evelyn Peters, 2 December 2016 Winnipeg; "Passages," *Winnipeg Free Press*, 28 May 2013, http://www.passagesmb.com/passage-details/id-202934/VAN%20WALLEGHEM_OMER.

73   1943 City of Winnipeg Building Permits, Ward 1, no. 2294, CWARC.

74   1944 City of Winnipeg Building Permits, Ward 1, no. 37, CWARC.

75   1949 City of Winnipeg Assessment Rolls, Ward 1, no. 3432, CWARC.

76   1943 City of Winnipeg Building Permits, Ward 1, no. 2342, CWARC; 1943 City of Winnipeg Assessment Rolls, Ward 1, no. 3441, CWARC.

77   1942 City of Winnipeg Building Permits, Ward 1, no. 1912, CWARC; City of Winnipeg Property Assessment Details, 1004 Weatherdon Avenue, http://www.winnipegassessment.com/asmttax/english/propertydetails/; 1948 City of Winnipeg Assessment Rolls, Ward 1, no. 3438, CWARC.

78   1943 City of Winnipeg Building Permits, Ward 1, no. 2262, CWARC; City of Winnipeg Property Assessment Details, 992 Weatherdon Avenue, http://www.winnipegassessment.com/asmttax/english/propertydetails/.

79   1943 City of Winnipeg Building Permits, Ward 1, no. 2350, CWARC; Manitoba Vital Statistics, Birth registration no. 1901,006008.

80   1922 City of Winnipeg Building Permits, Ward 1, no. 801, CWARC; City of Winnipeg Property Assessment Details, 937 Lorette Avenue, http://www.winnipegassessment.com/asmttax/english/propertydetails/;

81   1948 City of Winnipeg Building Permits, Ward 1, no. 1046, CWARC; City of Winnipeg Property Assessment Details, 935 Lorette Avenue, http://www.winnipegassessment.com/asmttax/english/propertydetails/.

82   Natural Resources Canada Photo A11320_205. Air Photo Taken by Energy, Mines and Resources 1948.

83   1941 City of Winnipeg Building Permits, Ward 1, no. 3838, CWARC.

84   "Between Lorette and Scotland," *Winnipeg Tribune*, 10 July 1948, 10.

85   1941 City of Winnipeg Building Permits, Ward 1, no. 3451-1, CWARC.

86   "Fate's Cruelest Blow," *Winnipeg Free Press*, 22 June 1947, 18.

87   1937 City of Winnipeg Building Permits, Ward 1, no. 3388, CWARC; Manitoba Vital Statistics, death registration no. 1938,048229, Adeline Fisher Gosselin.

88   1949–56 City of Winnipeg Assessment Rolls, no. 3438, CWARC.

89   Sandra Monro (née Birston), (Rooster Town resident). Interview by Evelyn Peters, 23 August 2012, Winnipeg.

CHAPTER FIVE: STEREOTYPING, DISSOLUTION, AND DISPERSAL: ROOSTER TOWN 1951–1961

1   "Deaths and Funerals, Marie Smith," *Winnipeg Free Press*, 12 June 1951, 7.

2   In his obituary, Mab Hogg is listed as "Mark Hough" but his residency at 1145 Weatherdon Avenue identifies him. "Deaths and Funerals, Mark Hough," *Winnipeg Free Press*, 28 December 1951; "Deaths and Funerals, Alice Hogg," *Winnipeg Free Press*, 22 January 1952.

3   "Deaths and Funerals, Joseph Henry," *Winnipeg Free Press*, 10 Sepember 1952, 22. We assume this is Patrick because he lives at 1141 Lorette Avenue, Julia's house. He mentions all of his other Henry siblings in his obituary, and the age is correct.

4   1955 City of Winnipeg Assessment Rolls, Ward 1, no. 4149, CWARC.

5   "Deaths and Funerals, Xaver [sic] Frank Gosselin [sic]," *Winnipeg Free Press*, 14 June 1958, 47.

6   "Deaths and Funerals, Patrick Conway," *Winnipeg Free Press*, 19 December 1956, 30.

7   Joan Cohen, "No Fuss, No Excitement, Squatters 'Just Moving,'" *Winnipeg Free Press*, 8 April 1959, 3.

8   Frank Sais (Rooster Town resident), remarks at a lecture at the Millennium Library, Winnipeg, 11 October 2016.

9   Frank Sais (Rooster Town resident), personal phone communication with Evelyn Peters, 13 March 2017.

10   Frank Sais (Rooster Town resident), remarks at a lecture at the University of Winnipeg, Winnipeg, 13 October 2016.

11   Warren Mills (Winnipeg resident who grew up near Rooster Town), interview with Evelyn Peters, 1 December 2016, Winnipeg.

12   Ibid.

13   "Deaths and Funerals, Julia Hogg," *Winnipeg Free Press*, 24 November 1973, 39.

14   When we first talked to Frank Sais, his son mentioned that he had been reluctant to contact us because he was afraid we would repeat the newspaper stories. Darrell Sais, Frank's son, at the interview with Frank Sais, 28 September 2012, Brandon, Manitoba.

15   Dennis Guest, *The Emergence of Social Security in Canada* (Vancouver: UBC Press, 1997), 123.

16   Alvin Finkel, *Our Lives: Canada After 1945* (Toronto: James Lorimer, 1997), 9–10.

17   Ibid., 15.

18   Guest, *The Emergence of Social Security*, 137.

19   Ibid.

20   Ibid., 140.

21   Finkel, *Our Lives*, 41

22   City of Greater Winnipeg, Committee on Public Health and Welfare, "Report of the Thirty-Fourth Annual Survey of Vacant Houses and Vacant Suites and a Statement of New, Completed Dwelling Units in the City ALSO Total Housing Accommodation and Remarks on Housing in General – January 1st, 1952." Retrieved from the City of Winnipeg Archives, Box A 727.

23   City of Greater Winnipeg, Committee on Public Health and Welfare, "Report of the Thirty-Fifth Annual Survey of Vacant Houses and Vacant Suites and a Statement of New, Completed Dwelling Units

in the City ALSO Total Housing Accommodation and Remarks on Housing in General – January 1st, 1953." Retrieved from the City of Winnipeg Archives, Box A 728, 3.

24   Ibid.

25   City of Greater Winnipeg, Committee on Public Health and Welfare, "Report of the Thirty-Sixth Annual Survey of Vacant Houses and Vacant Suites and a Statement of New, Completed Dwelling Units in the City ALSO Total Housing Accommodation and Remarks on Housing in General – January 1st, 1954." Retrieved from the City of Winnipeg Archives, Box A 729, 3.

26   Jim Silver, *Poverty and Public Housing in Canada* (Winnipeg: Fernwood Press, 2011), 117–18.

27   Burley, "Rooster Town," 33.

28   Ibid., 18.

29   David G. Burley, "Winnipeg's Landscapes of Modernity, 1945–1975," in *Winnipeg Modern, 1945–1975*, ed. Serena Keshavjee (Winnipeg: University of Manitoba Press, 2006), 37–40.

30   "Pupil Dental Decay Great: Seek Remedy," *Winnipeg Free Press*, 19 December 1951, 3.

31   "Village of Patched-Up Shacks Scene of Appalling Squalor," *Winnipeg Free Press*, 20 December 1951, 1, 8.

32   Bill MacPherson, "Heard of Rooster Town? It's Our 'Lost Suburb,'" *Winnipeg Tribune*, 20 December 1951, 1, 8.

33   MacPherson, "Heard of Rooster Town?," 1.

34   John Dafoe, "Shack-Towners to Lose Homes," *Winnipeg Free Press*, 4 March 1959, 1; John Dafoe, "Rooster Town Is Dying—but It Had Its Wild Days," *Winnipeg Free Press*, 11 April 1959, 1.

35   Leader, "Winnipeg's Rooster Town . . . Remembrance of Things Past," 3.

36   "Village of Patched-Up Shacks," 1.

37 MacPherson, "Heard of Rooster Town?" 1.

38 Dafoe, "Shack-Towners to Lose Homes," 1.

39 Ibid.

40 Dafoe, "Rooster Town Is Dying," 1.

41 Leader, "Winnipeg's Rooster Town . . . Remembrance of Things Past," 3.

42 Ibid.

43 "Village of Patched-Up Shacks," 8.

44 Dafoe, "Rooster Town Is Dying," 1.

45 "Village of Patched-Up Shacks," 8.

46 Dafoe, "Rooster Town Is Dying," 1.

47 Leader, "Winnipeg's Rooster Town . . . Remembrance of Things Past," 3.

48 Ibid.

49 "Village of Patched-Up Shacks," 8.

50 MacPherson, "Heard of Rooster Town?" 8.

51 Dafoe, "Rooster Town Is Dying," 1.

52 MacPherson, "Heard of Rooster Town?" 8.

53 Frank Sais (Rooster Town resident), interview with Evelyn Peters, 28 September 2012, Winnipeg.

54 Darrell Sais (Rooster Town descendant), personal communication with Evelyn Peters, 29 December 2017.

55 "Four Generations of Laramees," Winnipeg Free Press, 27 October 1950, 10.

56 Manitoba Vital Statistics, Marriage Registration no.1921, 026461, [Adolph Joseph] Delfis Pilon and [Marie] Josephine Laramee.

57 Frank Sais (Rooster Town resident), comments at a lecture at the Millennium Library, Winnipeg, 11 October 2016.

58 Frank Sais (Rooster Town resident), interview with Evelyn Peters, Winnipeg, 29 October 2012.

59 Donald Laramee (Rooster Town descendant), interview with Evelyn Peters, Winnipeg, 9 June 2016.

60 Frank Sais (Rooster Town resident), personal phone communication with Evelyn Peters, 13 March 2017.

61 "Four Generations of Omands," Manitoba Free Press, 20 September 1927, 7.

62 "Deaths and Funerals, James Omand," Winnipeg Tribune, 12 April 1912, 8.

63 "Burial Today of Pioneer Railroader, William Peppin," Winnipeg Free Press, 1 February 1932, 2.

64 "Deaths and Funerals, Louis Parisien," Winnipeg Tribune, 7 May 1941, 8.

65 "Deaths and Funerals, Joseph Noel Laramee," Winnipeg Free Press, 6 December 1988, 39

66 Doreen Pound (Frank Pound's daughter), interview with Evelyn Peters, Winnipeg, 31 November 2016.

67 Warren Mills (Winnipeg resident who grew up near Rooster Town), interview with Evelyn Peters, Winnipeg, 14 October 2016.

68 "Village of Patched-Up Shacks," 1; Dafoe, "Rooster Town Is Dying," 1.

69 Dafoe, "Shack-Towners to Lose Homes," 1.

70 This is calculated from our database.

71 "Nail Tinting 'No Good to Do,'" Winnipeg Tribune, 8 March 1937, 3.

72 "Four generations of Omands," Manitoba Free Press, 20 September 1927, 7.

73 "Gran'mere Poitras' Colorful Life Ends," Winnipeg Free Press, 4 October 1939, 7; "Funeral Service for Centenarian," Winnipeg Tribune, 5 October 1939, 7; "Life Still Full of Interest for Gran'mere Poitras, 105," Winnipeg Tribune, 16 May 1938, 3.

74 "Funeral Held for Mrs. K. Parisien, Pioneer of the West," Winnipeg Free Press, 5 June 1932.

75 "Burial Today of Pioneer Railroader, William Peppin."

76 Natural Resources Canada Photo A12650_145 from National Air Photo Library. Aerial Photo Taken 06-07-1950. Scale 1:9000.

77 City of Winnipeg, Committee of Finance. Letter of F.D. Bond, City Solicitor to Mr. G.L. Gardner, Secretary, Committee on Finance, "Squatters on City Property in South Winnipeg," Folder 9633. 22 April 1952, CWARC, n.p.

78 City of Winnipeg, Committee of Finance, "Squatters on City Property in South Winnipeg," n.p.

79 Ibid.

80 "CNR Ready to Rip Up Tracks on Branch Line, City Learns," *Winnipeg Free Press*, 17 June 1953, 3.

81 "More About Big Centre," *Winnipeg Free Press*, 8 May 1954, 7.

82 "Shopping Site Tops Barrier," *Winnipeg Free Press*, 4 August 1955, 1.

83 "Building Grant Park. Your Choice of Lots Now," *Winnipeg Free Press*, 4 May 1957, 52.

84 City of Winnipeg, Committee of Finance, "Squatters on City Property," n.p.

85 Burley, "Rooster Town," 16.

86 "Plan to Develop Housing Scheme," *Winnipeg Tribune*, 9 October 1952.

87 Bob Cardinal (former Rooster Town resident), interview with Lawrie Barkwell, Winnipeg, 2 February 2016.

88 The city had begun its first housing project in the North End, but it was not complete by the time Rooster Town was destroyed.

89 1927 City of Winnipeg Assessment Rolls, Ward 1, no. 3546, CWARC; 1927 City of Winnipeg Building Permits, Ward 1, no. 3373, CWARC.

90 1954–56 City of Winnipeg Assessment Rolls, Ward 1, roll no. 3546, CWARC.

91 "He Escapes Taxes for Seven Years. Tussle with City Finally Comes to Eviction," *Winnipeg Free Press*, 18 February1956, 3.

92 J.K. Morton, Solicitor, The School District of Winnipeg No. 1 to G.L. Gardiner, Esq., City Clerk, March 5, 1959, n."Removal of squatters from land sold to Winnipeg School Division," No. 1. File F. 1451 (253). Winnipeg: City of Winnipeg Archives and Record Centre (CWARD) n.p.

93 Fraser, W., Q.C., City Solicitor to Mr. G.L. Gardner, Secretary, Committee on Finance, re: High School Site – Grant-Nathaniel Streets, 24 March, 1959, City Council Minutes, April 6, 1959, item 417, 220, "Removal of squatters from land sold to Winnipeg School Division No. 1. File F. 1451 (253). Winnipeg: City of Winnipeg Archives and Record Centre (CWARD) n.p.

94 Frank Sais (Rooster Town resident), remarks at a lecture at the Millennium Library, Winnipeg, 11 October 2016.

95 Dafoe, "Shack-Towners to Lose Homes," 1.

96 Ibid.

97 Ibid.

98 Wade, "Home or Homelessness?" 26.

99 Dafoe, "Rooster Town Is Dying," 1; "Slaw Slugs Again at Finance Group," *Winnipeg Free Press*, 2 June 1959, 17.

100 Dafoe, "Rooster Town Is Dying," 1; "Shack-Towners to Lose Homes," 1; "$75 Lures Shacktown Families," *Winnipeg Free Press*, 29 May 1959, 1.

101 Frank Sais (Rooster Town resident), interview with Evelyn Peters, Winnipeg, 28 September 2012.

102 Frank Sais (Rooster Town resident), remarks at a lecture at the Millennium Library, Winnipeg, 11 October 2016.

103 Burley, "Rooster Town," 20.

CONCLUSION

1   "Shacktown," *Winnipeg Free Press* Negative, 4 March 1959, Provincial Archives of Manitoba. Lagassé, *A Study of the Population of Indian Ancestry*, 66.

2   Ibid., 69.

3   Frank Tough, *As Their Natural Resources Fail: Native Peoples and the Economic History of Northern Manitoba, 1870–1930* (Vancouver: UBC Press, 1997).

4   This is documented in Chapter 2.

5   Tyler McCreary, personal communication with Evelyn Peters, September 2015.

APPENDIX A

1   *1870 Census of Manitoba*, Library and Archives Canada, http://www.bac-lac.gc.ca/eng/census/1870/Pages/about-census.aspx. These population counts may slightly underestimate the population of the area that became Fort Rouge. The census does not identify the river lots that families were settled on. Census returns for St. Boniface were matched to HBC lists of individuals who received patents to their land and this comparison established that census takers travelled north in conducting the census. David Champagne received title to lot 14, which represents the southern boundary of Fort Rouge, so the Champagne household and all of the population to the north were counted as resident in Fort Rouge.

2   Ens, *Homeland to Hinterland*, 155.

3   Ibid., 173.

4   Ibid., 33.

5   *The Royal Commission on Aboriginal Peoples* (RCAP), *Volume 4: Perspectives and Realities* (Ottawa: Canada Communication Group — Publishing Ottawa, 1996), 342.

6   Flanagan and Ens, "Métis Land Grants in Manitoba," 68–71.

7   John M. Bumsted, *Dictionary of Manitoba Biography* (Winnipeg: University of Manitoba Press, 1999), 183.

8   Begg and Nursey, *Ten Years in Winnipeg*, 7.

9   Bumsted, *Dictionary of Manitoba Biography*, 159–60.

10   Begg and Nursey, *Ten Years in Winnipeg*, 157.

11   "Memorable Manitobans: Archibald Francis Wright," Manitoba Historical Society, October 2015, http://www.mhs.mb.ca/docs/people/index_a.shtml.

12   Ens, *Homeland to Hinterland*, 166, 168.

13   Flanagan and Ens, "Métis Land Grants in Manitoba," 77.

14   Ibid., 74.

15   Ibid., 76.

16   Ibid., 74.

17   Canada, Department of Labour, "Wages and Hours in the Building Trades," 8405.

18   Struthers, *No Fault of Their Own*, 3–4.

19   MS Census 1891, Manitoba, District 3 (Provencher), Subdistrict B (de Salaberry), 10 #40 for Emanuel Champagne; MS Census 1891, Manitoba, District 3 (Provencher), Subdistrict B (de Salaberry), 17 #72 for Moise Carriere; MS Census 1891, Manitoba, District 3 (Provencher), Subdistrict B (de Salaberry), 43 #79 for Philiberte Laderoute; MS Census 1891, Manitoba, District 8 (Provencher), Subdistrict h-1 (St. Norbert) Parish 37 #169 for Charles Genthon; MS Census 1891, Manitoba, District 1 (Lisgar), Subdistrict O (St. François Xavier) 31 #139 for Jean Baptiste Morin; MS Census 1891, Northwest Territories, District 200 (Saskatchewan), Subdistrict C (St. Laurent) 6 #22 for heir of Vital Turcotte; MS Census 1891, Manitoba, District 1 (Lisgar), Subdistrict A (Assiniboia), 32 #135 for Chrysosteme Laderoute;

MS Census 1891, Manitoba, District 1
(Lisgar), Subdistrict P (St. Laurent), 5
#22 for Paul Boucher; MS Census 1891,
Manitoba, District 10 (Winnipeg), Sub-
district Subdistrict 1 (Ward 1), 2 #112
for heir of Andre Harkness; MS Census
1891, Northwest Territories, District 199
(Assiniboia West), Subdistrict C (Moose
Jaw), 5 #10 for Joseph Caplet; MS Census
1891, Manitoba, District 3 (Provencher),
Subdistrict L (St. Boniface), 44 #78 for
Baptiste Berard.

20   MS Census 1891, Manitoba, District
      8 (Provencher), Subdistrict l (St.
      Boniface), 44 #78.

21   Begg and Nursey, *Ten Years in Winnipeg*,
      189.

BIBLIOGRAPHY

....

Primary Sources

GOVERNMENT OF CANADA DOCUMENTS

Canada. The Census Office. *Fourth Census of Canada, 1901*. Ottawa: King's Printer. http://www.bac-lac.gc.ca/eng/census/1901/Pages/about-census.aspx.

———. The Census Office. *Census of the Northwest Provinces: Manitoba, Saskatchewan, Alberta, 1906*. Ottawa: King's Printer. http://www.bac-lac.gc.ca/eng/census/1906/Pages/census-districts-sub-districts.aspx.

———. The Census Office. *Fifth Census of Canada, 1911*. Ottawa: King's Printer. http://www.bac-lac.gc.ca/eng/census/1911/Pages/about-census.aspx.

———. The Census Office. *Census of the Prairie Provinces, 1916*. Ottawa: King's Printer. http://www.bac-lac.gc.ca/eng/census/1916/Pages/about-census.aspx.

———. Department of Agriculture. *Census of Manitoba, 1870*. Ottawa: Queen's Printer. http://www.bac-lac.gc.ca/eng/census/1870/Pages/about-census.aspx.

———. Department of Agriculture. *Census of Manitoba, 1885–86*. Ottawa: Queen's Printer. http://www.bac-lac.gc.ca/eng/census/Pages/census.aspx.

———. Department of Agriculture. *Census of Canada, 1890-91*. Ottawa: Queen's Printer. http://www.bac-lac.gc.ca/eng/census/Pages/census.aspx.

———. Department of Indian Affairs. *Annual Report*. Ottawa: King's Printer, 1911.

———. Department of Labour. *The Labour Gazette*. Ottawa: King's Printer, 1905–26.

———. Dominion Bureau of Statistics. *Sixth Census of Canada, 1921*. Ottawa: King's Printer. http://www.bac-lac.gc.ca/eng/census/1921/Pages/introduction.aspx.

———. Dominion Bureau of Statistics. *Census of Canada 1941: Winnipeg Housing Atlas*. Ottawa: E. Cloutier, Queen's Printer, 1944.

———. Dominion Bureau of Statistics. *Population and Housing Characteristics by Census Tracts: Winnipeg, 1951*. Ottawa: E. Cloutier, Queen's Printer, 1953.

———. Energy, Mines & Resources Canada. *Aerial Photograph of part of Winnipeg*. Photo A11320_205. Ottawa: Natural Resources Canada, 1948.

———. Ministry of the Overseas Military Forces of Canada. Personnel Records of the First World War. RG150. Ottawa: Library and Archives Canada, various dates.

———. Natural Resources Canada. *Aerial Photograph of Part of Winnipeg*. Photo FA809_034. Ottawa: National Air Photo Library, 17 October 1927.

———. Natural Resources Canada. *Aerial Photograph of Part of Winnipeg*. Photo A1221_009. Ottawa: National Air Photo Library, 15 July 1929.

———. Natural Resources Canada. *Aerial Photograph of Part of Winnipeg*. Photo A12650_145. Ottawa: National Air Photo Library, 7 July 1950.

Library and Archives Canada. https://www.flickr.com/photos/manitobamaps/2079199096.Supreme Court of Canada Manitoba Metis Federation Inc. v. Canada (Attorney General) 2013 SCC 14.

Office of the Electoral Officer for Canada. 1935 Voters Lists, Winnipeg, Federal Elections, 1935–1980. R1003-6-3-E (RG113-B). Ottawa: Library and Archives Canada. http://www.bac-lac.gc.ca/eng/census/Pages/voters-lists.aspx.

Sinclair, D., and G. McPhillips. "Plan of the Red River Lots in the Parishes of St. John, St. James, and St. Boniface" [map]. Scale not given. Ottawa: Dominion Lands Branch, 1874.

PROVINCE OF MANITOBA DOCUMENTS

Henderson's Directories, 1878–1961.

Lagassé, Jean H. *A Study of the Population of Indian Ancestry Living in Manitoba.* Winnipeg, Manitoba. Department of Agriculture and Immigration. Social and Economic Research Office, 1959.

Manitoba, Provincial Archives of Manitoba. *Land Register Book B, Describing Lots Granted by Lord Selkirk and the HBC to Various Individuals, Including the Name of the Grantee, the Measurement of the Lot in Acres, Rods and Poles, the Date of Grant and the Price per Acre.* Collection: 1830–1871 Land records of the Red River Settlement sent to the Governor and Committee.

———. "Shacktown," *Winnipeg Free Press Negative*, 4 March 1959. Manitoba, Vital Statistics Agency. http://vitalstatistics.gov.mb.ca/ Query.

CITY OF WINNIPEG DOCUMENTS

City of Winnipeg. Assessment Rolls, Ward 1. Winnipeg: City of Winnipeg Archives and Record Centre (CWARC) 1901–1961.

———. Building Permits, Ward 1. Winnipeg: CWARC, 1901–1961.

———. City Clerk's Department, Election Rolls, 1926–1956. Winnipeg: CWARC.

———. City Council Minutes. Winnipeg: CWARC, 1931–1961.

———. Committee of Finance. Letter of F.D. Bond, City Solicitor to Mr. G.L. Gardner, Secretary, Committee on Finance, "Squatters on City Property in South Winnipeg." Folder 9633. 22 April 1952, n.p. Winnipeg: City of Winnipeg Archives and Record Centre (CWARD).

———. Committee of Finance. Letter of Mr. G.L. Gardner, Secretary, Committee on Finance to Mr. G.F.D. Bond, Q.C., City Solicitor. Re Squatters in South Winnipeg. City of Winnipeg Archive, Folder 9633. 28 August 1952, n.p. Winnipeg: City of Winnipeg Archives and Record Centre (CWARD).

———. Committee on Public Health and Welfare. Annual Reports. Winnipeg: CWARC, 1909–1939.

———. Committee on Public Health and Welfare. Report of the Twenty-Third Annual Survey of Vacant Houses and Vacant Suites in the City ALSO Total Housing Accommodation and Remarks on Housing in General—January 1941. Winnipeg: CWARC, 1941.

———. Committee on Public Health and Welfare. Report of the Twenty-Seventh Annual Survey of Vacant Houses and Vacant Suites in the City ALSO Total Housing Accommodation and Remarks on Housing in General—January 1946. Winnipeg: CWARC, 1946.

———. Committee on Public Health and Welfare. Report of the Thirty-Fifth Annual Survey of Vacant Houses and Vacant Suites and a Statement of New, Completed Dwelling Units in the City ALSO Total Housing Accommodation and Remarks on Housing in General—January 1st, 1953. Winnipeg: CWARC, 1953.

———. Committee on Public Health and Welfare. Report of the Thirty-Sixth Annual Survey of Vacant Houses and Vacant Suites and a Statement of New, Completed Dwelling Units in the City ALSO Total Housing Accommodation and Remarks on Housing in General—January 1st, 1954. Winnipeg: CWARC, 1954.

———. Tax Collector's Rolls, Ward 1. Winnipeg: CWARC, 1901–1961.

Fraser, W., Q.C., City Solicitor to Mr. G.L. Gardner, Secretary, Committee on Finance, re: High School Site—Grant-Nathaniel Streets, 24 March 1959, City Council Minutes, 6 April 1959, item 417, p. 220, "Removal of Squatters from Land sold to Winnipeg School Division." No. 1. File F. 1451 (253), n.p. Winnipeg: City of Winnipeg Archives and Record Centre (CWARC).

Lawrence, A.G. "Keeping the People Healthy: A Radio Broadcast." City of Greater Winnipeg.

Committee on Public Health and Welfare. Annual Report for the year ending December 31, 1939. Box A 718, n.p. Winnipeg: CWARC, 1940.

Morton, J.K., Solicitor, The School District of Winnipeg No. 1 to G.L. Gardiner, Esq., City Clerk, March 5, 1959, n.p. "Removal of Squatters from Land Sold to Winnipeg School Division." No. 1. File F. 1451

(253), n.p. Winnipeg: City of Winnipeg Archives and Record Centre (CWARC).

INTERVIEWS AND PERSONAL COMMUNICATIONS

Cardinal, Bob (former Rooster Town resident). Interview with Lawrie Barkwell. Winnipeg, MB, 2 February 2016.

Hogue, Candace (Rooster Town descendant). Personal communication with Evelyn Peters. 23 November, 2017.

Laramee, Donald (Rooster Town descendant). Interview with Evelyn Peters. Winnipeg, MB, 9 June 2016.

McCreary, Tyler (researcher). Personal communication with Evelyn Peters. September 2015.

Mills, Warren (Winnipeg resident who grew up near Rooster Town). Interview with Evelyn Peters. Winnipeg, MB, 1 December 2016.

Monro, Sandra (nee Birston) (former Rooster Town resident). Interview with Evelyn Peters. Winnipeg, MB, 23 August 2012.

Morrissette, Larry (Rooster Town descendant). Interview with Evelyn Peters. Winnipeg, MB, 10 March 2014.

Pound, Doreen (daughter of Frank Pound, greenhouse owner and florist). Interview with Evelyn Peters. Winnipeg, MB, 30 November 2016.

Sais, Darrell (Rooster Town descendent). Conversation with Evelyn Peters, during an interview with Frank Sais. 28 September 2012. Manitoba Métis Federation Annual Meeting, Brandon, MB.

———. Personal communication with Evelyn Peters, 29 December 2017.

Sais, Frank (former Rooster Town resident). Phone communication with Evelyn Peters. Winnipeg, MB, 13 March 2017.

———. Remarks during a Lecture at the Millennium Library. Winnipeg, MB, 11 October 2016.

———. Remarks at a Lecture at the University of Manitoba, Winnipeg, MB, 13 October 2016.

————. Interview with Evelyn Peters, 28 September 2012. The Manitoba Métis Federation Annual Meeting in Brandon, MB.

Smith, Loretta (Rooster Town descendant). Interview with Evelyn Peters. Winnipeg, MB,17 February 2016.

Walder, Audrey (nee Halchakar) (former Rooster Town resident). Interview with Evelyn Peters. Winnipeg, MB., 12 November 2012.

Wiwcher, Dan (Winnipeg resident who grew up near Rooster Town). Interview with Evelyn Peters. Winnipeg, MB, 8 March 2012.

Wright, Sonya, and Dwili Burns (cousins of Rooster Town resident Kenny Campbell). Interview with Evelyn Peters. Winnipeg, MB, 3 November 2013.

NEWSPAPERS

Manitoba Free Press, 1901–1931.

Winnipeg Free Press, 1931–2017.

Winnipeg Tribune, 1890–1961.

Secondary Sources

Anderson, Kay. "Science and the Savage: The Linnean Society of New South Wales, 1874–1900." *Ecumene* 5, no. 2 (April 1998): 125–43.

Andrews, Richard B. "Elements in the Urban-Fringe Pattern." *The Journal of Land and Public Utility Economics* 18, no. 2 (April 1942): 169–83.

Artibise, Alan F.J. *Winnipeg: A Social History of Urban Growth, 1874–1914.* Montreal: McGill-Queen's University Press, 1975.

————. *Gateway City: Documents on the City of Winnipeg 1873–1913.* Winnipeg: Manitoba Record Society, 1979.

Bacher, John C. *Keeping to the Marketplace: The Evolution of Canadian Housing Policy.* Montreal: McGill-Queen's University Press, 1993.

Bacher, John C., and J. David Hulchanski. "Keeping Warm and Dry: The Policy Response to the Struggle for Shelter Among Canada's Homeless, 1900–1960." *Urban History Review* 16, no. 2 (October 1987): 147–63.

Barkwell, Lawrence J. "Early Law and Social Control Among the Metis." In *Struggle for Recognition: Canadian Justice and the Métis Nation,* edited by W. Corrigan and L.J. Barkwell, 7–37. Winnipeg: Pemmican, 1991.

———. "The Reign of Terror Against the Métis of Red River." Virtual Museum of Métis History and Culture. 12 February 2008. http:// www.metismuseum.ca/media/document.php/07260.THE%20 REIGN%20OF%20TERROR.pdf.

Barman, Jean. "Erasing Indigenous Indigeneity in Vancouver." *BC Studies* 155 (Autumn 2007): 3–30.

Barron, F. Laurie. "The Indian Pass System in the Canadian West, 1882–1935." *Prairie Forum* 13, no. 1 (Spring 1988): 25–42.

Begg, Alexander, and Walter R. Nursey. *Ten Years in Winnipeg: A Narration of the Principal Events in the History of the City of Winnipeg from the Year A.D. 1870 to the Year A.D. 1879 Inclusive.* Winnipeg: Times Printing and Publishing House, 1879.

Bellan, Ruben. *Winnipeg First Century: An Economic History.* Winnipeg: Queenston House, 1978.

Berkhoffer, Robert. *The White Man's Indian: Images of the American Indian from Columbus to the Present.* New York: Vintage, 1979.

Blomley, Nicholas. *Unsettling the City: Urban Land and the Politics of Property.* New York: Routledge, 2004.

Boek, Walter E., and Jean K. Boek. *The People of Indian Ancestry in Greater Winnipeg.* Winnipeg: Manitoba Department of Agriculture and Immigration, 1959.

Brown, Jennifer S. H. *Strangers in Blood: Fur Trade Company Families in Indian Country.* Vancouver: UBC Press, 1980.

Bumsted, John M. *Dictionary of Manitoba Biography.* Winnipeg: University of Manitoba Press, 1999.

Burley, David G. "Winnipeg's Landscapes of Modernity, 1945–1975." In *Winnipeg Modern: Architecture, 1945–1975,* edited by Serena Keshavjee, 29–85. Winnipeg: University of Manitoba Press, 2006.

———. "Rooster Town: Winnipeg's Lost Métis Suburb, 1900–1960." *Urban History Review* 42, no. 1 (October 2013): 3–25.

Casey, Stephen. *Greater Glory: Thirty-Seven Years with the Jesuits*. Montreal: McGill-Queen's University Press, 2007.

Cyr, A. Bryan. *Métis Veterans of Manitoba: From Buffalo to Battlefields*. Winnipeg: Manitoba Métis Federation, 2010.

Davis, Arthur K. *Edging into Mainstream: Urban Indians in Saskatchewan*. Bellingham: Western Washington State College, 1965.

Dobbin, Murray. *The One-and-a-Half Men: The Story of Jim Brady and Malcolm Norris, Metis Patriots of the Twentieth Century*. Vancouver: New Star Books, 1981.

———. "The Métis in Western Canada Since 1945." In *The Making of the Modern West: Western Canada Since 1945*, edited by A.W. Rasporich, 183–194. Calgary: University of Calgary Press, 1984.

Edmonds, Penelope. *Urbanizing Frontiers: Indigenous Peoples and Settlers in 19th Century Pacific Rim Cities*. Vancouver: UBC Press, 2010.

Ens, Gerhard J. *Homeland to Hinterland: The Changing Worlds of the Red River Metis in the Nineteenth Century*. Toronto: University of Toronto Press, 1996.

Epp, Stefan. "Class, Capitalism, and Construction: Winnipeg's Housing Crisis and the Debate Over Public Housing, 1934–1939." *Histoire Sociale/Social History* 43, no. 86 (2010): 393–428.

Evans, Mike, and Lisa Krebs. *A Brief History of the Short Life of the Island Cache*. Edmonton: University of Alberta Press, 2004.

Finkel, Alvin. *Our Lives: Canada After 1945*. Toronto: James Lorimer, 1997.

———. *Social Policy and Practice in Canada: A History*. Waterloo: Wilfrid Laurier University Press, 2006.

Flanagan, Thomas, and Gerhard Ens. "Métis Land Grants in Manitoba: A Statistical Study." *Histoire Sociale/Social History* 27, no. 53 (May 1994): 65–87.

Foster, John E. "The Plains Metis." In *Native Peoples: The Canadian Experience*, edited by R. Bruce Morrison and C. Roderick Wilson, 297–319. Toronto: Oxford University Press, 2004.

Gaudry, Adam. "Kaa-tipeyimishoyaahk—'We are those who own ourselves': A Political History of Métis Self-Determination in the North-West, 1830–1870." PhD diss., University of Victoria, 2014.

Giraud, Marcel. *The Métis in the Canadian West,* vol I and II. Translated by George Woodcock. Edmonton: University of Alberta Press, 1986.

Goldie, Terry. *Fear and Temptation: The Image of the Indigene in Canadian, Australian, and New Zealand Literatures.* Montreal: McGill-Queen's University Press, 1989.

Greenway, Harold F. *Housing in Canada (A Study Based on the Census of 1931 and Supplementary Data).* Ottawa: Edmond Cloutier, 1941.

Guest, Dennis. *The Emergence of Social Security in Canada.* Vancouver: UBC Press, 1997.

Hamer, David. *New Towns in the New World: Images and Perceptions of the Nineteenth-Century Urban Frontier.* New York: Columbia University Press, 1990.

Harris, Cole. "How Did Colonialism Dispossess? Comments from an Edge of Empire." *Annals of the Association of American Geographers* 94, no. 1 (2004): 165–182.

———. *Making Native Space: Colonialism, Resistance, and Reserves in British Columbia.* Vancouver: UBC Press, 2002.

———. "The Lower Mainland, 1820–81." In *Vancouver and its Regions,* edited by G. Wynn and T. Oke, 38–68. Vancouver: UBC Press, 1992.

Harris, Richard. Personal communication. 2 October 2015.

———. *Unplanned Suburbs: Toronto's American Tragedy, 1900 to 1950.* Baltimore: Johns Hopkins University Press, 1996.

———. "Self-Building in the Urban Housing Market." *Economic Geography* 67, no.1 (January 1991): 1–21.

Hogue, Michel. *Metis and the Medicine Line: Creating a Border and Dividing a People.* Regina: University of Regina Press, 2015.

Horn, Michiel, ed. *The Depression in Canada: Responses to Economic Crisis.* Toronto: Copp Clark Pitman, 1988.

Jacobs, Jane M. *Edge of Empire: Postcolonialism and the City*. New York, Routledge, 1996.

Johnson, Jay T. "Dancing into Place: The Role of the Powwow within Urban Indigenous Communities." In *Indigenous in the City: Contemporary Identities and Cultural Innovation*, edited by Evelyn Peters and Chris Andersen, 216–30. Vancouver: UBC Press, 2013.

Leacy, F.H., and M.C. Urquhard, eds. *Historical Statistics of Canada*. Ottawa: Statistics Canada and Social Science Federation of Canada, 1983.

Little, Margaret Jane Hillyard. *'No Car, No Radio, No Liquor Permit': The Moral Regulation of Single Mothers in Ontario, 1920–1997*. Toronto: Oxford University Press, 1998.

Mawani, Renisa. "'Half-breeds,' Racial Opacity, and Geographies of Crime: Law's Search for the 'Original' Indian." *Cultural Geographies* 17, no. 4 (October 2010): 487–506.

———. "Genealogies of the Land: Aboriginality, Law, and Territory in Vancouver's Stanley Park." *Social and Legal Studies* 14, no. 3 (September 2005): 315–339.

———. "Legal Geographies of Aboriginal Segregation in British Columbia: The Making and Unmaking of the Songhees Reserve, 1850–1911." In *Isolation: Places and Practices of Exclusion*, edited by Carolyn Strange and Alison Bashford, 163–180. London: Routledge, 2003.

McClintock, Anne. *Imperial Leather: Race, Gender and Sexuality in the Colonial Context*. New York: Routledge, 1995.

McWilliams, Margaret. *Manitoba Milestones*. Toronto: J.M. Dent and Sons, 1928.

Metropolitan Planning Committee and Winnipeg Town Planning Commission. "Greater Winnipeg Tax Forfeited Lands (1946)." In *Metropolitan Planning Committee and Winnipeg Town Planning Commission, Background for Planning Greater Winnipeg* (Winnipeg: Metropolitan Planning Committee and Winnipeg Town Planning Commission, 1946), plate 9, http:www.flickr.com/photos/manitobamaps/3130341037/in/set-72157611557215976.

Miller, Jaimy. "The Papaschase Band: Building Awareness and Community in the City of Edmonton." In *Aboriginal Peoples in Canadian Cities: Transformations and Continuities*, edited by Heather Howard and Craig Proulx, 53–68. Waterloo: Wilfrid Laurier University Press, 2011.

Milne, Brad. "The Historiography of Métis Land Dispersal, 1870–1890." *Manitoba History* 30 (Autumn 1995): 30–41.

Morin, Gail. *Métis Families: A Genealogical Compendium*. Pawtucket, RI: Quintin Publications, 2001.

Morse, Bradford, and Robert K. Groves. "Canada's Forgotten Peoples: The Aboriginal Rights of Métis and Non-Status Indians." *Law and Anthropology* 2 (1987): 139–67.

Morton, Desmond. *Fight or Pay: Soldiers' Families in the Great War.* Vancouver: UBC Press, 2004.

Morton, William L. *Manitoba: A History*. Toronto: University of Toronto Press, 1967.

Newhouse, David. "The Invisible Infrastructure: Urban Aboriginal Institutions and Organizations." In *Not Strangers in These Parts: Urban Aboriginal Peoples*, edited by David Newhouse and Evelyn J. Peters, 243–54. Ottawa: Policy Research Initiative, 2003.

———. "From the Tribal to the Modern: The Development of Modern Aboriginal Societies." In *Expressions in Canadian Native Studies*, edited by Ron F. Laliberte, et al., 395–409. Saskatoon: University of Saskatchewan Extension Press, 2000.

Paquin, Todd, Patrick Young, and Darren Prefontaine. *Métis Farmers.* Saskatoon: Gabriel Dumont Institute's The Virtual Museum of Métis History and Culture, 2003. http://www.metismuseum.ca.

Perera, Nihal. "Indigenising the Colonial City: Late 19th-century Colombo and Its Landscape." *Urban Studies* 39, no.9 (August 2002): 1703–21.

Perrun, Jody. *The Patriotic Consensus: Winnipeg, 1939–1945*. Ottawa: Library and Archives Canada/Bibliothèque et Archives Canada, 2010.

Peters, Evelyn J. "Conceptually Unclad? Feminist Geography and Aboriginal Peoples." *Canadian Geographer* 48, no. 3 (October 2004): 251–65.

———. "'Urban' and 'Aboriginal': An Impossible Contradiction." In *City Lives and City Forms: Critical Research and Canadian Urbanism*, edited by John Caulfield and Linda Peake, 47–62. Toronto: University of Toronto Press, 1996.

Peters, Evelyn J., and Carol Lafond. "'I Basically Mostly Stick with My Own Kind': First Nations Appropriation of Urban Space in Saskatoon, Saskatchewan, Canada." In *Indigenous in the City: Contemporary Identities and Cultural Innovation*, edited by Evelyn J. Peters and Chris Andersen, 123–153. Vancouver: UBC Press, 2013.

Peters, Evelyn J., and Chris Andersen. "Introduction." In *Indigenous in the City: Contemporary Identities and Cultural Innovation*, edited by Evelyn J. Peters and Chris Andersen, 1–25. Vancouver: UBC Press, 2013.

Peterson, Jacqueline, and Jennifer S.H. Brown. *The New Peoples: Being and Becoming Métis in North America*. Winnipeg: University of Manitoba Press, 1985.

Raby, Stewart. "Indian Land Surrenders in Southern Saskatchewan." *Canadian Geographer* 17, no.1 (March 1973): 36–52.

Rea, J.E. *The Winnipeg General Strike*. Toronto: Holt, Rinehart, and Winston of Canada, 1973.

Robson, Hugh Amos. *Royal Commission to Enquire into and Report upon the Causes and Effects of the General Strike Which Recently Existed in the City of Winnipeg: For a Period of Six Weeks, Including the Methods of Calling and Carrying on Such Strike*. Winnipeg: Government of Manitoba, 1919.

Ross, Alexander. *The Red River Settlement: Its Rise, Progress, and Present State: With Some Account of the Native Races and Its General History to the Present*. Edmonton: Hurtig Publishers, 1972.

Rostecki, Randolph R. *Crescentwood: A History*. Winnipeg: Crescentwood Home Owners Association, 1993.

RCAP (The Royal Commission on Aboriginal Peoples). *Volume 4: Perspectives and Realities* Ottawa: Canada Communication Group — Publishing Ottawa, 1996.

Sautter, Udo. "Measuring Unemployment in Canada: Federal Efforts Before World War II." *Histoire sociale/Social History* 15, no. 30 (November 1982): 475–87.

Sealey, D. Bruce, and Antoine S. Lussier. *The Métis: Canada's Forgotten People*. Winnipeg: Manitoba Métis Federation Inc., 1975.

Sharpe, Christopher. "Recruitment and Conscription (Canada)." In *1914–1918-online: International Encyclopedia of the First World War*, edited by Ute Daniel, Peter Gatrell, Oliver Janz, Heather Jones, Jennifer Keene, Alan Kramer, and Bill Nasson. Berlin: Freie Universität Berlin, 2015. http://dx.doi.org/10.15463/ie1418.10670.

Shore, Fred J. "The Emergence of the Metis Nation in Manitoba." In *Metis Legacy: A Metis Historiography and Annotated Bibliography*, edited by Lawrence J. Barkwell, Leah Dorion, and Darren R. Préfontaine, 71–78. Winnipeg: Pemmican Publications, 2001.

Silver, Jim. *Good Places to Live: Poverty and Public Housing Policy in Canada*. Winnipeg: Fernwood Publishing, 2011.

———. *North End Winnipeg's Lord Selkirk Park Housing Development: History, Comparative Context, Prospects*. Ottawa: Canadian Centre for Policy Alternatives, 2006.

Solonecki, Joyce. *Fort Rouge Through the Years: Souvenir Booklet*. Winnipeg: Fort Rouge Centennial Brochure Committee, 1974.

Sprague, Donald N., and R.P. Frye. *The Genealogy of the First Metis Nation*. Winnipeg: Pemmican Press, 1983.

Spry, Irene M. "The Métis and Mixed-bloods of Rupert's Land before 1870." In *The New Peoples: Being and Becoming Métis in North America*, edited by Jacqueline Peterson and Jennifer S.H. Brown, 95–118. Winnipeg: University of Manitoba Press, 1985.

St-Onge, Nicole. "Memories of Metis Women of Saint-Eustache, Manitoba—1910–1980." *Native Studies Review* 17, no. 2 (2008): 45–68.

————. "Race, Class and Marginality in a Manitoba Interlake Settlement, 1850–1950." *Socialist Studies/Etudes Socialistes.* Annual No. 5 (1989): 116–132.

Stanger-Ross, Jordan. "Municipal Colonialism in Vancouver: City Planning and the Conflict over Indian Reserves, 1928–1950s." *Canadian Historical Review* 89, no. 4 (2008): 541–80.

Stanley, George F.G. *The Birth of Western Canada: A History of the Riel Rebellions.* Toronto: University of Toronto Press, 1961.

Strikwerda, Eric. *The Wages of Relief: Cities and the Unemployed in Prairie Canada, 1929–39.* Edmonton: Athabasca University Press, 2013.

Struthers, James. *No Fault of Their Own: Unemployment and the Canadian Welfare State, 1914–1941.* Toronto: University of Toronto Press, 1983.

Tatrie, Jon. 2014. "Africville." *The Canadian Encyclopedia.* http://www.thecanadianencyclopedia.ca/en/article/africville/.

Thompson, W.P., ed. *Fort Rouge Neighbourhood Walking Tour.* Winnipeg, 1994. http://www.winnipeg.ca/ppd/historic/pdf/Fort_Rouge_Walking_Tour_1994.pdf.

Thrush, Coll. "The Crossing-Over Place: Urban and Indian Histories in Seattle." PhD diss., University of Washington, 2002.

Tough, Frank. "Race, Personality and History: A Review of Marcel Giraud's *The Métis in the Canadian West.*" *Native Studies Review* 52, no. 2 (1989): 55–93.

————. *As Their Natural Resources Fail: Native Peoples and the Economic History of Northern Manitoba, 1870–1930.* Vancouver: UBC Press, 1997.

Troupe, Cheryl L. "Métis Women: Social Structure, Urbanization and Political Activism, 1850–1980." MA thesis, University of Saskatchewan, 2009.

Van Kirk, Sylvia. "'What if Mama is an Indian?' The Cultural Ambivalence of the Alexander Ross Family." In *The New Peoples: Being and Becoming Métis in North America,* edited by Jacqueline Peterson and Jennifer S.H. Brown, 207–217. Winnipeg: University of Manitoba Press, 1985.

Wade, Jill. "Home or Homelessness? Marginal Housing in Vancouver, 1886–1950." *Urban History Review / Revue d'histoire urbaine* 25, no. 2 (March 1997): 19–29.

Walker, Ryan, and Sarem Nejad. "Urban Planning, Indigenous Peoples, and Settler States." In *Urbanization in a Global Context*, edited by Allison Bain and Linda Peake, 136–54. Toronto: Oxford University Press, 2017.

Wilson, Kathi and Evelyn J. Peters. "'You Can Make a Place for It': Remapping Urban First Nations Spaces of Identity." *Society and Space* 23, no. 3 (2005): 395–413.

Winnipeg Council of Social Agencies. *Housing in Winnipeg: Report of Committee on Housing.* Winnipeg: The Committee on Housing, 1943.

Wood, Patricia K. "Pressured from All Sides: The February 1913 Surrender of the Northeast Corner of the Tsuu T'ina Nation." *Journal of Historical Geography* 30, no. 1 (2004): 112–129.

Woodsworth, James S. *My Neighbour: A Study of City Conditions, A Plea for Social Services.* Toronto: The Missionary Society of the Methodist Church, 1911.

INDEX

W